Sustainable Growth in a Post-Scarcity World

Sustainable Growth in a Post-Scarcity World

Consumption, Demand, and the Poverty Penalty

PHILIP SADLER

Routledge
Taylor & Francis Group

LONDON AND NEW YORK

First published 2010 by Gower Publishing

2 Park Square, Milton Park, Abingdon, Oxon OX14 4RN
711 Third Avenue, New York, NY 10017, USA

Routledge is an imprint of the Taylor & Francis Group, an informa business

First issued in paperback 2016

Gower Applied Business Research
Our programme provides leaders, practitioners, scholars and researchers with thought provoking, cutting edge books that combine conceptual insights, interdisciplinary rigour and practical relevance in key areas of business and management.

British Library Cataloguing in Publication Data
Sadler, Philip, 1930-
    Sustainable growth in a post-scarcity world : consumption,
    demand, and the poverty penalty.
    1. Production (Economic theory) 2. Technological
    innovations--Economic aspects. 3. Technological
    innovations--Social aspects. 4. Social responsibility of
    business. 5. Distributive justice.
    I. Title
    338.5-dc22

ISBN: 978-0-566-09158-2 (hbk)
ISBN: 978-1-138-25562-3 (pbk)

Library of Congress Cataloging-in-Publication Data
Sadler, Philip, 1930-
    Sustainable growth in a post-scarcity world : consumption, demand, and the poverty
    penalty / by Philip Sadler.
       p. cm.
    Includes bibliographical references and index.
    ISBN 978-0-566-09158-2 (hardback) -- ISBN 978-0-566-09159-9
    (ebook) 1. Wealth. 2. Poverty. 3. Technological innovations. 4. Sustainability. 5. Social
    responsibility of business. I. Title.
    HC79.W4S23 2010
    338.9'27--dc22

                                                                              2010016296

Contents

Preface

In his preface to *The Age of Discontinuity* (1968) Peter Drucker described the book as a 'handcar'. 'In guerrilla country a handcar, light and expendable, rides ahead of the big, lumbering freight train to detonate whatever explosives might have been placed on the track. This book is such a handcar. For the future is, of course, always "guerrilla country" in which the unsuspected and apparently insignificant derail the massive and seemingly invincible trends of today.'

This analogy struck me as particularly apt, possibly because some years earlier, as a young soldier, I had travelled through the length of Malaya – at that time under serious threat from communist guerrillas – in a train preceded by just such a handcar, albeit one manned by fierce-looking Sikh warriors.

It is my hope, therefore, that this book in turn might serve as just such a handcar and that it might help alert today's big lumbering freight trains – the multinational corporations – to the discontinuities which may derail them.

I have lived through a period of time that has seen enormous change in every aspect of our world – political, social, economic and technological.

Since I became involved in executive education in the 1960s I have followed two interests. On the one hand I have tried to understand why relatively few business organizations have followed the path of 'doing well by doing good'. I have also tried to understand why politicians the world over have continued to put their trust in economists – a profession which has so signally failed to proffer useful and timely advice

In 1953 when I started my first job, a reliable wrist watch was a scarce good and was priced accordingly; today reliable wrist watches exist in abundance and are cheap. This book is about the shift from scarcity to abundance and its implications – particularly its implications for the sustainability of the planet and the relief of poverty.

Reviews for
Sustainable Growth in a
Post-Scarcity World

Philip Sadler's latest book focuses on the next big global shift from scarcity to abundance – the 'post-scarcity economy' – and its critical implications for sustainability of the planet and relief of poverty. He pulls no punches in demonstrating that so few multinational corporations and the economists who advise them, have pursued a strategy of 'doing well by doing good'. He highlights how the economics of abundance and sustainability are in increasing conflict, in such areas as climate change, food and water shortages, and human rights. Sadler provides an excellent historical perspective coupled with a deep and thoughtful analysis of future economic trends. His challenging book should be read by all those who genuinely care about every aspect of sustainability and believe that the market cannot be relied upon to provide the planet with a safe landing.

Professor Michael Osbaldeston, Emeritus Professor,
Cranfield University School of Management

Philip Sadler excels at combining foresight with hindsight. He makes sense of all the important changes around us. He takes us into important new territory and challenges us to think systemically and laterally about the shift from scarcity to abundance.

Mark Goyder, Founder Director, Tomorrow's Company

PART 1

The Coming of Post-scarcity Society

1

The Post-Scarcity Paradox

Introduction

This book is about the next big shift in the nature of the economic and social system within which we live and work, and about its causes and its consequences. In particular it is about its implications for sustainability.

It will be a bigger shift than we have previously experienced; bigger than the industrial revolution, bigger than the digital revolution that has brought us the internet and connected us all together. It will unravel between now and 2050, but it is already under way. Politicians and business leaders who are trapped in the mindsets of today's world will not be fully aware of this shift until it is well advanced. Once they become aware many will resist it strongly.

As individuals and as members of institutions of many kinds we have strong vested interests in the present system – it provides us with jobs; it offers a good return on our savings even if it does not consistently fulfil that promise; it gives the majority of people in the developed countries a lifestyle that their grandparents would have not even imagined to be possible; and it enables a few to become extremely wealthy. Businesses, particularly large global corporations and financial institutions have particularly strong vested interests in the existing arrangements, which protect their markets and their profits.

As the shift gathers pace, however, it will involve what Schumpeter (1942) described as 'creative destruction' on a larger scale than has been seen previously. As in previous waves of change great companies will fail, whole industries will disappear, regions that were once prosperous will become depressed, new elites will emerge and existing ones will be obliterated.

At the same time the change will give rise to whole new industries, new fields of employment, new investment opportunities and new entrants to the group of the world's top one hundred companies.

The new system will be known as the post-scarcity society. It will, in many respects, be an age of abundance. It will bring mankind huge benefits but at the same time a whole new set of threats and dilemmas.

The Main Challenges

In what follows I will explain what is meant by a post-scarcity society and provide the evidence for the fact that it is coming about. Among the many issues it will give rise to I will address five:

1. As the abundance of goods and services continues to grow, how do we deal with the economic and social consequences?

2. How do we spread the enjoyment of the fruits of greater abundance to the poorer countries of the world?

3. Given the growing levels of consumption implied by the above, how do we cope with the impact on the environment generally and on the world's climate in particular?

4. What response to these issues can we expect from business organizations?

5. What are the prospects for system change?

A Dysfunctional System

In those parts of the world where it has prevailed, the market economy has driven economic growth, lifting the living standards of millions of people. But the world is now undergoing a period of unprecedented change. In some respects it is nearing a tipping point and it is becoming clear that the current institutions and practices which the market facilitates are leading to unsustainable outcomes. There are major issues which the market has not resolved – particularly climate change, areas of persistent poverty, water shortages, exhaustion of fishing stocks and abuse of human rights.

The market operates within a wider system – a system which incorporates three sub-systems: the economic, the social-political and the environmental. The London-based think tank Tomorrow's Company (2008) has coined the term 'the triple context' to refer to this overarching system. It is a way of expressing the fact that there are three distinct but interdependent systems – environmental, socio-political and economic – which continually interact to create, on a global scale, an all-encompassing system resulting from the complex feedback loops existing between the three sub-systems.

Zadek (2001) makes a similar point. 'Social, environmental and economic gains and losses arising from particular business processes cannot simply be added up. We do not know, for example, whether an additional four weeks of employee training, minus a dozen or so trees, plus a ton of profit, add up to more or less sustainable development ... In fact we do not and probably cannot know enough about the system to understand in this sense the relationship between the activities of one organization and the whole system.'

As Elkington (1998) has pointed out, 'Systems thinking tells us that sustainability cannot be defined for a single corporation. Instead, it must be defined for a complete economic-social-ecological system, and not for its component parts.'

The Components of the System

THE GLOBAL ECONOMY

The global economy can be viewed as consisting of three inter-related sub systems:

1.   The 'real economy' – producing goods and services that meet human needs and wants.

2.   The financial services industries, which facilitate the provision of capital for the real economy on the one hand and the provision of credit for consumers on the other.

3.   What Professor Susan Strange (1997) has dubbed the 'casino economy', the largely speculative activities of those in the financial sector which are unrelated to the production of goods and services.

As the so-called credit crunch crisis of 2008–2009 developed, many commentators around the world attributed blame to the operations of the casino economy and the use of derivatives in particular, coupled with the fact that financial services institutions such as retail banks and mortgage societies became involved in casino-type operations.

THE SOCIAL AND POLITICAL SYSTEMS

Social and political systems are the human element: the people on the Earth and the political and social institutions that govern their interaction. There is, of course, no global socio-political system in the same way that there is a global economy or a global natural world. Each society has its own set of values, characteristic lifestyles, traditions, mores and institutions. Unsustainable systems are characterized by oppression, corruption, crime, extremes of inequality and poor human rights. They also tend to have weak, fragile economies and poor records in such matters as pollution, conservation of species and deforestation. Economic activity is in many cases sustained only by virtue of rich natural resources – oil or diamonds, for example.

Within the past few decades we have seen the collapse of a number of unsustainable systems such as the Soviet bloc and the former Yugoslavia. Currently Zimbabwe is close to collapse. Within the foreseeable future we can expect the breakdown of the existing socio-political systems in a number of countries, including North Korea, Iran and Burma (Myanmar).

THE NATURAL ENVIRONMENT

The natural environment can be defined as landscapes, flora and fauna, freshwater and marine environments, geology and soils. It is persistently under pressure from a range of threats, many of which have been evident for more than a century. These include the sheer pressures created by population increases, the clearance of woodland for settlements or for agriculture, the various forms of pollution produced as one country after another has industrialized, the mindless harvesting of fishing stocks and the unthinking exploitation of a wide range of non-renewable resources. Further economic growth, if it is to be sustainable, needs to be accompanied by deliberate action to protect the structure, functions and diversity of the world's natural systems on which our own species depends.

Currently, however, the main focus under this heading is on global warming, not only because of its possible consequences for almost every other aspect of the natural world but also because of its implications for the future path of economic growth and socio/political stability

Changing the System

Today, beyond any doubt, the necessity to change in the interests of sustainability is increasingly widely accepted. Changing the global system, however, cannot be brought about by the isolated actions of nations acting alone or of individual companies trying to be a force for good. Nor does it result from advocacy, however persuasive. If efforts to achieve sustainability are to be effective, governments, international agencies, multinational companies, NGOs and other bodies must work together.

> What history teaches us is that man does not change arbitrarily; he does not transform himself at will on hearing the voices of inspired prophets. The reason is that all change, in colliding with the inherited institutions of the past, is inevitably hard and laborious; consequently it only takes place in response to the demands of necessity. For change to be brought about it is not enough that it should be seen as desirable; it must be the product of changes within the whole network of diverse causal relationships which the determine the situation of man. (Durkheim, 1984)

The Shift to a Post-Scarcity World

The world's most highly developed economies are now capable of producing huge amounts of material wealth in the form of goods and services with the aid of a relatively small percentage of the population and are moving at an accelerating pace towards a state of post-scarcity, an age of abundance, a state in which an ever wider range of economic goods and services are available in abundant supply and at extremely low cost.

In the early days of industrialization most goods and services were expensive relative to average earnings and were produced by the masses of the working class for consumption primarily by the middle and upper classes.

However, huge strides in productivity growth have led to greatly reduced costs of production, while markets have expanded well beyond national boundaries, creating greater economies of scale. In recent years the impact of productivity has been augmented by the globalization of manufacturing and the accompanying very rapid increase in the supply of cheap labour as a result of the rapid industrialization of Asian countries. The consequent intensification of competition is causing prices of a wide range of goods to fall to the marginal cost of production. At the same time, rises in real wages in the developed countries have placed an increasing range of goods and services which until relatively recently were restricted to the middle and upper classes within the reach of ordinary working people. Obvious examples include air travel, foreign holidays, cruises, eating out, sound systems, home cinemas, central heating and personal computers.

This shift, from relative scarcity to relative abundance, has been progressing steadily for many years. It was first pointed out in America before the Second World War, notably by John Maynard Keynes (1963) and Stuart Chase (1934) whose ideas, along with those of others are described in the next chapter.

A consequence of the development of abundance over the past few decades has been the shift in emphasis from managing production to managing consumption. In modern manufacturing enterprises the numbers of employees directly engaged in production is remarkably small. The majority are employed in functions such as sales, marketing, public affairs, human resources, finance and accounting, and, more recently, in corporate social responsibility. As productivity has grown, jobs have not only shifted from production to other functions, but they have also shifted from the private sector to the public sector.

Henry Ford's great vision was that he saw mass production and its impact on productivity merely as a means to the end of mass consumption; hence the model T, designed so that every American family would be able to afford a motor car.

I hold that it is better to sell a large number of cars at a reasonably small profit … I hold this because it enables a larger number of people to buy and enjoy the use of a car and because it gives a larger number of men employment at good wages. Those are the two aims I have in life. (Ford, 1929)

Huge reductions in costs have been achieved despite the fact that the supply of most things involves massive expenditure on distribution. As well as wholesalers' and retailers' mark-ups there are the costs of building brand identity, advertising, marketing, packaging and promotion and the costs of physical movement of goods. For most goods today the costs of distribution far outweigh the costs of production.

Companies, either individually or acting in concert, engage in a variety of practices to create a degree of artificial scarcity with the aim of maintaining prices. These include restriction of production, (for example in diamond mining, agriculture, and oil extraction), branding, (particularly in relation to fashion goods), and patents, (most noticeably in software and pharmaceuticals) and planned obsolescence. Some things remain relatively expensive artificially because of taxes imposed by governments – Scotch whisky, for example. What companies are doing in the face of growing abundance will be discussed in Chapter 10.

The Future Development of Abundance

We are in the early stages of a new era that has the potential to be one of even greater abundance. Its growth is being driven by new technologies which are developing at an exponential rate. These technologies include the development of computing power and speed, biotechnology, nanotechnology and technologies as yet dimly perceived that are the result of convergence of the aforementioned. At some point in the second half of this century, molecular manufacturing may well have become a reality.

The coupling of molecular manufacturing with appropriate programming tools could ultimately bring about a revolution that is being termed 'personal manufacturing.' Personal nanofactories (PNs) already have been envisioned and are likely to be similar in look and ease of use to a printer or microwave oven. 3D printers, which can produce three-dimensional objects in colour, are already in use. They cost now about $20,000 dollars. If mass-produced they could sell for about £1,000 each.

Meanwhile, computing power – information management – continues to expand exponentially even as its cost drops precipitously. Today, an increasing range of 'intelligent' products contain greater and greater information content at lesser and lesser cost. These developments are discussed in Chapter 5.

The Post-Scarcity Paradox

POVERTY IN THE DEVELOPED COUNTRIES

The paradox is that in those countries which are foremost in creating post-scarcity conditions, millions still exist in poverty. These include those of working age who for one reason or another are unemployed, those who exist on minimum-wage levels, single parents and the elderly who depend on state benefits. The modern developed economy has the capacity to produce goods faster than it can generate incomes to consume them. This gap between the supply of goods and services and the ability to consume them is increasingly filled by consumer credit offered at high rates of interest, the long-term effect of which is to reduce consumers' incomes still further, while building up a mountain of debt. This is particularly the case with respect to the actions of companies that specialize in loans to the very poor. Such companies justify very high rates of interest on the grounds that the default rate is very high. This, of course, is a circular argument, in that the very high interest rates themselves lead to borrowers defaulting. It was reported in *The Times* (9 July 2009) that Barnardos, the UK children's charity, accused Provident Financial, one of the biggest home-credit providers in the UK and Ireland, of driving poor families into 'worrying levels of debt' and called for an inquiry into the company's lending practices. It said that Provident charged 'extortionate' annual percentage rates of up to 545 per cent to borrowers on low incomes.

Provident Financial made a profit of £53.1 million in the first half of 2009, up 3.5 per cent on the previous year. On its website it gives an example of a loan of £300, to be repaid by a weekly payment of £10.50 for 50 weeks, making a total of £525, with an APR of 254 per cent.

There is a growing gap in living standards between the poor and those on higher incomes which is dangerously socially divisive and will become more so. It is also economically inefficient in that it stifles the demand needed to sustain economic growth.

Some years ago an American car manufacturer introduced a new assembly line largely manned by robots. Showing a union leader around, the company's chairman said 'Do you know what I like about these robots? They will never ask for a pay rise and they will never go on strike.' 'Yes,' replied the union leader, 'but how many cars will they buy?'

This anecdote illustrates the point that in the modern advanced economy consumers have become more important than producers. The main engine of the growth is a high level of effective demand rather than a high level of supply.

WORLD POVERTY

The gap between rich and poor in the developed world is, of course, greatly magnified on the global scene.

The World Bank has warned that world poverty is much greater than previously thought. It has revised its previous estimate and now says that 1.4 billion people live in poverty, based on a new poverty line of $1.25 per day. This is substantially more than its earlier estimate of 985 million people living in poverty in 2004. ... The new estimates suggest that poverty is both more persistent, and has fallen less sharply, than previously thought. However, given the increase in world population, the poverty rate has still fallen from 50 per cent to 25 per cent over the past 25 years.

Poverty and some potential solutions are discussed in Chapters 8 and 9.

Resolving the Paradox

The growing wealth of nations will not resolve the paradox of poverty unless there are radical changes in the global economic system and in the social and political systems within countries.

THE REFORM OF THE ECONOMIC SYSTEM

In 2007 a group of business leaders from global companies such as BP, ABB, Ford, SUEZ, Infosys, Anglo-American, McKinsey and Alcan set out their views in forthright fashion. 'We believe that we are entering a period of history in which it is becoming clear that the operation of the current system is unsustainable and that to progress further tomorrow's global companies need to redefine success and help to create better frameworks for the working of the market' (Tomorrow's Company, 2007).

The report argued that the response should not be to turn our backs on the market economy – because the market has driven human progress and economic growth for centuries. Instead, we need to harness the power of the market and global businesses to be a force for good. The authors emphasized that global businesses have unique power to deliver practical solutions. For example, they can bring electricity, telephones and medicines to low-income communities. They can bring about advances in energy efficiency and low carbon power to address climate change. They can set high standards in working conditions.

This much we must believe as a starting point:

That the earth produces, or is capable of producing, enough to give decent sustenance to everyone – not of food alone, but of everything else we need. For everything is produced from the earth.

That it is possible for labour, production, distribution, and reward to be so organized as to make certain that those who contribute shall receive shares determined by an exact justice.

That regardless of the frailties of human nature, our economic system can be so adjusted that selfishness, although perhaps not abolished, can be robbed of power to work serious economic injustice.

Henry Ford (1929)

SOCIAL/POLITICAL REFORM

There is a clear need to develop a stable social/political framework within which the reduction of inequality can take place. This means tackling the causes of international conflict, civil war, civil disturbance, genocide and terrorism. By comparison the tasks of dealing with climate change or the collapse of the global financial system may pale into insignificance. There are clearly huge problems under this heading which greatly affect mankind's prospects for survival and in regard to which the growing powers of technology may be relatively impotent.

The prospects for system change are discussed in Chapter 13.

2

The Prophets of Abundance

Introduction

The system within which we currently carry on our economic activity, whether as individuals or as corporations, is a system based on assumptions of scarcity. Most people, including most economists, still believe that the primary function of the free market is to allocate scarce resources. Despite the fact that many eminent thinkers have challenged the validity of such assumptions, the economic system remains intact, albeit increasingly fragile, as does the dominant paradigm of scarcity.

By contrast, the basic proposition on which post-scarcity abundance is based is that, over time, more and more goods and services will become less and less scarce and in consequence be available to consumers at very low cost or will, indeed be free. It is perfectly understandable that this concept is a difficult one to come to terms with, but it is by no means a new idea –yet there remains a surprising lack of awareness of it. This chapter looks at how a number of forward-thinking and influential economists and others have considered the concept of abundance, and its implications for society.

Noticeably, they understood right from the beginning that it is important to consider the social as well as the economic implications of abundance. Most of those who have written about abundance take the view that a post-scarcity society would also be a utopian one. This is a very big assumption. Abundance is likely to bring as many problems as it solves; as Keynes (1963) said, 'man may solve its economic problem. Man's social problems will take a lot longer to resolve.'

However, setting aside any moral judgements and eschewing both a utopian vision and a dystopian nightmare, the point is that in large areas of the world a post-scarcity society is already in its early stages and mankind needs to adapt to it. The implications for business and for the major global companies in particular, are likely to be profound – in an environment in which a wide range of goods can no longer be profitably sold, new business models will be needed; as will fresh approaches to the creation of and satisfying of consumer demand in the poorer parts of the world.

The Early Pioneers

The rapid growth of productivity and the spread of mechanization and mass production in the early years of the twentieth century, particularly in the United States, led some visionary economists and thinkers to look far into the future and speculate about the longer-term consequences for society of sustained economic growth. Some of those who did look ahead, such as John Maynard Keynes (1963), Stuart Chase (1934) and Buckminster Fuller (1972) took a highly optimistic, positive attitude, emphasizing the benefits of growth, and envisaging a utopian future of abundance and equality, while others, such as J. K. Galbraith, (1969) Vance Packard (1960) and Robert Theobald (1961), stressed the more problematic aspects and the darker side of abundance, such as waste and materialistic values.

JOHN MAYNARD KEYNES

In 1931 Keynes published a book of essays, one of which was titled *Economic Possibilities for Our Grandchildren* (Keynes 1963). This was written in the context of the great depression, so it is not surprising that he began by commenting on the prevailing mood of pessimism regarding the economy.

> We are suffering just now from a bad attack of economic pessimism. It is common to hear people say that the epoch of enormous economic progress which characterized the nineteenth century is over; that the rapid improvement in the standard of life is now going to slow down – at any rate in Great Britain; that a decline in prosperity is more likely than an improvement in the decade that lies ahead of us.

> The prevailing world depression, the enormous anomaly of unemployment in a world full of wants, the disastrous mistakes we have made, blind us to what is going on under the surface – to the true interpretation of things.

The latter paragraph is as apposite today as it was then.

Keynes argued that the world was not suffering from 'the rheumatics of old age', but from the growing pains of over-rapid changes, from the painfulness of readjustment from one economic period to another.

He went on to say that his purpose in the essay was not to examine the present or the near future, but to ask the question: 'What can we reasonably expect the level of our economic life to be a hundred years hence? What are the economic possibilities for our grandchildren?'

Dismissing the depression as a temporary phase of maladjustment he made the dramatic assertion that 'in the long run man is solving his economic problem.' He predicted that the standard of life in 'progressive countries' in one hundred years' time would be between four and eight times as high as it was in 1930. The economic problem '*Is not the permanent problem of the human race*' (Keynes' italics).

Keynes prediction of the rate of growth appears to have been pretty accurate. By 1998, UK GDP per capita was approximately four times higher than in 1930. Between 1930 and 1998 GDP per capita grew five and a half times in the USA and Germany, six times in France and fourteen times in Japan.

The needs of human beings, he went on to argue, fall into two classes. There are needs that are absolute, in the sense that we feel them whatever the situation of our fellow human beings may be. There are also needs that are relative, in that we feel them only if their satisfaction lifts us above or makes us feel superior to our neighbours. These latter needs, he stated, might well be insatiable, but this was not so in the case of the former. 'A point may soon be reached, much sooner perhaps than we are all of us aware of, when these needs are satisfied in the sense that we prefer to devote our further energies to non-economic purposes.' (He clearly did not anticipate the rise in obesity that would follow the solving of the economic problem in a number of countries as far as food is concerned.)

Keynes, having reached this conclusion, then asks the question – will this state of affairs be of benefit? Man has struggled throughout history for subsistence; this struggle has been his primary purpose. If the economic problem is solved, how will man occupy his time? Keynes thought with dread of the problem of readjustment of the instincts and habits of ordinary people, bred into them over countless generations.

He went on to speculate about some of the social consequences that might follow such an increase in abundance. He expressed the hope that people would be free to return to some of the most sure and certain moral principles, regarding avarice as a vice, usury as a misdemeanour and the love of money as detestable.

Finally, he pointed out that this would all happen gradually; that there would be ever larger groups and classes of people from whom the problems of economic necessity have been practically removed. The pace of change would, in his view, be affected by four things:

1. the ability to control population growth

2. the ability to avoid wars

3. willingness to entrust to science the direction of those matters which are properly the concern of science

4. the rate of capital accumulation as determined by the margin between production and consumption.

STUART CHASE

Stuart Chase (1888–1985) was an American economist and engineer. His life and work won him international acclaim as a critic of unethical corporate practices, an innovator in consumer protection, a promoter of altruistic economic policies, an advocate of adult learning and mass public education, and an activist for responsive government and ecological stewardship. He advised presidents and interpreted contemporary issues for ordinary men and women in 35 books and hundreds of pamphlets and articles, seeking to help people improve their lives.

He attended MIT briefly and then Harvard, graduating cum laude in 1910. After several years as an accountant in his father's firm he joined the Federal Trade Commission. There he worked to hold corporations to his own high standards. When his study of the meatpacking industry revealed corporate accounting irregularities, congressional Republicans (including then senator and future president Warren G. Harding) successfully pressured the commission to fire him in 1920.

He subsequently began collaboration with the economic philosopher Thorstein Veblen to bring greater efficiency and enhanced managerial and fiscal integrity to government and industry. His growing influence attracted the attention of Franklin D. Roosevelt (FDR), then governor of New York. The men first met in 1931, shortly before the publication of Chase's book *A New Deal*. Franklin D. Roosevelt made use of its economic arguments and made a 'New Deal' the focal point of his 1932 speech accepting the Democratic presidential nomination. Chase later served in FDR's 'kitchen cabinet'; in 1937, the president told Chase's father that his son was teaching the American people more about economics than all the others combined.

Writing in 1934 (Chase, 1934), he defined the 'economy of abundance' as 'an economic condition where an abundance of material goods can be produced for the entire population of a given community'. However, he went on to point out that the smooth operation of such an economy is seriously disturbed when 'we set technological abundance into a background of prevailing financial habits. These habits were laid down in an 'economy of scarcity', and clash bitterly with the facts of plenty.'

He went on to give a more extended definition of abundance, as follows.

- A condition where the bulk of economic work is performed, not by people, but by inanimate energy.

- A point at which living standards per head reach an average at least twice as high as that which existed under scarcity conditions.

- A point at which the curve of invention, increasing geometrically, becomes the dominant factor in economic life.

- A point at which much of the industrial plant has been constructed, requiring relatively smaller outlays for capital goods in the future.

- A point at which the scientific method supersedes the work of craftsmen in producing material goods.

- A point at which specialization has destroyed local self-sufficiency.

- A point at which output per man hour becomes so great that the total of productive labour must thereafter decline, while output continues to grow.

- A point at which labour productivity ceases to be a useful measure of output.

- A point at which over-production becomes a more serious threat to the financial system than shortages.

- A point at which consumption becomes a greater problem than production. Here Chase quotes F.L. Ackerman: 'Our economy is so set up that it creates goods at a higher rate than it produces income with which to purchase them.'

- A point at which, due to technological progress, costs, prices, interest rates, debts, begin a descent with descent to zero as their objective.

Chase was somewhat premature in his opinion that these conditions were largely fulfilled in the United States by 1920. Yet today, some 90 years later, the concept of the economics of abundance still lies outside the frames of reference of the world's leading policy makers and their economic advisers.

Taken together, Chase's points sum up the characteristics of a society in the process of moving to a post-scarcity condition. The final three points are amazingly insightful, considering when they were written.

In order to solve the problem that the economy was producing goods at a faster rate than it was creating incomes with which to purchase them, businesses invented mortgages, hire-purchase schemes and the credit card. Using credit in one form or another, people could consume more goods and services than their incomes would allow. In this way, at least for a time, the problem appeared to be solved. However, as governments used interest rates as a means of controlling inflation, at times interest rates were very high, making it difficult for people to service their indebtedness, and debt mountains began to build up.

Chase quoted a number of eminent US authorities in support of his view that the dream of unlimited wealth for all could be achieved. However, he was cautious in extrapolating such projections beyond the borders of the USA.

The energy, materials and technical training required effectively to raise the living standards of the population … of China and India, present a problem which staggers me … To give Chinese and Indians, for instance, as many automobiles per capita as Americans now drive would mean 140 million cars. At only 5000 miles per year and twenty miles per gallon of gasoline this fleet would demand thirty-five billion gallons of gasoline, which alone would take far more than the whole world production of petroleum in recent years.

Chase's analysis of what he calls 'The march to zero' is extraordinarily visionary, particularly given the depression era in which he was writing and predates the ideas of Chris Anderson (discussed later in this chapter) by some 80 odd years.

He quotes statistics showing that at that time over 80 per cent of industries in the USA were characterized with diminishing costs. 'In any five- and ten-cent store you will find scores of articles which used to cost dollars; articles that our ancestors prized and carefully saved. We fling them about carelessly, valuing them little more than air or water.'

He points out that in the struggle to avoid being put out of business by falling prices and falling margins the practice had grown of deliberately trying to create scarcity – for example, by creating a monopoly, *de facto* if not *de jure*, by the deliberate destruction of goods, dumping of goods in foreign markets at lower prices, building in obsolescence, protective tariffs, suppressing invention and adding distribution costs with such things as advertising, branding and packaging. Each of these strategies and their struggle to remain effective will be discussed in Chapter 10.

J.K. GALBRAITH

Born on a farm in Ontario, Canada, J.K. Galbraith graduated from an agricultural college in the depths of the Depression in the 1930s. He went to the United States for graduate study and remained there to teach at the University of California-Berkley, at Princeton, and, most notably, at Harvard, retiring in 1973. He was one of the most influential economists of the twentieth century. His more than 40 books bridge the gap between academic economic theorists and the common reader. He is credited with having coined key phrases now in common parlance, most notably 'conventional wisdom'. Galbraith was a liberal who, in addition to writing and teaching, played an active role in American politics. He held various government posts and worked as a speech writer for United States Presidents Franklin D. Roosevelt, John F. Kennedy and Lyndon B. Johnson.

In *The Affluent Society* (1969) he argued that the problem that has traditionally been of primary concern to economists, how to increase production, was no longer the most important problem in industrially advanced countries like the USA. He maintained that the problem of production had been so well solved that all citizens could have enough to satisfy their needs if output were distributed more equally. Furthermore, he said, a lot of what we produced was intentional waste, such as oversized cars. He noted that most of the American population ate too much, not too little.

He argued that economic theory is based primarily on societies characterized by poverty and was, therefore, inadequate to addressing the economic condition of the United States in the twentieth century. He asserted that 'conventional wisdom' is based primarily on tradition and does not accommodate changes in society and so must be viewed with scepticism. He pointed out that the early economic theorists of the previous centuries (Smith, Ricardo and Malthus) based their theories in a world economy characterized by poverty. He then gave an overview of major currents in economic theory since the mid nineteenth century, including what he called 'the central tradition'' of economic theory – which was that financial crises, such as the depression, are a normal occurrence of economic cycles.

Galbraith traced the major themes of American economic thought in the twentieth century, particularly the influence of Social Darwinism and Marxism, and argued that the issue of inequality in the distribution of wealth had become less and less of a concern. Focus had moved instead to the benefits of increased production at all levels of society. He pointed out that since the 1930s economic security, both for the business owner and the worker, had steadily increased, alongside overall production. With the decrease in concern for economic inequality and the relative elimination of extremes of economic insecurity, he argued, production had become the foremost concern in economic thought, and the essential measure of economic vitality. However, he argued that this concern with production was irrational and inappropriate to the realities of the economy.

He also pointed out that the conventional economic thinking deemed private sector production to be good for the economy while social services provided by the government were considered bad for the economy. He argued that an affluent society is dependent, for the public good, on state expenditures in the areas of the police force, education, public sanitation, public transportation, roads, and the regulation of safety standards for air and water. Public education, he asserted, is an area of government expenditure that is ultimately an investment in private-sector industry. In an age of technology, citizens with a higher education in the areas of science and engineering are necessary to the advance of industry. However, the conventional wisdom, Galbraith observed, did not consider public education to be a valuable investment in economic prosperity.

He observed that with the steady increase in wages in the United States, luxury items had come to be considered consumer 'needs', equivalent to the need for food and shelter in less affluent societies. He asserted that it is inaccurate to claim that the production of these luxury items is determined by the 'needs' of the consumer; rather, it is the extensive advertising efforts that accompany production, which create the 'need' in the consumer. Contemporary economic theory, in his view, failed to take this factor, which he calls the 'dependence effect,' into account.

He conceded that although in recent times the focus on production as a measure of economic vitality has given way to a broader range of concerns it remained, in the conventional wisdom, the be-all and end-all of national prosperity. He went on to describe the steady increase in consumer debt from the 1920s to the time of writing, warning that massive consumer debt which was encouraged in the United States as a corollary to high rates of production and consumption was potentially hazardous to the economy.

VANCE PACKARD

Vance Packard was born to a farming family. He was educated at Pennsylvania State College, gaining a degree in English in 1936.

In 1937 he obtained his masters degree at Columbia University and joined the reporting staff of the *Boston Daily Record*. After a number of other jobs he moved to the magazine *Colliers*, where he worked as a writer. When *Colliers* closed in 1956 he began to devote his life to writing. In 1957 his best-selling book *The Hidden Persuaders* was published and established his reputation. The book that is most relevant to the issues being discussed here is *The Waste Makers* published in 1960.

Both he and Galbraith were writing at a time when GDP per capita was significantly higher in the USA than in Europe or Japan. In consequence, growing abundance and its future implications were more evident.

Packard opened his argument with the bold statement that marketing experts were 'grappling with a problem that would frighten the wits out of less resolute people. That problem is the spectre of glut for the products they are already endeavouring to sell.'

Whereas throughout recorded history man had struggled to cope with material scarcity, the great challenge now 'is to cope with a threatened overabundance of the staples and amenities and frills of life'. The United States was finding that 'the challenge of coping with its fabulous productivity is becoming a major national problem and is inspiring some ingenious responses and some disquieting changes'.

America, he wrote, had become a 'hyperthyroid society' that could only be sustained by constant stimulation of the people and their leaders to be more prodigal with the nation's resources.

Packard pointed out that large numbers of citizens had a direct stake in maintaining the momentum of growth in production and consumption – small business owners, employees anxious to hold onto their jobs, small investors and so on.

He was one of the earliest commentators to take account of the impact of growth on natural resources. He warned of 'the dangerous decline in the USA of its supply of natural resources'.

Nor was he unaware of the problem of global imbalance. 'United States industrial firms are grinding up more than half of the natural resources processed each year on this planet for the benefit of six per cent of the planet's people.'

He was also acutely aware of the paradox that, alongside this profusion of material wealth, millions of families remained unquestionably ill-fed, ill-clothed and ill-housed. 'And the television set may be substituting for adequate food in the family budget.'

Packard's work is associated mainly with domestic consumption and private sector productivity growth. However, he also pointed to conspicuous waste in the public arena, particularly in defence spending. 'The landscape of the globe is becoming strewn with armaments and other *materiel* abandoned by employees of the United States government.'

He went on to describe the various strategies being adopted by the marketing experts to stimulate demand. These included:

- Encouraging a throw-away culture – from razors to watches, things were to be used a few times, then disposed of. Food scraps were to be thrown away instead of using them to feed the pet dog.

- Functional obsolescence – the new product on the market could do a better job.

- Built in obsolescence – the product is designed to break down after a certain period. (As was once alleged in the case of the tendency of some makes of motor car to rust after a year or two.)

- Obsolescence of desirability – persuading customers that a given product was now out of fashion.

- Encouraging people to own more than one of a given product – a second car, a second home. The latter carried the advantage that it meant a second stove, a second freezer and so on.

- Encouraging people to buy on credit. Second mortgages, hire purchase agreements, credit cards, store charge cards were proliferating at the time he was writing.

- Simply encouraging hedonism – an approach reflected today in television advertising for expensive cosmetics branded by L'Oreal, using the slogan 'Because you're worth it!'

ROBERT THEOBALD

An Englishman who moved to the United States in the late 1950s, Robert Theobald was an economist, lecturer, teacher, and author of more than 20 books, including *The Rapids of Change, Turning the Century*, and *Reworking Success*. In

The Challenge of Abundance (1961) Theobald pointed out that the old rules were breaking down 'Our economic system has depended upon the assumption of scarcity … We can now look forward to the day – whether it be twenty, fifty, or a hundred years off – when these conditions will no longer exist.'

He argued that the stage of abundance is reached when the increase in the production of material goods raises new problems even while meeting the traditional goal of a higher material standard of living. In his view the development of a high-production, high-consumption economy makes it necessary to re-examine certain basic theories by which we have lived in the past. 'In an economy of abundance, economic growth would not need to be given top priority; science could be used in such a way that it could increase rather than decrease the validity of human life. Similarly we would need to re-examine the belief that the "invisible hand" of economic forces will automatically lead to a coincidence between private and social goals.'

In response to the argument that the present system should not be changed because of its success in the past, he asserts that it is the very success of the system that has made change necessary. Although the developed countries are committed to growth, Theobald points out that it has not been well understood that if economic growth is to be achieved, then continuous change must be accepted as its inevitable concomitant. Economic theory has consistently understated the unpleasant side of growth and has tended to write off the hardships that are the necessary outcome of economic progress. At the same time economic theory has itself a failed to adjust to changed conditions. While it is the case that Keynesian theory of the causes of slumps and the development of unemployment has come to be accepted as valid, this has not led to the abandonment of neo-classical theory, since neo-classical economics has absorbed Keynsian ideas. 'Unfortunately the resulting synthesis must necessarily be unsatisfactory, for the two theories are incompatible.' One reason for the survival of neo-classicism, according to Theobald, is the formal beauty of the neo-classical model. Also, the formal assumptions of the model free the economist from having to take account of the erratic nature of human behaviour or the multiplicity of human motives. Another is the fact that it is based on and supports an ideology that is deeply embedded in Western philosophy, that of the importance of the individual.

Theobald's ideas were extremely radical for his time. For example, he challenged the conventional wisdom that government debt created during a recession by running a budget deficit should be paid back during boom conditions. He also anticipated quantitative easing. 'It seems possible that, with progress towards an abundant society, private demand may become insufficient to absorb the potential supply and that government should create funds to fill the gap.'

He was well in advance of his peers in recognizing that, whereas in the past when there was a shortage of goods the main factor controlling growth was the amount of saving and investment, in conditions of abundance it is the effective demand for goods that is the main factor. 'America has both the productive capacity and the unemployed labour that would allow it to produce additional goods. It is the lack of demand for these goods that prevents the economy from expanding.'

Although Theobald envisaged the continuation of economic growth that has in fact occurred since the 1960s, he had reservations about the desirability of making the rapid expansion of material wealth the major goal of society. He referred to increasing doubt that this policy would augment happiness and also expressed the fear that it would disrupt society.

BUCKMINSTER FULLER

Fuller was descended from a long line of New England nonconformists, the most famous of whom was his great-aunt, Margaret Fuller, the critic, teacher, woman of letters and cofounder of *The Dial*, organ of the Transcendentalist movement. He was twice expelled from Harvard University and never completed his formal education. He saw service in the US Navy during the First World War as commander of a crash-boat flotilla.

A construction company in which he was a partner encountered financial difficulties in 1927, and Fuller was forced out, with the consequence that he found himself stranded in Chicago, without any source of income. At this point in his life, Fuller resolved to devote his remaining years to a non-profit search for design patterns that could maximize the social uses of the world's energy resources and its evolving industrial complex. The inventions, discoveries, and economic strategies that followed and for which he became famous were all intended to contribute to that end.

He is best known for designing the geodesic dome, a frame the total strength of which increases in logarithmic ratio to its size. Many thousands of geodesic domes have been erected in various parts of the world, the most publicized of which was the United States exhibition dome at Expo 67 in Montreal.

Fuller did not regard himself as primarily an inventor or an architect. All of his innovations, in his view, were accidental or interim incidents in a strategy that aimed at a radical solution of world problems by finding the means to do more with less. The work which is most relevant in this context is *Utopia or Oblivion* (1969).

He held that comprehensive and anticipatory design initiative alone – rather than the actions of politicians or political theories – could solve the problems of human shelter, nutrition, transportation, and pollution; and could do so with a fraction of the materials now inefficiently used. Moreover, he believed that energy, ever more available, directed by cumulative information stored in computers, would be capable of synthesizing raw materials, of machining and packaging commodities, and of supplying the physical needs of the total global population.

He was a sharp critic of conventional economics which, he said, 'Starts with Malthus' assumption that there is and always will be only enough of the essentials of life to support a minority of mankind.'

He understood that the solution to the problem of scarcity would need to be a global solution. 'It is now scientifically clear that we have the ability to make all of humanity physically successful. But it can be done only on the basis of making all of humanity successful. We cannot remain just half successful or with just a minority successful.'

Although he did not use the term 'post-scarcity' Fuller had a clear vision of what a post-scarcity world would be like. 'What we will do … is to invest escalatingly in the successful potential of all human beings. We will start that investing by sending almost everybody back to school … For the first time in the history of man we are going to ask "What would you like to do? In what direction do you have some spontaneous urge to develop or to make a social contribution?"'

He saw in California of the 1960s a kind of embryonic version of the abundant society of the future. 'In California I find a powerful latent awareness of the significance of this great moment of human transition. I find in this community a spontaneous desire to cease backing up into our future and enthusiasm for a general forward facing of society.'

THE LIMITS OF THEIR VISION

All the previously mentioned writers had great vision but, not surprisingly, none of them had the foresight to predict the emergence of the digital or e-economy. The arrival of the web and its various linked technologies have enabled completely different business models, driven by low production costs and low, or free, pricing structures and have greatly accelerated the advance to the post-scarcity society.

Two Contemporary Commentators

Recently Brink Lindsey (2007) has celebrated the role of the market economy in bringing about abundance in the USA, a condition which he sees as wholly beneficial, while Chris Anderson, (2009) editor-in-chief of *Wired* magazine has attracted widespread attention as the author of *Free: The Future of a Radical Price*, in which he analyses why so many things are now either free to the consumer or are offered at very low prices.

BRINK LINDSEY

The vice-president of the libertarian Cato Institute, Brink Lindsey is a right-wing free-market advocate whose economic ideals and personal values influence his understanding of American history. His *The Age of Abundance* (2007) is a celebration of the shift from scarcity to abundance. The founding premise for Lindsey's exuberant interpretation of American history is that abundance is the prerequisite for freedom. 'Liberation from material necessity marks a fundamental change in the human condition.' He aims to show how the unprecedented prosperity that the United States has enjoyed since the 1940s has allowed Americans to become the first people in history to find out what freedom really is.

In a swift summary of twentieth-century American cultural and social progress Lindsey tells how American culture moved from a 'scarcity-based mentality of self-restraint' to an 'abundance-based mentality of self-expression.' That move, in turn, he argues has enabled Americans to uncover, explore and exploit entirely new dimensions of freedom.

Capitalism, by generating abundance, Lindsey argues, has made it possible for Americans to climb Abraham Maslow's motivational pyramid, a 'hierarchy of needs' that begins with basic physiological requirements (food, sleep, air), passes through safety (security of body, family, property) and belonging (love, family, intimacy), rises to emotional needs based on esteem (self-respect, respect for others, the respect of others), and culminates in self-actualization (personal growth based on morality, creativity, awareness, trust, fairness, love and individualistic expression). In other words, as health improved and lives grew longer, as disposable income increased and daily life came to involve more choice, Americans began to be able to devote themselves to the pursuit of happiness that was so central to the Founding Fathers' conception of independence.

In Lindsey's terms, mass affluence triggered a 'mirror-image pair of cultural convulsions' in which movements we now associate with the left and the right were born. The left, Lindsey notes, embraced the personal freedoms created by wealth, but rejected the engine of wealth itself, capitalism. The result was its romantic preoccupation with collectivism and its emphasis on tolerance, rights and free expression. By contrast, Lindsey observes, the right embraced capitalism but rejected the manner in which a thriving market inevitably opens up new choices and broadens the range of acceptable behaviour. Each movement was, and is, urgently felt and relentlessly advanced, Lindsey notes, but each is ultimately misguided in its failure to comprehend that mass affluence involves both a free market and a free society. As such, they offer conflicting half-truths about what America is and ought to be.

After the First World War in America, Lindsey argues, material well-being finally made people free enough to find their own idiosyncratic paths to contentment. He is dismissive of the paradox of poverty amidst such abundance. 'There has been no mass immiseration of the poor and working classes.' While accepting that growth in wages and household income slowed and even reversed in the middling and lower levels of the income distribution, he argues that income measures do a poor job of capturing changes in what can be bought for a given amount of money. 'It is beyond serious argument that most Americans have made significant gains in material welfare over their counterparts a generation ago.' He also states that the statistics would look rosier if the great wave of Hispanic immigration had somehow been prevented. 'Yet most of the poor immigrants who came here from Mexico and Central America surely bettered their lot in doing so.'

CHRIS ANDERSON

Anderson, editor of *Wired* magazine, first came to the attention of a wider public with his book *The Long Tail: Why the Future of Business is Selling More of Less* (2006), in which he argued that consumption patterns were being fundamentally altered by the abundant, low-cost shelf-space provided by digital technology. As a result, thousands of niche products would become economical to stock and the revenue from these would be as significant as the revenue from the 'hits'.

In 2009 he followed that up with *Free: The Future of a Radical Price*, setting out the case for giving away products to consumers rather than charging for them. He describes the main features of the 'free economy'. It includes:

- Radio and television advertising which, in the USA, amounted to $45bn in 2006, together with online advertising-supported media, which Anderson estimated at $21bn to $25bn annually, totalling to some $80bn.

- The value of 'freemium' internet and software products (estimated to be about $1bn), and open-source software and consulting services at $30bn. (Freemium is where a company allows people to use their products free of charge, but makes a charge for a premium version.)

Anderson also argues that the free total should include the 'gift economy', including the songs on iPods downloaded illegally or between peers.

Extrapolating from the US figures, he concludes that the global figure (not including non-monetary benefits) for the free economy is about $300bn.

He makes the strong assertion that 'The new form of Free is not a gimmick, a trick to shift money from one pocket to another [like razors and blades]. Instead, it's driven by an extraordinary new ability to lower the costs of goods and services close to zero. While the last century's Free was a powerful marketing method, this century's Free is an entirely new economic model.'

As companies compete vigorously, prices fall to just above the marginal cost of production. Since the marginal cost of making a piece of software is zero, and the cost of digital distribution is zero, prices ought to fall to zero.

He weakens his argument by over-emphasizing 'free', since the most important issue is not that some things such as newspapers or videos on the internet are free to the end-user, but the underlying one that greatly reduced marginal costs make it possible for an ever wider range of goods and services to be provided at prices ever closer to zero.

Anderson argues that now a feast of internet material has been made available without fee, companies must find ways to adapt to the new reality. 'The way to compete with Free is to move past the abundance to find the adjacent scarcity,' he writes. And *Free* is full of specific examples of how to do just that.

Anderson eventually acknowledges that, despite the radical message sent by the title of his book, he doesn't envision an economy based entirely on zero pricing. 'Free may be the best price, but it can't be the only one,' he says. He advocates the balancing of differently priced versions of a product for different markets, acknowledging that this balance is not easily achieved. He also recognizes that when making buying decisions, consumers think not only about money but also about intangibles like convenience, access, quality and time.

Some of the implications of Anderson's ideas will be discussed in Chapter 4.

3

A Short History of System Change

Previous Big Shifts

Over thousands of years the social and economic structure of human society has developed through a number of stages, each of which is characterized by its predominant technologies, its primary economic activity and its form of social organization and governance.

THE HUNTING/GATHERING SOCIETY

In the first phase, the typical human community was a tribal grouping based on kinship and depending upon hunting and gathering for subsistence. Such communities were usually nomadic, continually moving to find fresh hunting grounds. Sometimes they followed their food supply in the form of migrating herds, as the Lapps do today, following herds of reindeer. Tools were limited to primitive axes and spears.

THE AGRARIAN SOCIETY

Gradually, however, and beginning about 12,000 years ago in the fertile lands of the Middle East, this type of society gave way to settled communities or villages where the growing of crops and the husbandry of livestock marked the beginning of what we now regard as civilization. The agricultural way of life provided a more secure livelihood, even to the extent of enabling surpluses to be accumulated. In the centuries that followed, inventions multiplied – the needle, the spade, the sickle, the nail and the screw, the bellows, the loom and of course, the wheel and the plough. The process of making a hard metal, bronze, from copper and tin, was discovered about 3800 BC; iron was being smelted by about 1500 BC, and steel was being made in India by about 1000 BC.

The domestication of animals, which began with the dog, progressed through sheep, goats and cattle, reaching its zenith with the horse about 5,000 years ago.

The growing productivity resulting from technological progress led to the freeing up of peoples' hands and minds from the daily task of securing the food supply, enabling the development of the institutions of governance, the construction of great cities, the emergence of scientific thought, art and literature – all the elements of culture.

The earliest civilizations were established by the late fourth and the third millennia BC in parts of Asia and north Africa. The three large alluvial systems of the Tigris–Euphrates, the Nile and the Indus supported three great ancient civilizations. These communities formed part of a unified economic system, in which markets and trade, communications, currency and a range of services were all present.

These early civilizations were followed by those of Greece (where a form of democratic governance emerged) and Rome in Europe, and the great civilizations of Central and South America. Power and wealth accrued mainly to the landowners and particularly to those who could draw upon a cheap labour supply of slaves or serfs.

Agriculture remained by far the main basis of economic activity, employment and social life in most countries well into the twentieth century.

THE INDUSTRIALIZED SOCIETY

The growing prosperity that followed agricultural improvements led to population growth and there began to be fears that yet further population growth would in the end negate the growth in productivity. Malthus's essay *The Principles of Population*, first published in 1798, expressed these anxieties. However, it was at this same point in time, starting in Britain, that a new form of society began to emerge – the industrial society, one that was eventually to draw millions of people from the countryside into newly developing towns and cities and which would depend primarily on manufacturing and the factory system for both wealth creation and employment. The population of Manchester in 1801 was some 75,000. By 1851 it was over 300,000.

The enormous scope for productivity improvement that industrialization would bring about was foreseen by Adam Smith. Both the science of economics and the theoretical basis of free market capitalism were invented by him in the *Wealth of Nations*, published in 1776. The most quoted sentence in his great work, and the one which most pithily sums up the spirit of the market is 'By pursuing his own self interest he frequently promotes that of society more effectually than when he really intends to promote it. I have never known much good done by those who affected to trade for the public good.'

Smith foresaw that productivity gains would stem from three factors under the factory system:

- The division of labour and the consequent dexterity of highly specialized workpeople.

- Not wasting time in moving from one task to another as in agriculture, coupled with the benefits of working in a confined space.

- New machinery and tools.

Countless volumes of economic and social history have been devoted to seeking the answers to three questions. What were the causes of the industrial revolution? Why did it begin to emerge in the late eighteenth century, and why in England? The answers are largely to do with the way in which earlier social and political reform in Britain had created an educated middle class, members of which joined scientific and learned societies and engaged in innovation and its practical application to their affairs. People like Coke and Tull in agriculture and Newcomen, Watt and the Stephensons in industry set in train a process which was to transform productivity and generate a rate of economic growth which would ultimately invalidate Malthus's thesis. In the early part of the eighteenth century Britain was unmistakeably an agrarian society. By the middle of the nineteenth century, and following the Representation of the People Act of 1832, it was clear that an economic and social revolution had taken place. Great Britain was without doubt the leading the way in both technology and governance.

The Great Exhibition of 1851 in London was conceived to symbolize and celebrate the industrial, military and economic superiority of the country. Just representing the feats of Britain itself would have excluded many of the technological achievements pioneered by the British in its many colonies and protectorates, so it was decided to make the exhibit truly international with invitations being extended to almost the entire colonized world. The British also felt that it was important to show their achievements right alongside those of what they regarded as 'less civilized' countries.

The Great Exhibition was held in Hyde Park in London in the specially constructed Crystal Palace. This magnificent building was designed by Sir Joseph Paxton in only 10 days and was a huge iron and glass structure with over a million feet of glass. It was important that the building used to showcase the country's achievements be grandiose and innovative. Over 13,000 exhibits were displayed and viewed by over 6,200,000 visitors. They marvelled at the products of the industrial revolution that was propelling Britain into becoming the greatest power of the age. Among the exhibits from all around the world were the Jacquard loom, an envelope machine, tools, kitchen appliances, steel-making displays and a reaping machine from the United States. The objects on display came from India and the countries with recent white settlements, such as Australia and New Zealand, which constituted the new empire. Many of the visitors who flocked to London came from European cities.

Power and wealth were now shifting to the capitalist class, people like Robert Owen and Titus Salt who successfully entered the world of manufacturing and who within a generation or two would rival the traditional landed aristocracy. The latter remained wealthy and politically powerful, however, particularly if the land they owned concealed rich deposits of coal, tin or other raw materials waiting to fuel the growth in output of manufactures.

One such was Francis Egerton, the third and last Duke of Bridgewater, who was born on 3 May 1736. After a failed attempt at marriage he busied himself in the running of his vast estates. He owned copious reserves of coal in the North of England and had a ready market for that coal in Manchester and Salford, where the demand for fuel was even by the late eighteenth century becoming insatiable, but the cost of transport from one to the other was prohibitive. The Duke's land agent, John Gilbert, proposed building a canal straight into the mines, simultaneously solving the problem of draining the mine shafts and providing a consistent supply of water for the canal. The Duke's engineer, James Brindley, helped to turn what might have been a useful but limited idea into a nationwide canal network. The result was the largest private fortune of the age.

In the period before the Second World War the industrialized society was well-developed in Britain, the USA, Germany and, to a lesser extent, Japan and by most economists and policy makers was assumed to be the ultimate stage of economic and social development. It was just a question of perfecting it by means of incremental changes in productivity and quality.

The theoretical backing at this stage of development was supplied by neo-classical economics, a school of thought in economics in the twentieth century, enormously influential, especially in the United States, for which the allocation of resources is the major focus of attention. (The term neo-classical simply means that the body of theory differs in important ways from the 'classical' economics of the previous century.)

Neo-classical economists share some of the following points:

- Economics is the study of the allocation of scarce resources. In this school of thought, economics is defined as 'the study of how people and society choose to employ scarce resources that could have alternative uses in order to produce various commodities and to distribute them for consumption' (Samuelson and Nordhaus, 1985).

- Neo-classical economists believe that free markets usually bring about an efficient allocation of scarce resources.

- In those more or less rare cases when markets fail to bring about an efficient allocation of resources, it is appropriate for the government to intervene to correct the situation.

Neo-classical economists have not as a rule based their assumptions on psychological views of the human motivation. Rather, most economists have begun from an assumption few modern psychologists would endorse, the assumption that human beings are highly rational and self-interested.

Strictly speaking, neo-classical economics does not assume that real human beings are rational and self-interested. Rather, most economists assume that economic systems work *as if* they consisted of rational, self-interested persons. After all, it is averages that count for these purposes. People have all sorts of motives and differ in their capacity for rational decision-making, but if the average is a person who is rational and self-interested, then the system will function *as if* people in general were rational and self-interested. It is assumed that resources of all kinds are scarce and that there are not enough resources to produce all of the goods and services that people might like to have. This leaves some basic questions to be answered – what resources will be used to produce which goods and services? In a planned economy, resources are allocated by the state; in a capitalist economy resources are partly allocated by the state, but for the most part are allocated by market forces. Resources are defined as land, natural resources, labour and capital.

THE POST-INDUSTRIAL SOCIETY

In the immediate post-Second World War years Britain and the United States were mature industrial societies. Employment was dominated by the steel and chemical industries, engineering, vehicles and coal mining. Manufacturing industry was the main component in gross domestic product (GDP). By the late 1960s and early 1970s, however, a number of visionary thought-leaders, and in particular Peter Drucker, (1969), Daniel Bell (1972) and Alvin Toffler (1980) drew attention to some 'weak signals' or early warning signs of trends which, they argued, would result in radical economic and social change in the developed nations.

Drucker pointed out that the economic growth that had taken place in the years following the Second World War had been carried largely by industries that were already big business before the First World War, and had been based for the most part on technologies developed by the Victorians. Also, no new country had joined the 'club' of major industrial powers other than the 'satellite' economies of Canada and Australia.

The most important change, which in Drucker's view was about to disrupt this continuity, was the emergence of knowledge as the key factor in economic growth. 'Knowledge, during the last few decades, has become the central capital, the cost center, and the crucial resource of the economy.' He pointed to early indications of massive changes – changes which did indeed take place in the last three decades of the twentieth century.

- The *relative* decline of the great 'smokestack' manufacturing industries such as steel, textiles, automobiles, chemicals and the 'metal bashing industries' coupled with the corresponding growth of the service industries, particularly professional and financial services, both in terms of share of employment and percentage of gross domestic product. (The word *relative* is particularly important here. According to an article in *The Times* by Philip Whyte (13 March 2009), 40 years after Drucker was writing, Britain was producing more manufactured goods than it had been doing in 1950 when the economy was dominated by manufacturing. Until the global collapse in output triggered by the financial crisis in late 2008, manufacturing output in the UK was higher than it had ever been. In 2007 it was two and a half times higher in real terms than it was in 1950. And despite the surge in imports from China, production was 7.1 per cent higher in 2007 than it was in 1995. The reason for the relative decline was, of course, the fact that the output of the service sector was growing much faster than that of the manufacturing sector.)

- The growing proportion of women in the active workforce. This trend was partly a function of the growth of service-sector jobs which offer more employment opportunities to women compared with the physically exacting work of mining, steel-making or shipbuilding. It also reflected social change, as more and more women sought escape from the kitchen sink, both to enjoy a more fulfilled life and to enjoy the goods and services that the economy was now producing in huge, affordable quantities.

- The increase in the proportion of the workforce who could be described as 'knowledge workers' creating a new category of employees (sometimes referred to as gold-collar workers) alongside traditional white-collar and blue-collar workers. This trend was linked to some extent to the growth of London, Tokyo and New York as global centres for the rapidly growing financial services industries and also to the growing range of skills required as computers and the related software programs grew in economic significance.

- The way in which information technology was already beginning to transform communications and information processing in virtually every aspect of peoples' working lives and leisure time.

- The increasing globalization of markets, both in terms of goods and of capital flows, and the emergence of the truly multinational corporation.

Bell predicted a vastly different society developing – one that would rely on the economics of information rather than the economics of goods. Bell argued that the new society would not displace the older one but rather co-exist with some of the previous layers. He prophetically stated that we should expect 'new premises and new powers, new constraints and new questions – with the difference that these are now on a scale that had never been previously imagined in world history'.

Toffler (1980), who described this shift in the system as the 'third wave' of change, pointed out that whereas the agricultural phase of society took thousands of years to play out, the development of the industrialized society took a mere 300 years to reach its zenith. He predicted that the Third Wave would 'sweep across history and complete itself within a few decades.'

Bell and his peers were able to see the way in which the industrial society would give way to a post-industrial era at a time when most politicians, economists and industrialists were firmly of the belief that strengthening the manufacturing sector and defending the status quo was the essential key to future prosperity.

One strong advocate of resisting the decline in manufacturing was the flamboyant chairman of Britain's ICI plc, John Harvey Jones. In his 1986 Dimbleby Lecture for the BBC, he famously remarked: 'If we imagine the UK can get by with a bunch of people in smocks showing tourists around medieval castles, we are quite frankly out of our tiny minds.' He could not envisage a world in which a wider and wider range of service industries would become the major engines of the nation's wealth creation. He questioned whether the City could ever provide enough extra overseas earnings to replace more than a modest part of the huge slice of the UK economy represented by manufacturing.

The UK Royal Society of Arts designated 1986 'Industry Year' in an attempt to reverse the tide and bring about a revival of manufacturing's pre-eminence in the UK economy 'in order to change Britain's position from bottom of the major industrial league'. Industry Year had the full support of the government, the Confederation of British Industries (CBI), the Trades Union Congress (TUC), the British Institute of Management (BIM) and the Engineering Council

The post-industrial society led to the emergence of new elites in terms of wealth and power. These were of two kinds. On the one hand were the key players in the service sectors which replaced manufacturing companies as the 'commanding heights' of the new economy – investment banking, venture capital, hedge funds and commercial law. On the other hand, elites of a different kind were emerging, often from the working class – pop stars, professional footballers, TV personalities and other celebrities. Between 1970 and 2000 an international footballer's weekly wage rose from a few hundred pounds a week to tens of thousands of pounds.

Knowledge as a Factor in Growth

Since the early 1990s one of the business techniques seen as 'the latest big idea' is 'knowledge management'. The important role it plays in business success is well summed-up in the following statement by the chairman of one of Britain's major companies.

Unilever, he said, had competitors with similar access to capital, who faced lower taxes and enjoyed government subsidies. What they lacked, however, was the 'immense body of varied knowledge and commercial skills which Unilever has built up over the years.'

> *In every aspect of the business knowledge is vital; and much of the knowledge which is important to a firm like Unilever cannot be found in books; it has to be acquired often expensively, sometimes painfully, by experience and deliberate enquiry.*
>
> *Knowledge is not cheap. Around the world we spend many millions in acquiring it. But without this expenditure we could not survive against competition.*
>
> *The economies of using knowledge over and over again, everywhere adapting it to local needs, are very great. Knowledge has no marginal cost. It costs no more to use it in the 70 countries in which we operate than in one. It is the principle which makes Unilever economically viable. The knowledge Unilever has is both extensive and complex. It is the source of your profits and of the main benefits Unilever brings to the peoples of the countries in which it operates.*

Quite so. But the point of including this quote is that the statement was made by the then chairman of Unilever in the company's annual report in 1972! Why did it take over 20 years for this essential truth to percolate through into mainstream management thinking, let alone the thinking of traditional economists? The answer is that most of us are mental prisoners of old mindsets. We were brought up to believe, (particularly those who became accountants) that a company's assets consist of its *tangible* property such as its premises, plant and equipment and cash at the bank. Today, that thinking is seen as belonging to the past. The market valuation of companies is more and more based on the judgement of investors as to the prospects for future earnings and this in turn is based on an assessment of the extent to which the company's knowledge base is being updated, exploited and renewed.

Nevertheless, the ability to exploit this understanding for competitive advantage would have been very much greater back in the 1970s, when the central role of knowledge management had not become an accepted part of management thinking. Today, superior knowledge management may no longer serve as a key source of competitive advantage.

New Growth Theory

Bell, Drucker and Ernest Woodruffe, the chairman of Unilever, were anticipating New Growth Economics by some 30-odd years. New Growth Theory emphasizes that economic growth results from the increasing returns associated with new knowledge. Knowledge has different properties from other economic goods (being non-rival, and partly excludable). The ability to grow the economy by increasing knowledge rather than labour or capital creates opportunities for nearly boundless growth. And because knowledge can be infinitely reused at zero marginal cost, firms using knowledge in production can earn quasi-monopoly profits. All forms of knowledge, from big science to better ways to sew a shirt, exhibit these properties and contribute to growth.

Similar ideas about the sources of economic growth were, in fact, propounded in the 1940s by Schumpeter (Schumpeter, 1942). Schumpeter argued that innovation by entrepreneurs leads to creative destruction as innovations cause old inventories, ideas, technologies, skills, and equipment to become obsolete. The question is not how capitalism administers existing structures, but how it creates and destroys them. This creative destruction, he believed, causes continuous progress and improves the standard of living for everyone.

Growth, Schumpeter argued, results not from price competition but from competition that is brought about by new technology, the new product and the new type of organization. Today we would add the new business model. This competition strikes not so much at the profit margins of the existing firms but at their foundations and their very sustainability.

Schumpeter never made completely clear whether he believed innovation is sparked by monopoly per se or by the prospect of getting a monopoly as the reward for innovation. Most economists accept the latter argument and, on that basis, believe that companies should be able to keep their production processes secret, have their trademarks protected from infringement, and obtain patents. The economy of the future is likely to be 'Schumpeterian,' with creative destruction the norm and innovation the main driver of wealth. Products based on ideas – music, software, pharmaceuticals – require an enormous investment to develop but incur relatively small expenditure to keep producing. Together, these factors – high cost to create, minimal cost to produce, and a winner-take-all environment – tend to generate natural monopolies, at least until the next significant innovation comes along.

Schumpeter's ideas have no place for economists' smooth graphs of long-run growth trends and economic evolution. Growth produces progress and wealth, but in unforeseeable ways and in discrete steps that create many small winners (for example, the people who can now fly from London to Nice for £25 on easyJet rather than for £250 on a traditional airline) and a few huge winners, for example, Bill Gates of Microsoft, and notable substantial losers such as British Airways or the music industry.

The challenge for the government in managing the market thus becomes not just the task of securing property rights, enforcing contracts, and providing civil order, but also the tremendously difficult job of managing the creative destruction so that the pain is alleviated and the benefits more equitably delivered.

Today's leading advocate of New Growth Theory is Professor Paul Romer, Professor of Economics at Stanford University's Graduate School of Business and a senior Fellow of the Hoover Institution. He was recently elected a Fellow of the American Academy of Arts and Sciences. *Time* magazine has described him as 'One of the 25 most influential Americans.'

Romer has had a profound impact on modern economic thinking and policymaking. New Growth Theory argues that economic growth is not a function of simply adding more labour to more capital, but results primarily from new and better ideas expressed as technological progress. It transforms economics from a 'dismal science' that describes a world of scarcity and diminishing returns into a discipline that points to constant improvement and unlimited potential, that is, an economics of abundance. Before New Growth Theory, economists recognized that technology contributed substantially to growth, but they had difficulty in incorporating that insight into economic theory. Romer's innovation, expressed in technical articles with titles such as Increasing Returns and Long-Run Growth (Romer, 1986) and Endogenous Technological Change, (Romer, 1990) has been to analyse rigorously how technological progress brings about economic growth.

In Romer's view the process of technological discovery is supported by a unique set of institutions which are most productive when they are closely linked to the institutions of the market. The Soviet Union had very strong science in some fields, but because its application was not driven by the market the benefits of scientific discovery were very limited for the population. In the Capitalist countries the combination of strong scientific institutions and strong market institutions has resulted in very considerable benefits.

Romer defines institutions as much more than just organizations. He includes conventions and rules about how things are done. He points to a basic distinction between science and the market. In the market, the fundamental institution is the notion of private property, that an individual owns a piece of land or a barrel of oil, and that individual has considerable scope in deciding how that resource should be used.

In the world of science there is a very different convention. When somebody discovers some new piece of knowledge, the convention in science is that he should not claim ownership of that idea, he should publish it. Science is about the dissemination as well as the creation of ideas. The reward is the prestige and respect accorded to the person who first publishes an idea.

Yet, to the extent that the market system is used to refine and bring ideas into practical application, there needs to be some kind of control over the idea – through patents, or copyright, or just through secrecy. Such control mechanisms create opportunities for people to make a profit developing ideas. The government doesn't pay drug companies to develop AIDS drugs. The companies incur huge costs in developing such drugs, so if they succeed, they feel justified in charging a high price for selling that drug. The result has been the prolonging of life of people with AIDS, but the high price is also denying many people access to those drugs.

At the same time there are some kinds of ideas where, once those ideas are uncovered, the scientists concerned would like to make them as widely available as possible, so everybody in the world can benefit. But if an idea is to be given away there is a need for a system to finance it, and that's where government or charitable foundation support for research comes in.

Romer points out that because everybody can use the idea at the same time, there's no 'tragedy of the commons' in the intellectual sphere.

From Post-Industrial to Post-Scarcity

The emergence of the post-industrial society took place within the living memory of the 'baby boomer generation' but it is already giving way to a new phase of social and economic development that is widely referred to as the 'post-scarcity society'. This central fact about economic life today is not widely recognized or understood for the reason that once more people's perception of the world is imprisoned in old, inappropriate mindsets. The past was characterized by scarcity. We find it very difficult to envisage a future world characterized by abundance. The system we have grown up with is based on the assumption of scarcity; the function of the market is to allocate scarce goods and resources via the pricing mechanism. We view the problems facing the world – poverty, health, climate change and human rights – through the lens of scarcity. In what follows these issues will be revisited through the lens of abundance.

Productivity growth and technological change are radically reducing the cost of supplying a wide range of goods and services, shifting them from a state of relative scarcity to one of relative abundance. On the basis of a simple extrapolation from about 1850 to now, the average economic growth rate on the planet was about 3 per cent per year. Extrapolating that until about 2100 world gross domestic product (GDP) would be about $550 trillion, ten times bigger than the current world economy of $47 trillion, and the average per capita income on the planet would be $70,000.

The trend to post-scarcity conditions is taking place particularly rapidly in relation to goods and services that can be delivered digitally, such as books, magazines, newspapers, music, film, telecommunications, and knowledge of very many kinds.

It is also taking place, albeit more slowly, in respect of other goods and services such as air travel, electrical goods, white goods, clothing, furniture, and so on.

In the most highly developed economies of the world the economy of scarcity is being replaced by the 'economy of abundance' that was foreseen by the visionary writers whose work was discussed in the previous chapter. It is now becoming a lively topic of debate, albeit within a relatively narrow circle and is the subject of an increasing number both of learned articles and blogs.

The study of economics arose in the context of scarcity and focused on the allocation of scarce resources. Adam Smith, the founder of the 'dismal science', nevertheless pointed to the power of productivity in his famous example of the division of labour in the manufacturing of pins. From the eighteenth century onwards, the world has been moving at an increasing rate to an economy of abundance. Our economic and financial institutions and ideas, however, are rooted in conditions of scarcity. Even more important is the fact that the mindsets of our business and government policy-makers are also locked in the past.

Abundance and scarcity are relative terms. Some things and will remain absolutely scarce, such as a Van Gogh painting, but in the everyday world of economic behaviour things are subject to degrees of scarcity or abundance. Between the hours of 8 a.m. and 6 p.m. parking places in London are relatively scarce and are priced accordingly, obeying the laws of the market so as to balance supply and demand. Too high a price and people will leave their cars at home. Too low a price and the streets will be choked with cars seeking parking places. However, between the hours of 6 p.m. and 8 a.m. parking slots are relatively abundant, to the extent that the market mechanism does not apply and the places are free. Today, relative to the past, more and more things are becoming abundant; fewer things are characterized by scarcity. The balance is changing; the tipping point is very close.

The Key Role of Talent

Meanwhile the foundation of economic success is shifting from the management of knowledge to the management of talent. There is a need for fresh thinking about what we understand by the word talent. At present many employers reserve the word 'talent' for the few high fliers who are destined to become top executives or high-level specialists. This is too narrow a view for a world with multiple challenges – needing people with a wide range of capabilities. Talent of very many kinds is all around us waiting to be unleashed. 'Talent' should not be seen as a rare quality, but a diverse, multifaceted one that exists, to some degree and in some form, in everyone – it is abundant. It is a nice quirk of the English language that *talent* is an anagram of *latent*, underlining the fact that so much talent remains hidden and undiscovered.

The post-scarcity society is better described as a 'talent-intensive society' than as a 'knowledge-intensive society'. Its wealth-creators and high earners are not only scientists, engineers, bankers and lawyers; they are artists, sports players, rock stars, fashion designers, chefs, interior decorators, therapists, landscape gardeners.

Sooner or later all knowledge is obsolete and in the world of the internet, a world in which China is producing engineers and scientists on a colossal scale, it is sooner rather than later. In corporate circles there is talk of the 'war for talent'. Business leaders understand that without an adequate supply of fresh talent their business has no future, regardless of its existing assets, whether in terms of cash, property or patents. Fortunately, talent is abundant; it is just a matter of recognizing it and removing existing barriers to its development and application. Over the next few decades millions of people who even in quite recent times would have been employed as farm workers or in other jobs involving relatively very low wealth creating potential will become graduate engineers, scientists, surgeons, lawyers and managers.

Abundance and Sustainable Consumption

As incomes rise and extreme poverty is gradually eliminated, falling real prices will encourage the consumption (and waste) of goods and raw materials in ways which are unlikely to be sustainable, either because of the impact on climate change or possibly because sources of energy and a range of non-renewable resources get used up. The first law of the economics of abundance is: whatever is abundant will be wasted.

Table 3.1   Stages in the development of human society

Stage of development	Key technologies	Principal economic activity	Key resource	Social system	Governance
Pre-agrarian	Stone-age tools	Hunting and gathering	The natural environment	Tribal, nomadic	Heredity chieftain
Agrarian	Iron tools, weapons, wind power	Cultivation of crops, animal husbandry	Fertile land	Rural settlements, linked to markets and centres of governance	Kingdoms, feudal system
Industrial	New sources of power and transportation. Chemicals and steel	Manufacturing	Capital	Large conurbations, suburbia	Limited democracy, leading to universal suffrage
Post-industrial	Computing power	Services	Knowledge	Inner city decay, depressed former manufacturing and mining regions	Full democracy
Post-scarcity	The internet, nanotechnology, biotechnology	Health, education, the arts	Talent	Globally mobile, highly ethnically diverse	Considerable devolution

In the final analysis the whole market system will have to adapt as the economics of abundance comes into collision with the economics of sustainability. That adaptive process will of necessity involve intervention, both by governments and by global institutions, if catastrophic, albeit transitional, shortages of food, raw materials and energy are to be avoided. The mechanisms of the market cannot be relied upon to provide the planet with a safe landing.

4

Abundance and Waste in Today's Economy

Introduction – the Real and Digital Economies

The phrase 'economy of abundance' implies that there is such a thing as 'the economy' and that within it goods and services are so abundant as to create post-scarcity conditions. In reality, the world is much more complex than this.

Activity that falls under the general heading 'economic' can be sub-divided into a number of different categories. Setting aside activities of a purely speculative nature, (the 'casino economy'), firstly there is a set of activities usually referred to as the 'real' or 'traditional economy':

- food production

- production of manufactured goods

- construction and civil engineering

- transport and distribution, including traditional retail distribution

- professional services

- health and education

- public administration

- financial services that support other elements of the real economy, for example banking, insurance

- personal services

- miscellaneous services.

Secondly there is the so-called digital or 'e-economy' which includes:

- a wide range of services delivered digitally via the internet – entertainment, information, games, news, and so on

- online commercial transactions of various kinds.

This chapter first explains the abundance that already exists in the real or traditional economy, and then looks at how the digital revolution is already paving the way to abundance on an altogether different scale.

However, it is important to stress that 'abundance' and 'scarcity' are relative, not absolute terms. In many areas of the world scarcity and deprivation continue to be self-evident. The 'poverty trap' affecting millions of people in both developed and developing economies is discussed in detail in Chapter 8. Clearly, resolving this issue must lie at the heart of a successful transition to a post-scarcity global economy.

In most of today's highly developed societies, however, the term 'abundance' can be reasonably applied to the wide availability and affordability of such things as staple foodstuffs, a wide range of manufactured goods and many services. Within the lifetime of today's elderly citizens, ordinary working families in European countries ate chicken only on feast days, rarely owned cars, had no central heating, no refrigeration, no washing machine, no television, no bathroom and never travelled outside their own country. Conditions in the USA were better for white families in the industrial and commercial centres, but rather worse for coloured families in the deep South or immigrant sweat-shop workers in the New York slums. These conditions of relative scarcity bred values associated with thrift and frugality – saving for a rainy day, re-using wrapping paper and string, meals conjured from left-overs and walking to save the bus fare. There was little need, at the lower levels of income, for lectures on recycling or energy conservation.

Today, not only have many things become more affordable to ordinary working people but the range of things and variants of things available has expanded enormously. The number of new products launched on the market in just the last two decades is considerable. These include mobile phones, iPods, digital cameras, a wide range of computerized interactive games, and satellite navigation systems.

As for variants of a basic product, in the modestly-sized supermarket in the small British town in which I live there are over 180 different types of cereal on display; when I was a child the corner grocer's shop offered a choice between porridge and cornflakes.

Abundance of Food

In 2010, ordinary working people in the world's developed countries can consume as much food as they wish. Indeed, the availability of foodstuffs at very low prices is leading to serious health problems. Obesity is a disease that affects approximately 60 million people in the United States, where women are especially affected. Over one-third of American women between the ages of 20 and 74 are obese, the majority of them being African–American or Mexican–American. With more and more pre-packaged food and less and less activity, the number of obese people in America has steadily increased since the 1960s.

In 1980, fewer than 10 per cent people in Britain were obese. Twenty years on, and the proportion is 20 per cent. Ten years from now it could be over 25 per cent. These figures apply only to those at the extreme end of being overweight – those who qualify as obese. Many more have less serious weight problems. Nearly two thirds of men and over half of women in England are now overweight or obese.

What is not eaten is thrown away. According to a study by the University of Arizona Garbage Project, the average American throws away 1.3 pounds of food every day, or 474.5 pounds per year. This is more than twice the US Environmental Protection Agency's (EPA) estimates. In response to this and a previous US Department of Agriculture (USDA) study, the EPA has revised its data methodology from the late '90s to present.

In the UK in 2008, research by The Waste and Resources Action Programme (WRAP) found that people were needlessly throwing away 3.6 million tonnes of food each year. The study analysed the waste disposed of by 2,138 households. Environment Minister Joan Ruddock said the findings were 'staggering' at a time of global food shortages.

Food consumption can be seen as a test case of how people react to abundance. Do they abuse it or see it as something that frees them to pursue other goals in life than consumption? The answer can be seen in landfill.

The Paradox Exemplified – Bottled Water

The steady growth of the practice of consuming water in bottles promoted as branded goods is an interesting case of the impact of growing abundance. It also provides a good example of the darker side of a post-scarcity world.

Estimates variously place worldwide bottled water sales at between $50 and $100 billion each year, with the market expanding at the startling annual rate of 7 per cent.

In 1976, the average American drank 1.6 gallons of bottled water a year, according to Beverage Marketing Corp. Last year, they each drank 28.3 gallons of bottled water – 18 half-litre bottles a month. Americans drink more bottled water than milk, or coffee, or beer. Only carbonated soft drinks are more popular than bottled water, at 52.9 gallons annually.

The water aisle in a US suburban supermarket typically stocks a dozen brands of water – not including those enhanced with flavours.

Pepsi's Aquafina™ or Coca-Cola's Dasani® bottled water are sold in 20-ounce sizes and can be purchased from $1 vending machines alongside soft drinks – and at the same price. That works out to 5 cents an ounce. Most municipal water costs less than one cent per gallon.

Petrol has to be pumped out of the ground in the form of crude oil, shipped to a refinery (often halfway across the world), and shipped again to a local filling station. In the USA, the average price per gallon is hovering around $3. There are 128 ounces in a gallon, which puts the current price of gasoline at fraction over 2 cents an ounce.

Bottled water produces up to 1.5 million tons of plastic waste per year. According to the website *Food and Water Watch*, that plastic requires up to 47 million gallons of oil per year to produce. And while the plastic used to bottle beverages is of high quality and in demand by recyclers, over 80 per cent of plastic bottles are simply thrown away. Plastic waste is now at such a volume that vast quantities of plastic trash now spin endlessly in the world's major oceans. This represents a great risk to marine life, killing birds and fish which mistake the waste for food. And, owing to its slow decay rate, the vast majority of all plastics ever produced still exist – somewhere. One billion bottles of water a week are transported in ships, trains, and trucks in the United States alone. That represents a weekly convoy equivalent to 37,800 18-wheelers delivering water.

Bottled water has become accepted as a part of Western culture. It will be found in lunch boxes; on the table at every meeting; students carry it into lectures; travellers on the London Underground are advised to a carry it in hot weather. Every hotel-room mini-bar offers bottled water for sale, while at the US upmarket supermarket Whole Foods, the bottled water is the number-one item by units sold. A generation that grew up drinking tap water is today raising a generation that views tap water with disdain.

When people buy a bottle of water they are not just buying water or the convenience of a bottle to carry the water around with them. They are also buying the brand image, the idea of naturalness, health and purity. Their choice of brand is a message about their sophistication and the success they have achieved in life.

Water is a perfect example of the post-scarcity paradox, poverty amidst plenty. Water is being called the 'Blue Gold' of the twenty-first century. Thanks to increasing urbanization and population, shifting climates, and industrial pollution, fresh, drinkable water is becoming humanity's most precious resource. Multinational corporations are stepping in to purchase groundwater and distribution rights wherever they can, and the bottled water industry is an important component in their drive to commercialize what many feel is a basic human right: the access to safe and affordable water.

Meanwhile, one in every six people in the world has no dependable, safe drinking water. The most fundamental element of life is denied to 1 billion people, while delivering to the richer countries a wide range of brands of water from around the globe. In Fiji, a state-of-the-art factory produces more than a million bottles a day of a leading brand of bottled water on the US market, while more than half the people in Fiji do not have safe, reliable drinking water.

Abundance of Goods

In the past, many categories of goods were expensive relative to average earnings. Such things as motor cars were produced by the working class for consumption by the middle and upper class. Over the years improvements in productivity have led to greatly reduced costs of production. At the same time, rises in real wages have placed an ever wider range of goods within reach of ordinary working people. The developed economies are now capable of producing huge amounts of products with the labour of a relatively small percentage of the population, just as they are able to produce enough food while employing less than 5 per cent of the working population in agriculture.

This is the realization of Henry Ford's vision, which was not so much about mass production as about enabling mass consumption; hence the model T. He looked forward to the day when every American worker would own an automobile.

In the developed world the great majority of households own automobiles, televisions (usually more than one), freezers, mobile phones and a wide range of gadgets. Increasingly the goods people own are 'intelligent' in that components from the digital world are built in.

Some goods which in the past were delivered as manufactured tangible packages such as music, film and books are increasingly being delivered at cost much closer to zero in digital form, creating considerable dilemmas for their producers and publishers.

The reduced costs of a wide range of goods have been achieved despite the fact that the supply of most things involves massive expenditure on distribution. As well as wholesalers' and retailers' mark-ups there are the costs of building brand identity, advertising, marketing, packaging and promotion and the costs of physical movement of goods. For a wide range of goods today the costs of distribution far outweigh the costs of production. The next step is, of course, to move from lean production to lean distribution.

Abundance in Services

Ordinary people can afford to have their hair done, they have bank accounts, they enjoy foreign holidays. The idea of near-free air travel would have been regarded as revolutionary a decade or so ago.

Working people and their families can afford to eat out. At McDonald's in the UK two 100-per cent beef patties with lettuce, onions, pickles, cheese, Big Mac sauce in a sesame seed bun cost a mere £2.95. In America, The Dollar Menu features some McDonald's favourite foods such as two beef patties and a slice of cheese in a bun for only a dollar.

Many previously costly service activities are being cheapened by relatively simple rationalisation and industrialization – for example 'production line' operations for hernias or hip joint replacements. Other, more complex things like heart and brain surgery will increasingly be performed by robots.

In regard to services, however, the major increases in abundance take the form of services delivered publicly.

In most progressive societies – but not yet in the USA – basic health services are free for the most part, as, of course, is education up to school-leaving age. In many developed societies tertiary education is also free. Even where a university education is not free an increasingly large percentage of the population are now able to access such tuition through a multiplicity of grants and bursaries available on a means-tested basis.

In other fields scarcity remains the norm. In some instances this is just a matter of time. In others, scarcity will persist.

There are chronic shortages of affordable housing in many societies. Transport facilities are scarce at the times of peak travel, abundant at other times. The same is true of road space on major routes and of parking places in cities.

Services that will remain scarce and hence command relatively high prices include those which involve the employment of highly educated, skilled, talented people – legal and financial services, for example, or a place at a world-class university.

Some scarcities are due to absolute limitations on supply. There is only one Mona Lisa. Some scarcities, however, are contrived as businesses or governments restrict supply or use other approaches that result in prices remaining relatively high. The sources of contrived scarcity will be discussed in Chapter 10.

Hirsch (1976) argues that as well as absolute scarcity there is also something he calls social scarcity. As the average level of consumption rises, an increasing proportion of consumption takes on a social as well as an individual aspect, meaning that the satisfaction an individual derives from goods and services depends increasingly not only on his or her own consumption but on consumption by others as well.

He points out that there are two extremes in distinguishing between private and public goods. For instance, a meal consumed by a hungry man is a pure private good, while at the other extreme, city parks, street lighting and defence are pure public goods. In between, however are goods and services the consumption of which includes a social element. The utility of an individual's spending on achieving a given level of educational qualification will decline as more and more people acquire that same level of qualification. Traffic congestion reduces the satisfaction an individual obtains from ownership of an automobile.

It is this social element in some aspects of consumption that gives rise to Hirsch's concept of social scarcity. This arises when an abundance of supply of a good or service results in a reduction in the satisfaction derived from its consumption. This, Hirsch argues, is equivalent to a limitation in the absolute physical supply of a product or service of a given quality.

Jeff Jarvis, in his book, *What Would Google Do*? (2009), wonders if there is a revenue-generating 'free' model for automobile manufacturers. Could they adopt the Google model and give away advertising-supported cars? There is no reason that cars should not be free, with the driver then paying for fuel and servicing. He quotes Professor Werbach of Wharton, who gives an account of a start-up manufacturer of electric cars, called Better Place, which is looking at making its cars available at a low price and charging for new batteries, just as printer manufacturers offer low-cost printers and put a high price on ink cartridges.

The appeal of 'free' has been shown to be huge, such that the demand you get at a price of *zero* is many times higher than the demand you get at a very low price. Josh Kopelman, a venture investor and entrepreneur who founded Half.com, has written about what he dubbed 'the penny gap'. Even charging one cent for something dramatically lessens the demand created by a price of zero cents. In Britain 'pound shops' are being put out of business by shops where the maximum price is 99p.

The 'Spectre' of Deflation

The term deflation is used to describe a general decline in prices. It can be caused by a reduction in the supply of money or credit or a decrease in government, personal or investment spending. According to traditional economic teaching, declining prices, if they persist, generally create a vicious spiral of negatives such as falling profits, closing factories, shrinking employment and incomes, and increasing defaults on loans by companies and individuals. To counter deflation, central banks can use monetary policy to increase the money supply and deliberately induce rising prices, causing inflation. Rising prices, it is argued, provide an essential lubricant for any sustained recovery because businesses improve their profitability and take some of the depressive pressures off wages and debtors. Deflationary periods can be either short or long, relatively speaking. Japan, for example, had a period of deflation lasting decades starting in the early 1990s. The Japanese government lowered interest rates to try and stimulate inflation, to no avail.

The weakness in this theory is that in today's world there is increasingly no such thing as a general level of prices. For some time now we have been living in a world in which whole classes of goods and services have been subject not only to falling prices, but to prices which have been falling radically. These goods and services include most electrical and electronic goods, a wide range of relatively simple manufactures such as clothing, white goods and furniture. At the same time other prices have been rising – some very rapidly – such as housing, local taxes, heating and transportation costs. Given such a wide divergence in price trends any index of the cost of living, however weighted, has lost all real meaning since the expenditure patterns of individuals determine their individual cost of living. For example, until recent developments the retail price index in the UK was around 2.0 per cent, indicating a modest level of inflation. For those living on the state pension, however, spending a higher proportion of their income on such things as heating (and facing local taxes above the general rate of inflation), the annual increase in living costs was in the region of 8 per cent.

The main point, however, is that manufacturers and retailers of personal computers, refrigerators, sofas and pairs of jeans have by and large managed to remain profitable in the face of falling prices. Technology companies, in particular, have learned to live with the problem by creating compelling reasons for people to buy today rather than wait for a better and cheaper version. Manufacturers in other industries have survived through a combination of productivity improvement and moving production to parts of the world where production costs are lower. Moreover these falling prices have taken place in boom years and have not resulted from a reduction in the supply of money or credit or a decrease in government, personal or investment spending. The underlying force is the shift from scarcity to abundance.

Digital Abundance

It is clearly the case that the emerging digital economy is a driver of abundance rather than of scarcity, creating new industries and radically new business models even whilst it destroys traditional companies and ways of life.

Digital has the potential to make a much greater impact on economies, because of the nature of the difference between tangible goods and 'informational' goods. When you consume tangible goods – eat a chocolate bar, or buy a car – there is one less of that good in the marketplace. But when you consume an informational item – download an application, or an mp3 – you copy it and there is now one more of that good, not one less. This, indeed, is how the success of an informational product is measured – by the number of times it has been reproduced; the number of books bought, the number of music CDs purchased, and so on. In the case of informational goods, therefore, the shift from scarcity to abundance is obvious.

The 'Decline to Zero' in the e-Economy

Chris Anderson (2009) cites King Gillette as a pioneer of free goods. By giving away his razors, which were useless by themselves, he was, of course, creating demand for disposable blades. A few billion blades later, this business model is now the foundation of entire industries: cell phones are given away in order to sell a monthly plan; video consoles are sold cheaply so as to sell more expensive games.

However, Anderson points out, until recently, practically everything 'free' was really just the result of what economists would call a cross-subsidy: one was offered free if you bought another, or a product was free only if you paid for a service.

Over the past decade, however, he argues that a different sort of 'free' has emerged. The new model is based not on cross-subsidies — the shifting of costs from one product to another — but on the fact that the cost of the product or service is itself falling very rapidly.

A prime example of this new type of free is to be found on the internet, where can be found free information, free news, free films and free music. Offering free music proved successful for Radiohead, Trent Reznor of Nine Inch Nails, and a swarm of other bands on MySpace that grasped the audience-building merits of zero pricing. Virtually everything Google does is free to consumers.

The rise of this type of free is being driven by the underlying technologies that power the web.

Just as Moore's law dictates that a unit of processing power halves in price every 18 months, the price of bandwidth and storage is dropping even faster. As a result, the factors that determine the cost of doing business online are all moving prices closer and closer to zero.

The web is all about scale, finding ways to attract the most users for centralized resources, spreading those costs over larger and larger audiences as the technology gets more and more capable. It's not about the cost of the equipment at the data centre; it's about what that equipment can do. And every year it does more and more for less and less, bringing the marginal costs of technology in the units that individuals consume closer to zero. For example, in 2007 Yahoo announced that Yahoo Mail, its free webmail service, would provide unlimited storage. So the market price of online storage for email has now fallen to zero.

Anderson asserts that practically everything web technology touches starts down the path to becoming free, at least as far as consumers are concerned. When Google turned advertising into a software application, a classic labour-intensive services business in which things get more expensive each year, they switched to a digital business model in which things get cheaper every year.

Anderson argues that when a company's primary expenses become things based in silicon, free becomes 'not just an option but the inevitable destination'.

Anderson points out that 40 years ago, Professor Carver Mead of Caltech identified the corollary to Moore's law of ever-increasing computing power. Every 18 months, Mead observed, the price of a transistor would halve. And so it did, going from tens of dollars in the 1960s to approximately 0.000001 cents today for each of the transistors in Intel's latest product. This, Mead realized, meant that we should start to 'waste' transistors.

Alan Kay, working at Xerox's Palo Alto Research Center, began to use cheap transistors to do things such as draw icons, windows, pointers, and even animations on the screen. The result was ease of use of computers for the general public, including children. Kay's work on the graphical user interface became the inspiration for the PC and the Apple Macintosh, which changed the world by opening computing to the public at large.

Anderson points out that transistors (or storage, or bandwidth) do not have to be completely free to invoke this effect. At a certain point, they are cheap enough to be safely disregarded. If the unitary cost of technology ('per megabyte' or 'per megabit per second' or 'per thousand floating-point operations per second') is halving every 18 months, in the end it comes close enough to zero to make it possible to round it down to nothing.

'Even though they may never become entirely free, as the price drops there are great advantages to be had in treating them as if they *were* free'.

However, just because products are free to the consumer doesn't mean that someone, somewhere, isn't making money. Google is the prime example of this. According to Anderson, you have to shift from a basic view of a market as a matching of two parties — buyers and sellers — to a broader sense of a network with many parties, only some of which exchange cash.

The most common of the economies built around free is the three-party system. Here a third party pays to participate in a market created by a free exchange between the first two parties.

In the traditional media model, a publisher provides a product free (or nearly free) to consumers, and advertisers pay to ride along. Radio broadcasts are free and so is much of television. Likewise, newspaper and magazine publishers don't charge readers anything close to the actual cost of creating, printing, and distributing their products. They're not selling papers and magazines to readers; they're selling readers to advertisers. It's a three-way market. (Many newspapers are now, of course, completely free).

In a sense, what the web represents is the extension of the media business model to industries of all sorts. This is not simply the notion that advertising will pay for everything. There are other ways that media companies make money around free content, from selling information about consumers to brand licensing, 'value-added' subscriptions, and direct e-commerce. Now an entire ecosystem of web companies is growing up around the same set of models.

Anderson's 'Taxonomy of Free'

FREEMIUM

This term, coined by venture capitalist Fred Wilson, is the basis of one of the most common web business models. It sounds like the traditional free sample. But whereas the free chocolate bar is the bait to tempt you into making many subsequent purchases, for digital products, this ratio of free to paid is reversed. A typical online site follows the 1 per cent rule — 1 per cent of users support all the rest. In the freemium model, that means for every user who pays for the premium version of the site, 99 others get the basic free version. The reason this works is that the cost of serving the 99 per cent is close enough to zero to treat it as nothing.

ADVERTISING

This is the Google business model. A related example is lead generation, where a third party pays for the names of people interested in a certain subject. All such approaches are based on the principle that free offerings build audiences with distinct interests and expressed needs that advertisers will pay to reach.

CROSS-SUBSIDIES

Google has used profits from web-search ads to finance moves into other free online applications, confounding competitors who had grown accustomed to charging money for similar products. Google Docs, a free suite of office applications (word processor, spreadsheet, and so on,) competes with software for which Microsoft normally charges hundreds of dollars. Microsoft has been forced to respond by promising that free web versions of its software suite will be available.

Adobe gives away its Adobe Reader software for displaying documents that use the company's PDF electronic document format, but charges corporations for the Adobe Acrobat software needed to create the documents.

ZERO MARGINAL COST

The most frequently quoted example is online music. The real cost of distributing music has become extremely small. This is a case where the product has become free because of sheer economic gravity, with or without a business model. That force is so powerful that all the measures to prevent piracy the music publishers can think of have encountered problems. Some artists now give away their music online as a way of marketing concerts, merchandise, licensing, and other paid fare. Consumers' sense of entitlement to free content online has had a catastrophic effect on the music industry. Music CD sales have gone from $13 billion in the USA to about $7 billion since 2001 while legal digital downloads generated about $1.5 billion in sales.

In August, 2009, *The Times* reported a study by the University of Hertfordshire that found that 14- to 24-year-olds in the UK had on average more than 8,000 songs on their computers, knew that file sharing was illegal, but would exploit every technological possibility to enable them to add to their music collections without payment. The research also found that despite the emergence of new, legal music download services and threats of legal action, 61 per cent of young people are still illegally swapping music.

Spotify is a new way to enjoy music. Subscribers simply download and install, after which they can listen to the artist or song of their choice. There are no restrictions in terms of what subscribers can listen to or when. Although it is not possible to save the music for use outside the application, a link is provided which allows the listener to purchase the material via partner retailers.

'We want to connect millions of people with their favourite songs by creating a product that people love to use. We respect creativity and believe in fairly compensating artists'. Spotify was launched for public access in October 2008. Free accounts were initially available only on invitation in order to manage the growth rate of the service. In February 2009 Spotify opened free registration in the UK. The service in its free version is only available in parts of Western Europe although the subscription version is available more widely.

LABOUR EXCHANGE

For example, by using Google's 411 service, the act of using the service creates something of value, either improving the service itself or creating information that can be used elsewhere.

GIFT ECONOMY

This covers Freecycle (free secondhand goods for anyone who will take them away), open source software and Wikipedia.

Anderson concludes by relating the idea of 'free' to the concept of the economics of abundance. He quotes Milton Friedman's famous dictum 'there's no such thing as a free lunch'.

However, he argues, Friedman was wrong in two ways. First, a free lunch doesn't necessarily mean the food is being given away or that you'll pay for it later — it could just mean someone else is paying. Second, in the digital realm the main components of the information economy — storage, processing power, and bandwidth — are getting cheaper by the day. Two of the main scarcity functions of traditional economics — the marginal costs of manufacturing and distribution — are moving rapidly to zero. 'It's as if the restaurant suddenly didn't have to pay any food or labour costs for that lunch'. Finally, he claims that we are entering an era when free will be seen as the norm, not an anomaly.

How Do Companies Make Money When So Much is Given Away?

From his study of the network economy Kelly (2008) identified eight categories of intangible value that people buy when they pay for something that could be free. He calls these things generatives, meaning that they are qualities or attributes that must be generated, grown, cultivated or nurtured. They cannot be copied, replicated or counterfeited.

Kelly's generatives are:

- *Immediacy* – Getting a copy delivered to your inbox the moment it is released or produced.

- *Personalization* – For example, a free movie you buy may be cut to reflect the rating a person requires (no violence, dirty language okay).

- *Interpretation* – For example, providing paid support for free software.

- *Authenticity* – Getting assurance that a key software application is bug-free, reliable, and warranted.

- *Accessibility* – People will pay Acme Digital Warehouse or similar companies to serve them any musical tune in the world, when and where we want it, as well as any movie, photo. Acme backs everything up, pays the creators, and delivers for a fee.

- *Embodiment* – For example, music in a live performance, with real performers. The music is free, but the performance is expensive.

- *Patronage* – Radiohead's recent high-profile experiment in letting fans pay them whatever they wished for a free copy is an excellent illustration of the power of patronage. The intangible between appreciative fans and the artist is worth something – in Radiohead's case it was about $5 per download.

- *Findability* – When there are millions of books, millions of songs, millions of films, millions of applications, millions of everything requesting our attention – and most of it free – being found is valuable. Companies such as Amazon and Netflix generate income by helping the audience find works they seek.

Kelly goes on to comment that advertisements are widely regarded as the solution, almost the only solution, to the 'paradox of the free'. However, in his view they will only be part of the new ways money is made selling 'the free'.

A Moral Issue?

One of the key objections people keep coming up with is that this whole concept of the economics of abundance makes no sense because it means the creators of content make no money and they have a right to make money for their creative output.

Masnik (2006) argues that this objection is wrong on two major points. First, is the idea that 'free' means creators of content can't make any money. In fact, nothing can be further from the truth. In his view, the opportunity for making money is even greater when people understand the economics, and don't rely on directly selling the non-scarce good. The second objection is that there's a right to make money. However, Masnik points out, economics is not a moral issue. The market does not take into consideration anyone's 'right' to make money from their creative output. Everyone has the right to *try* to make money out of their creative output, but if the market is not there, then there's no money to be made.

Masnik gives the example of somebody making a drawing and trying to sell it as fine art – but no one would buy it, because that person's drawing ability is undistinguished. The market would properly value the drawing at something close to zero because there would be no demand for it. Similarly, in a situation where there's a lack of scarcity, the market would properly value something at close to (or equal to) zero because there's infinite supply. It has nothing to do with the moral issue of the creators' right to profit from the creative output, and everything to do with the market.

Confusion arises because content creators have had a good run selling their content. As a result people have trouble understanding why they need to learn how to take the same content they've been selling for money and give it away free. It's not about a *choice* between being able to sell the content for money or giving it away for free, Masnik asserts, but a recognition of where the market is going. Historically, the content has been made scarce by connecting it to a specific medium (music on CDs, video on tape/DVD, and so on). What the internet is doing is breaking down that scarcity, and that's changing the market, pushing out the supply to infinite levels and putting pricing pressure on the content.

The term 'algamics' has been coined to describe an approach to (or more properly, perhaps, an alternative to) economics which acknowledges that non-scarce goods will always be copied, whether legally or illegally.

Red Hat – a Free Business Model

Red Hat will continue to pursue a business model under which it makes its software available at no cost and makes money selling services to businesses, according to its chief executive James Whitehurst.

'We are a mission-based company. Democratising information is a social good,' he said. 'We will be open source. We will be the leader in open source.'

Open source software makers invite the public to help in developing their computer programs, using the internet to collaborate. Proponents argue that this collaborative approach results in the creation of programs that are superior to software from companies such as Microsoft, which keep their code secret and generally require customers to pay a licence fee for each piece of software in addition to fees for any services.

But Red Hat's approach also gives rivals the ability to copy and resell its products.

Oracle started distributing a copycat version of Red Hat Linux in 2006 and offering support at prices that it initially said were cheaper than those of Red Hat.

A group of software developers have collaborated on a second copycat version of Red Hat's product, known as CentOS, that is available for free download over the internet.

While it is unclear how much business Red Hat has lost to Oracle or CentOS, analysts say the emergence of those products shows that open-source companies are constantly vulnerable to new competitors with low barriers to entry. In addition, Red Hat faces fierce competition from Microsoft, which is launching a new line of rival products.

Red Hat's existing customers are free to keep using the software once their service contracts have expired.

'There are frustrations with any model. It's part of the greater good' Whitehurst said. 'It's easier to copy what we do. We are not going to win by providing better bits. We are going to win by providing better service and better value.'

He said that businesses seek out Red Hat's products partly because the company has the most expertise in its field.

'Hemingway could talk better about his work than somebody who could just copy it,' he said. 'The same is true about software. We are built around core values about being open and being collaborative … We are enabled to provide better value because it is part of our culture.'

Free Knowledge

The most well-known source of free knowledge is the web site Wikipedia, founded in 2001, a free multilingual encyclopaedia which is written collaboratively by volunteers. There are more than 75,000 contributors working on some 13,000,000 articles in 260 languages. In 2009 the site was being visited by some 65 million people each month.

The Massachusetts Institute of Technology (MIT) has made nearly all of its courses available on the web, free of charge. Its Open Course Ware program, established in 2001, now offers some 1,890 courses, and is accessed by over 2 million visitors each month.

A Culture of Free

The result of all this has been a change in consumer expectations. A 'culture of free' has emerged – there are a lot of things for which people simply do not expect to pay. Forced to compete against free offerings, traditional businesses have suffered.

Consumers' sense of entitlement to free content online has had a catastrophic effect on music. Music CD sales have gone from $13 billion in the USA to about $7 billion since 2001 while legal digital downloads generated about $1.5 billion in sales.

The effects of the free culture online have had a hard impact on a range of traditional businesses. Many jobs once done by people are turning into software applications. What was a stockbroker is now a trading web site and the travel agent is being replaced by a search engine.

Chapter 5 describes how science and technology will continue to revolutionize the development and delivery of goods and services in every area of the traditional and emerging digital economy.

5

How Science and Technology are Creating Tomorrow's Abundance

Introduction

The pace of innovation has been very rapid in recent years bringing about huge changes both in the way we live and in the way business is conducted. Yet the surprising thing is how quickly new products and services have become taken for granted and quietly absorbed into our lifestyles and how quickly people in developed countries have come to take for granted their greatly increased living standards.

Nightly Business Report, the American PBS business program, and the Wharton Business School web bulletin, Knowledge@Wharton, set out to compile a list of the top 30 innovations of the last 30 years. The show's audiences and Knowledge@Wharton's readers from around the world were asked to name the innovations that have shaped the world in that period of time.

After receiving some 1,200 suggestions, a panel of eight judges from Wharton reviewed and selected the top 30, which were revealed on air and online on 16 February 2009.

Unsurprisingly, the internet – combined with broadband, browsers and HTML – was ranked first in the list, as an innovation that created an industry and subsequent new technologies as well as improving communications and enhancing the standard of living and working regardless of one's location.

The list included the other key features of the digital economy: PC/laptop computers, mobile phones, email, microprocessors, fibre optics, office software (spreadsheets, word processors), GPS systems, digital photography/videography.

In the medical field the main ones were DNA testing and sequencing/ human genome mapping, magnetic resonance imaging (MRI), non-invasive laser/robotic surgery (laparoscopy) and anti-retroviral treatment for AIDS.

Innovations affecting everyday life included online shopping/e-commerce (for example, eBay and Amazon), social networking via the internet, ATMs, and bar-code scanners.

Not surprisingly the list does not include the considerable number of innovations of financial products such as various types of derivatives – products which have proved to carry risks that were unforeseen by most bankers and economists.

Innovation in the Next Thirty Years

The first thing to say about innovation between now and 2040 is that it will almost certainly be even more radical and even more powerful in its impact on peoples' lives than that of the last 30 years.

Much of it, of course, is totally unpredictable at this point in time. However, there are several areas where trends and developments already in hand give some indication of where the major breakthroughs will occur. These include:

- Further step changes in the speed and power of computation, possibly leading to the realization of Turing's vision of artificial intelligence (AI).

- The application of genetic science to the elimination of a range of common sources of morbidity and mortality with a consequent increase in peoples' lifespan.

- The application of nanotechnology in a number of different fields.

- The development of a whole range of technologies stimulated by fears of climate change, and sustainability issues, including alternative energy sources, desalination of ocean waters, genetic modification of foods.

- 3D movies and television.

The range of possibilities is vast. The examples that follow have been selected on the basis of the strength of expert opinion regarding the significance of their economic and social impact.

Supercomputers

A newly built supercomputer, Jaguar, which is the most powerful ever dedicated to science is tackling questions about climate change, supernovas, and the structure of water. Jaguar is located at the National Center for Computational Sciences (NCCS), part of Oak Ridge National Laboratory, Tennessee, and can perform more than a million billion mathematical operations every second. First unveiled in 2008, after several months of testing, scientists at Oak Ridge recently started tasking Jaguar with its first research projects. The projects to be tackled by Jaguar were chosen in a peer-reviewed process designed to get the computer producing useful science even during the period when its performance is still being fine-tuned by engineers.

Environmental issues motivate many of the first wave of 21 projects. Three involve climate models – including one that models the global atmosphere down to grids of 14 kilometres instead of the more usual 55- or 100-km squares. Other environmentally inspired projects will simulate flames inside diesel engines with the aim of cutting fuel consumption, and the synthesis of biofuels from waste plant material. Subsequently the computer will be made available to the Intergovernmental Panel on Climate Change for a month or more.

Artificial Intelligence

Kevin Kelly (2009), writing on the *Edge* website, argues that it is hard to imagine anything that would result in radical change as much as a cheap, powerful, ubiquitous artificial intelligence. In his view, a very small amount of real intelligence embedded into an existing process would boost its effectiveness to another level, and the ensuing change would be hundreds of times more disruptive to our lives than was the transforming power of electrification. Not only would we apply AI to complex research problems like curing cancer, or solving intractable mathematical problems, but the real disruption would come from inserting intelligence into such everyday things as vending machines, our shoes, books, tax returns, automobiles, and email.

He points out that AI's capacity to bring about change is a not so much a function of how smart it is, or its variety, but how ubiquitous it could be.

Until recently it has been taken for granted that AI would at first be based on supercomputers and later on peoples' home computers. However the new thinking is that it will be based on the web. 'Instead of dozens of geniuses trying to program an AI in a university lab, there are a billion people training the dim glimmers of intelligence arising between the quadrillion hyperlinks on the web' (Kelly, 2009).

Biological Computers

Scientists are devising a new generation of fast and flexible biological computers built from DNA and neurons, which are so tiny that billions of them fit in a test tube and can perform more than a billion operations per second. Whereas ordinary computers need absolutely correct information every time to come to the right answer, biological computers seek to arrive at the correct answer based on partial information, by filling in some of the gaps themselves. Some of the biological computers being built can 'think for themselves' because the biological components – DNA and neurons – are able to form their own connections from one to another.

Cloud Computing

Cloud computing is another ongoing development in the information processing field. It is the process by which a company buys access to software on computers operated by a third party. Typically, the software is accessed over the internet using only a web browser. As long as the software performs properly, it doesn't matter where the systems that run it are located. They are 'out there somewhere' – in 'the cloud' of the internet. It is not just about using computers that are in distant locations. People have run IT for years in data centres they didn't own. In cloud computing there are no longer specific machines dedicated to specific software applications. Instead, a piece of software runs across a pool of machines, making optimal use of all the available hardware resources.

Cloud computing offers a number of advantages – lowered investment in hardware, more efficient use of computing systems in existing data centres, easier scale-up of the applications and services. As bandwidth has become cheap and readily available, and transmission speed is no longer an impediment, it's possible to store data and run software anywhere for users to access from wherever they want.

The easiest examples to understand are consumer web applications such as Microsoft's Hotmail, Google's Gmail and YouTube, and Yahoo's Flickr photo-sharing service. Consumers run only their browsers on local computers. The rest of the software, together with users' email messages, photos or videos is on remote machines the user can't see and doesn't have to know anything about.

Cloud computing applications encouraged the development of the market for netbooks – lightweight portable computers which contain minimal data storage and computing capacity, and carry price tags usually under $400. By taking advantage of online applications and storage, users have the option to spend less money on hardware.

Google offers a service called Google AppEngine that allows businesses to develop and run their own programs on Google's servers. Amazon has a similar offering called the Elastic Compute Cloud, or EC2. These services offer companies a place to host applications and data under a pay-for-usage model – called 'utility computing' because it is ready on demand.

Eventually IT may evolve to an almost completely external cloud. Companies in the health care business, or financial services or manufacturing would avoid spending hundreds of millions or billions of dollars on IT infrastructure.

Even more important for the future is the way cloud computing reduces the startup costs of new businesses. Entrepreneurs can begin by buying the relatively small amounts of computing they need and then ramp up usage as the business expands.

Fabbers

Fabbers (also known as 3D printers or rapid prototyping machines) are a relatively new form of manufacturing that builds 3D objects by depositing materials drop by drop, layer by layer. Slowly but surely, with the right set of materials and a geometric blueprint, it is possible to fabricate complex objects that would normally take special resources, tools and skills if produced using conventional manufacturing techniques. A fabber can make it possible to explore new designs, email physical objects to other fabber owners, and most importantly encourage innovation.

While several commercial systems are available, their price range – tens of thousands, to hundreds of thousands of dollars – is typically well beyond what an average home user can afford. Furthermore, commercial systems do not usually allow or encourage experimentation with new materials and processes. But more importantly, most – if not all – commercial systems are geared towards making passive parts out of a *single material*. The future holds the possibility of universal fabrication machines that can use multiple materials to fabricate complete, active systems.

RepRaps

RepRap is short for replicating rapid-prototyper. It is the practical self-copying 3D printer. A RepRap will make plastic, ceramic, or metal parts, and is itself made from plastic parts, so it will be able to make copies of itself. It is a three-axis robot that moves several material extruders. These extruders produce fine filaments of their working material with a paste-like consistency. If a RepRap was making a plastic cone, it would use its plastic extruder to lay down a quickly-hardening 0.5 mm filament of molten plastic, drawing a filled-in disc. It would then raise the plastic extrusion head and draw the next layer (a smaller filled disc) on top of the first, repeating the process until it completed the cone. To make an inverted cone it would also lay down a support material under the overhanging parts. The support would be removed when the cone was complete. Conductors can be intermixed with the plastic to form electronic circuits.

The RepRap build cost will be less than $400 for the bought-in materials, all of which have been selected to be as widely available everywhere in the world as possible. Also, the RepRap software will work on all computer platforms for free. Complete open-source instructions and plans are published on this website for zero cost and available to everyone.

Nanotechnology

The first use of the concepts in 'nano-technology' (but predating use of that name) was in a talk given by physicist Richard Feynman at an American

Physical Society meeting at Caltech on 29 December 1959 (Feynman, 1959). He described a process by which the ability to manipulate individual atoms and molecules might be developed, using one set of precise tools to build and operate another proportionally smaller set, so on down to the needed scale. In the 1980s the possibility of such a process was explored in depth by Dr. K. Eric Drexler (1986) who promoted the technological significance of nano-scale phenomena and devices through speeches and books. Work on nanotechnology and nanoscience started in the early 1980s with two major developments; the birth of cluster science and the invention of the scanning tunnelling microscope (STM). The atomic force microscope was invented six years later. In 2000, the United States National Nanotechnology Initiative was founded to coordinate federal nanotechnology research and development.

The standard unit of measurement, a nanometer, is a billionth of a metre – barely the size of 10 hydrogen atoms in a row. Researchers have discovered that matter at this tiny scale often behaves very differently. Familiar materials display useful new properties. Some transmit light or electricity. Others become harder than diamonds or turn into potent chemical catalysts. A tiny amount of nanoparticles can transform the chemistry and nature of far bigger things, creating everything from fortified car bumpers to superefficient fuel cells. Opaque substances become transparent, stable materials turn combustible, solids turn into liquids at room temperature, insulators become conductors. A material such as gold, which is chemically inert at normal scales, can serve as a potent chemical catalyst at nanoscales.

For now, the biggest markets for nanoparticles remain in familiar products. Consumers will encounter nanotechnology in the form of nick-proof trims on cars, tennis racquets with extra drive power, and golf balls that are designed to prevent a shift in weight as they spin. However, new nano-based products that could have a far bigger impact are only a few years away.

Instead of one new phenomenon, like the Internet, nano offers new possibilities for thousands of materials that already exist. Within the next few years, diagnostic machines with components built at the nano scale should allow doctors and nurses to carry miniature laboratories in their briefcases, perhaps to test for HIV or count white blood cells on the spot. Nano sensors at airports will detect traces of anthrax or sarin.

From 21 August 2008, the Project on Emerging Nanotechnologies estimated that over 800 manufacturer-identified nanotech products were publicly available, with new ones reaching the market at a pace of three to four per week. The project lists all of the products in a publicly accessible online inventory. Most applications are limited to the use of 'first generation' passive nanomaterials which include titanium dioxide in sunscreen, cosmetics and some food products; carbon allotropes used to produce gecko tape; silver in food packaging, clothing, disinfectants and household appliances; zinc oxide in sunscreens and cosmetics, surface coatings, paints and outdoor furniture varnishes; and cerium oxide as a fuel catalyst.

One example is DuPont's Voltron, a super-durable wire coating used in heavy-duty electric motors. Previous generations of such coatings, seen through a powerful microscope, would reveal the chemical components packed with irregular spaces between the molecules. This structure leads the material to break down more easily. Voltron's nanoscale particles fill in many of the voids, making a stronger insulator that lasts longer. In DuPont's tests on electric motors, a coating of Voltron extended the time between failures by a factor of 10 to more than 1,000 hours. And since such motors consume an estimated 65 per cent of US electric power, lengthening their life and efficiency promises big energy savings. This is a good illustration of how new technology will contribute to the sustainability of the environment.

LabNow Inc., an Austin (Texas) company, is developing technology to address the problem of AIDS. Using minute channels and sensors, the company has devised a blood laboratory on a chip the size of a business card. The patient places a single drop of blood on the chip, which is then inserted into a small electronic reader. Within minutes, HIV/AIDS patients can get a count of their white blood cells – a crucial metric for treatment. Currently that test takes weeks or months in poor regions of the world, where blood samples are trundled back and forth in slow trucks. Patients can die waiting for the results. LabNow's technology has the potential to speed AIDS treatment in much of the world.

Other potential applications in the medical field include targeted anti-cancer drugs and tumour-removal technologies, surgical implants with improved biocompatibility, anti-bacterial and anti-viral coatings for medical and medicinal equipment, high-specificity drug-delivery technologies, and theranostics (that is, combined diagnostics – therapeutics).

In other areas, possible applications include enhanced SPF sunscreens, high-efficiency fuel-borne catalysts, enhanced data-storage devices, stain-repellent fabrics, self-cleaning paints and windows, high-performance sports equipment, low-cost high-efficiency solar cells, exhaust-emission detection and absorption devices and improved water filtration technologies.

Nanotechnology has the potential to replace the silicon chip. This process has already started with memory chips, the least complicated kind. Hewlett-Packard recently disclosed a breakthrough in nanotechnology that, within a decade, could carry computing beyond today's silicon and transistors Within two or three years, developers hope to make viable memory chips from spaghetti-shaped carbon nanotubes, each one only 1 nm wide. Further out, engineers are learning how to replace minuscule metal circuits and gateways on today's chips with new nano-engineered materials. IBM researchers have built transistors with carbon nanotubes that promise a huge leap in performance while cutting heat loss.

Molecular Manufacturing

Molecular nanotechnology, sometimes called molecular manufacturing, is a term given to the concept of engineered nanosystems (nanoscale machines) operating on the molecular scale. It is especially associated with the concept of a molecular assembler, a machine that can produce a desired structure or device atom-by-atom using the principles of mechanosynthesis. Manufacturing in the context of productive nanosystems is not related to, and should be clearly distinguished from, the conventional technologies used to manufacture nanomaterials such as carbon nanotubes and nanoparticles.

Chris Phoenix, (2005), Director of Research at the Center for Responsible Nanotechnology, explains how existing technologies can be coordinated toward a reachable goal of general-purpose molecular manufacturing. 'Molecular manufacturing offers a fundamentally new approach to build things 'from the bottom up'; the idea is to use nanoscale machines to create structures with atomic precision. Ultimately, that can result in the ability to make complex products, both small and large, with unprecedented performance and value.'

The National Science Foundation (a major distributor for nanotechnology research in the United States) funded researcher David Berube (2006) to study the field of nanotechnology. He concludes that much of what is sold as nanotechnology is in fact a recasting of straightforward materials science, which is leading to a nanotech industry built solely on selling nanotubes, nanowires, and the like which will end up with a few suppliers selling low-margin products in huge volumes. Further applications which require actual manipulation or arrangement of nanoscale components await further research. Though technologies branded with the term 'nano' are sometimes little related to and fall far short of the most ambitious and transformative technological goals of the sort involved in molecular manufacturing proposals, the term still connotes such ideas. According to Berube, there may be a danger that a nano bubble will form, or is forming already, from the use of the term by scientists and entrepreneurs to garner funding, regardless of interest in the transformative possibilities of more ambitious and far-sighted work.

Concerns in Relation to Nanotechnology's Environmental Impact

Nanotechnology has the potential to create many new materials and devices with wide-ranging applications, such as in medicine, electronics, and energy production. On the other hand, nanotechnology raises many of the same issues as with any introduction of new technology, including concerns about the toxicity and environmental impact of nanomaterials, and their potential effects on global economics, as well as speculation about various doomsday scenarios. These concerns have led to a debate among advocacy groups and governments on whether special regulation of nanotechnology is warranted. On 10 December 2008, the US National Research Council released a report calling for more regulation of nanotechnolgy. The Center for Responsible Nanotechnology suggests that new developments could result in, among other things, untraceable weapons of mass destruction, networked cameras for use by the government, and weapons developments fast enough to destabilize arms races.

One area of concern is the effect that industrial-scale manufacturing and use of nanomaterials would have on human health and the environment, as suggested by nanotoxicology research. The Center for Responsible Nanotechnology has advocated that nanotechnology should be specially regulated by governments for these reasons. Others counter that overregulation would stifle scientific research and the development of innovations which could greatly benefit mankind. Longer-term concerns centre on the implications that new technologies will have for society at large, and whether these could possibly lead to either a post-scarcity global economy, or alternatively exacerbate the wealth gap between developed and developing nations.

In the UK a Royal Society report identified a risk of nanoparticles or nanotubes being released during disposal, destruction and recycling, and recommended that 'manufacturers of products that fall under extended producer responsibility regimes such as end-of-life regulations publish procedures outlining how these materials will be managed to minimize possible human and environmental exposure'. The Institute for Food and Agricultural Standards has proposed that standards for nanotechnology research and development should be integrated across consumer, worker and environmental standards. They also propose that NGOs and other citizen groups play a meaningful role in the development of these standards.

Technology and Future Energy Supplies

At present the there are several options for alternative means of power generation and propulsion. Each of these has strong support from experts and also each has strong critics. It is impossible for lay persons to assess their respective merits. It is to be hoped that the world's politicians are able to make the right decisions.

Power generation possibilities include:

- *Wind power*. This currently features strongly in the energy policy of the UK. Its opponents stress the visual pollution resulting from onshore installations and question the extent to which wind farms can supply a major part of a country's energy needs.

- *Nuclear power*. The nuclear route is strongly opposed by many environmental groups, mainly on the grounds of the problems associated with the disposal of nuclear waste. According to an article in *Wired*, January 2010, thorium oxide has the potential to revolutionize the nuclear power industry and is a safer alternative to uranium. Thorium oxide, which is three times more abundant than uranium, is also a radioactive material, but it is safe to hold in your hand. It can generate power without emitting greenhouse gases and thorium waste would only remain radioactive for 500 years, not the tens of thousands for which uranium by-products remain active.

- *Carbon capture and storage.* This solution would enable the vast coal deposits of China, the USA and Russia to be used without creating emissions. Initiatives to develop this technology began in the USA during the oil crisis in the 1970s but were dropped in the 1980s when the price of oil fell sharply. For more than a decade, Norwegian oil company Statoil Hydro has been stripping carbon dioxide (CO_2) from natural gas in its Sleipner West field and burying it beneath the seabed rather than venting it into the atmosphere. The company estimates that since 1996 it has stored more than 10 million-plus metric tons of CO_2 some 3,300 feet (1,000 metres) down in the sandstone formation from which it came – and all of it has stayed put, which means storage may be the simplest part of the carbon capture and storage (CCS) challenge.

- *Solar energy.* The total energy the earth receives each year from the sun is around 35,000 times the total energy used by man. However, about $1/3$ of this energy is either absorbed by the outer atmosphere or reflected back into space. Solar energy is presently being used on a smaller scale in furnaces for homes and to heat up swimming pools. On a larger scale use, solar energy could be used to run cars or aircraft as well as power plants.

- *Tidal or wave power.* The tidal process utilizes the natural motion of the tides to fill reservoirs, which are then slowly discharged through electricity-producing turbines. Hydroelectricity comes from the damming of rivers and utilizing the potential energy stored in the water. As the water stored behind a dam is released at high pressure, its kinetic energy is transferred onto turbine blades and used to generate electricity. This system has substantial costs up front, but has relatively low maintenance costs and provides power quite cheaply.

- *Geothermal power.* Geothermal energy is obtained from the internal heat of the planet and can be used to generate steam to run a steam turbine. This in turn generates electricity.

- *Incineration of waste.* Treatment plants operate by feeding wastes onto a moving grate where they are burned. The heat generated raises steam, driving turbines to generate electricity.

The main options for propulsion are:

- *Bio-fuels*. Since the 1970s Brazil has focused on an ethanol fuel programme. It is the world's second largest producer after the USA. Light vehicles in Brazil no longer run on petrol alone. Deriving alternative fuels from foodstuffs raises food prices on the one hand while having little impact on dependency on imported energy and even a negative impact on climate change. There are advocates for the use of algae rather than corn or wheat.

- *Electric vehicles and hybrid vehicles*. There are several models of electric and hybrid electric vehicles on the market today. These still have severe limitations, however, in terms of mileage between recharging, size and top speed.

- *Hydrogen powered vehicles*. Hydrogen-powered cars have already made their debut. Since hydrogen is the most abundant element in the universe it was inevitable that attempts would be made to produce hydrogen powered cars. Though hydrogen powered cars are not ready for primetime for consumers yet, many manufacturers are showing off their concept cars and prototypes to get consumers excited about the future. The biggest challenge now is developing less expensive technology and a refuelling infrastructure to support consumers. Many experts believe that hydrogen powered cars for the consumer are still 3–10 years away. Others believe they have no future.

Today it is far from clear which of these technologies will take hold in the marketplace – and which of them will wither. Nevertheless it is generally agreed that radical changes in the sources of energy are inevitable, although there is less agreement about the pace of change.

Change is driven by two main factors: first, the fact that sooner or later the supply of oil and gas is going to dry up (opinions about when 'peak oil' will be reached are also widely divergent); secondly, the scientific consensus that climate change is being driven by the use of fossil fuels.

However, the huge investments required to get the needed new infrastructures set up mean that the process of change will not be rapid, with the consequence that severe energy shortages might occur at some stage in the future. Companies are unlikely to risk the substantial capital sums involved without massive governmental support.

For example, the recent US government stimulus package, which allocates approximately $50 billion to a range of clean energy initiatives, might help some projects get off the ground.

Biotechnology

Biotechnology is a collection of technologies that capitalize on the attributes of cells, such as their manufacturing capabilities, and puts biological molecules, such as DNA and proteins, to work. Cells are the basic building blocks of all living things. The simplest living things, such as yeast, consist of a single, self-sufficient cell. Complex creatures such as plants, animals and humans, are made of many different cell types, each of which performs a very specific task. In spite of the extraordinary diversity of cell types in living things, what they share is a remarkable similarity. This commonality at the cellular level provides the foundation for biotechnology.

Biotechnology research has led to the formulation of more than 200 therapies and vaccines, including products to treat cancer, diabetes, HIV/AIDS and autoimmune disorders. There are very many more biotech drugs and vaccines currently in clinical trials targeting more than 200 diseases, including various cancers, Alzheimer's disease, heart disease, diabetes, multiple sclerosis, AIDS and arthritis.

In addition, biopesticides and other bio products also are being used to improve the food supply and to reduce dependence on chemical pesticides. Environmental biotechnology products have such uses as cleaning up hazardous waste more efficiently by pollution-eating microbes.

Industrial biotechnology applications have led to cleaner, less wasteful processes and ones that use less energy and water in industries such as chemicals, pulp and paper, textiles, food, energy, and metals and minerals. Laundry detergents contain biotechnology-based enzymes.

Nanobiotechnology

Nanobiotechnology joins the breakthroughs in nanotechnology to those in molecular biology. Molecular biologists are helping nanotechnologists understand and access the nanostructures and nanomachines designed by 4 billion years of evolutionary engineering, that is, cell machinery and biological molecules. Exploiting the properties of biological molecules and cell processes, nanotechnologists can achieve many things that would be difficult or impossible to achieve by other means.

For example, rather than build silicon scaffolding for nanostructures, DNA's ladder structure provides nanotechnologists with a natural framework for assembling nanostructures, and its highly specific bonding properties bring atoms together in a predictable pattern to create a nanostructure.

Nanotechnologists also rely on the self-assembling properties of biological molecules to create nanostructures, such as lipids that spontaneously form liquid crystals. Most appropriately, DNA, the information storage molecule, may serve as the basis of the next generation of computers.

DNA has been used not only to build nanostructures but also as an essential component of nanomachines. As microprocessors and microcircuits shrink to nanoprocessors and nanocircuits, DNA molecules mounted onto silicon chips may replace microchips with electron flow-channels etched in silicon. Such biochips are DNA-based processors that use DNA's extraordinary information storage capacity. Biochips exploit the properties of DNA to solve computational problems. Scientists have shown that 1,000 DNA molecules can solve in four months computational problems that would require a century for a computer to solve.

Other biological molecules are making it possible to store and transmit more information in smaller places, for example using light-absorbing molecules, such as those found in our retinas, to increase the storage capacity of CDs a thousand-fold.

Some applications of nanobiotechnology include increasing the speed and power of disease diagnostics, creating bio-nanostructures for getting functional molecules into cells, and improving the specificity and timing of drug delivery.

Technology and Sustainability

Vinod Khosla was a co-founder of Sun Microsystems. He has since become one of America's top venture capitalists, first at Kleiner Perkins, which funded Amazon and Google among others, and now at his own Khosla Ventures, one of the biggest investors in green technology.

Khosla's commitment has led to his becoming an adviser to President Barack Obama and Tony Blair's Climate Group, which aims to cut greenhouse-gas emissions.

Khosla is an optimist. In an interview in the *Sunday Times*, 30 March 2009, he stated his belief that we are on the verge of a technological revolution, with money and talent pouring into green technology, and more and more companies offering solutions to the energy crisis.

He argued that much of the debate on climate change is ill thought-out, and that the 'environmentalists' are wrong. Rather than use less energy, we need to find new solutions. Khosla is critical of what he sees as 'silly' solutions to climate change. He dismissed 'green' light bulbs, wind power and electric cars as niche products, too expensive or unreliable to become truly mainstream.

There are four main problems that need solving, according to Khosla – oil, coal, cement and steel which, between them, are responsible for 75 per cent of greenhouse-gas emissions. For technology to save the planet it must reach what he calls the 'Chindia' price – a level at which a new green product can compete fairly with existing products and can be adopted by India and China, whose energy needs now rival those of America. No matter what the environmental costs, Indian consumers won't buy a $22,000 Prius hybrid electric car when Tata makes the Nano for $2,000.

Khosla stressed the speed of change which in his view is going to catch many by surprise. He remarked that in 1990 when he put his email address on his business card, people laughed. The speed of change seems improbable before it happens.

Technology and science have the capacity both to change and to save the world, but can we do it in time, before we have done irretrievable damage to our planet and our society? Chapter 7 assesses the risks.

PART 2
Sustainability

6

Fifty Wasted Years

Chapter 2 traced the development of abundance as an economic concept, but although we are rapidly becoming able to produce as many goods and services as we need at very low, or even no cost, there remains the spectre of rapidly depleting natural resources and thoughtless pollution of our environment as a by-product of technological progress. As we enter the second decade of the twenty-first century the question of the future of human society is dominated by the issue of sustainability. This issue has had a long incubation period, and some of the key contributors to the debate are profiled here. However, this vital issue still has not reached the top of the agenda for many governments and business organizations.

The Pioneers

John Elkington (1997) credits Rachel Carson's *Silent Spring* (1962) with having sparked the 'environmental revolution'. She drew public attention to the massive destruction of wildlife caused by the use of chemical insecticides and other biocides. Organizations such as Friends of the Earth were founded; support for such bodies as the World Wildlife Fund grew rapidly.

Yet some 14 years earlier William Vogt in his prescient work *Roads to Survival* (1948) had drawn attention to the problems already discernible in respect of man's relationships with his environment, relationships which 'are inevitably exerting a gargantuan impact upon the human world of tomorrow. Disregarded they will almost certainly smash our civilization.' He went on to challenge the American people as follows:

> *Anyone reading this book should share the author's conviction, deepening ever more as the book was written, of how extremely fortunate we are to be Americans. I hope I may help this realization to grow, and*

that with it there will also grow the recognition of the opportunity and responsibility we all have, not only to be effective members of our own national community, but also of the world community. We have not treated our country well; only its lush bountifulness has made possible the richness of our lives in the face of our abusive wastefulness. We still have much wealth left; and as we prudently husband it to avert our own rainy day, we must, in human decency as well as in self-protection, use our resources to help less well-endowed peoples.

Fifty years before Carson's book appeared an English poet, Gordon Bottomley (1912) delivered a warning that was not heeded.

When you destroy a blade of grass
You poison England at her roots:
Remember no man's foot can pass
Where evermore no green life shoots.

You force the birds to wing too high
Where your unnatural vapours creep:
Surely the living rocks shall die
When birds no rightful distance keep.

In 1970 a book by a Yale professor of law appeared which topped the US best-sellers list for 13 weeks – *The Greening of America* (Reich, 1970). The opening sentence grabs attention with its stark message: 'America is dealing death, not only to people in other lands, but to its own people.' Reich went on to assert:

There is a revolution coming. It will not be like revolutions of the past. It will originate with the individual and with culture, and it will change the political structure only as its final act. It will not require violence to succeed, and it cannot be successfully resisted by violence. It is now spreading with amazing rapidity, and already our laws, institutions and social structure are changing in consequence.

In 1971, motivated by their vision of a green and peaceful world, a small team of activists set sail from Vancouver, Canada, in an old fishing boat. These activists, the founders of Greenpeace, believed a few individuals could make a difference. Their mission was to 'bear witness' to US underground nuclear testing at Amchitka, a tiny island off the West Coast of Alaska, which is one of the world's most earthquake-prone regions. Amchitka was the last refuge for

3,000 endangered sea otters, and home to bald eagles, peregrine falcons and other wildlife. Even though their old boat, the *Phyllis Cormack*, was intercepted before it got to Amchitka, the journey sparked a flurry of public interest. The USA still detonated the bomb, but nuclear testing on Amchitka ended that same year, and the island was later declared a bird sanctuary.

The Report of the Club of Rome

In 1972, the Club of Rome, an international think-tank, published a report which argued that depletion of the Earth's natural resources at the then current rate would eventually lead to severe economic collapse. The Club attracted considerable public attention with its report *Limits to Growth* (Meadows, 1972), which has sold 30 million copies in more than 30 translations. The report predicted that growth could not continue indefinitely because of the limited availability of natural resources, oil particularly. The oil crisis in 1973 intensified public concern.

A year later the Science Policy Research Unit of the University of Sussex (1973) published a critique of the Meadows report. Among the important points made were the following:

- The growth versus no growth debate was a sterile one since it did not take into account two very important issues – the composition of growth and the distribution of the fruits of growth. Some types of growth are consistent with or actually enhance the conservation of the environment.

- The report underestimates the possibilities of continued technological progress. The inclusion of technological progress in the Meadows model in sectors from which it was excluded would have the effect of indefinitely postponing some of the catastrophic outcomes predicted by the model. A forecast for the next 100 years made in 1870 would have omitted oil as a source of energy, along with nuclear power; it would probably also have excluded most synthetic fibres, aluminium and some other metals as well as the computer. Also such a forecast might well have cautioned that most cities in the developed countries would be brought to a halt within 50 years owing to the accumulation of horse manure.

- The Meadows study does not distinguish between the physical and the political and economic factors limiting growth. The main problems in providing food for a growing world population are political rather than physical.

- The model, which is at the global level, needs disaggregating, for example by distinguishing between the developed and developing nations.

However, even before *Limits to Growth* was published Pestel and Mestarovic (1974) had begun work on a far more elaborate model. (It distinguished 10 world regions and involved 200,000 equations compared with 1,000 in the original Meadows model.) The research had the full support of the Club of Rome and the final publication, *Mankind at the Turning Point*, was accepted as the official Second Report to the Club of Rome in 1974. In addition to providing a more refined regional breakdown, Pestel and Mesarović had succeeded in integrating social as well as technical data. The Second Report revised the predictions of the original *Limits to Growth* forecast and gave a more optimistic prognosis for the future of the environment, noting that many of the factors were within human control and therefore that environmental and economic catastrophe were preventable.

However, the world recession which followed the oil crisis of the early seventies diverted peoples' attention and saw concern for the environment relegated to the bottom of the agenda.

Critical Episodes

The following years saw a number of influential events which set alarm bells ringing again. One such was the Bhopal disaster in India, an industrial accident at a Union Carbide plant in the Bhopal. On 3 December 1984, the plant released 42 tonnes of toxic gas (MIC) gas, exposing more than 500,000 people to grave danger. The first official immediate death toll was 2,259. A more probable figure is that 8,000 died within two weeks, and it is estimated that an additional 8,000 have since died from gas-related diseases.

In 1985 the Antarctic ozone hole was discovered by British scientists Joseph Farman, Brian Gardiner and Jonathan Shanklin of the British Antarctic Survey. The ozone 'hole' is really a reduction in concentrations of ozone high above the earth in the stratosphere.

In April 1986 there was an explosion at the nuclear power plant at Chernobyl in the Ukraine, which at that time was part of Soviet Russia. The result was a significant release of radioactivity into the atmosphere which led to a number of deaths from radiation. The plume of radioactivity drifted over much of the western Soviet Union, eastern Europe, northern and western Europe and eastern North America, causing considerable public alarm. Large areas of the Soviet territory were contaminated and over 300,000 people had to be settled elsewhere.

In 1987 another influential publication helped trigger a new wave of concern. This was *Our Common Future* produced by the World Commission on Environment and Development (1987), under the leadership of Gro Harlem Brundtland, Prime Minister of Norway. This report brought the new concept of 'sustainable development' to the attention of a world-wide audience. The Brundtland Commission laid down the most well-known definition of what had by then become known as sustainable development:

> *Meeting the needs of the present without compromising the ability of*
> *future generations to meet their own needs.*

A fresh wave of public concern, from 1987 to 1990, was signalled by the adoption of policies for environmental protection by world politicians and by the activities of a resurgent 'green' consumer movement.

THE INTERGOVERNMENTAL PANEL ON CLIMATE CHANGE

1988 saw the setting up of the Intergovernmental Panel on Climate Change (IPCC) by the World Meteorological Organization (WMO) and by the United Nations Environment Programme (UNEP). The IPCC was established to provide the decision-makers and others interested in climate change with an objective source of information about the subject.

Its constituency is made up of:

- Governments: the IPCC is open to all member countries of WMO and UNEP. Governments participate in plenary sessions of the IPCC where main decisions about the IPCC work programme are taken and reports are accepted, adopted and approved. They also participate in the review of IPCC reports.

- Scientists: hundreds of scientists all over the world contribute to the work of the IPCC as authors, contributors and reviewers.

- People: as a United Nations body, the IPCC work aims at the promotion of the United Nations human development goals.

THE EXXON VALDEZ DISASTER

Fresh public concern for the environment was stimulated by the Exxon Valdez disaster. On 24 March 1989, the tanker *Exxon Valdez*, en route from Valdez, Alaska to Los Angeles, California, ran aground on Bligh Reef in Alaska. The vessel was travelling outside normal shipping lanes in an attempt to avoid ice. Within six hours of the grounding, the *Exxon Valdez* spilled approximately 10.9 million gallons of its 53-million-gallon cargo of oil. Eight of the eleven tanks on board were damaged. The oil would eventually impact over 1,100 miles of non-continuous coastline in Alaska, making it the largest spillage of oil to date in US waters.

The images that the world saw on television and descriptions they heard on the radio that spring were of heavily oiled shorelines, dead and dying wildlife and thousands of workers mobilized to clean beaches. These images reflected what many people felt was a severe environmental insult to a relatively pristine, ecologically important area that was home to many species of wildlife endangered elsewhere. In the weeks and months that followed, the oil spread over a wide area, resulting in an unprecedented response and cleanup – in fact, the largest cleanup of oil pollution ever mobilized. Many local, state, federal, and private agencies and groups took part in the effort. Even today scientists continue to study the affected shorelines to understand how an ecosystem like Prince William Sound responds to, and recovers from, an incident like the *Exxon Valdez* oil spill.

THE RIO SUMMIT

In 1992, more than 100 heads of state met in Rio de Janeiro, Brazil, for the first international Earth Summit convened to address urgent problems of environmental protection and socio-economic development. The assembled leaders signed two conventions, one on climate change and one on biological diversity. They also endorsed the Rio Declaration and adopted Agenda 21, a 300-page plan for achieving sustainable development in the twenty-first century.

The Commission on Sustainable Development(CSD) was created to monitor and report on implementation of the Earth Summit agreements. It was agreed that a five-year review of Earth Summit progress would be made in 1997 by the United Nations General Assembly meeting in special session.

In 1994, at the International Conference on Population and Development, 179 governments accepted a plan of action to achieve universal primary education, steep reductions in child and infant mortality, and, by 2015, universal access to reproductive health care, family planning, assisted childbirth and prevention of sexually transmitted diseases.

Human Rights and Poverty

The major focus of attention by activists in the mid 1990s shifted attention from a more or less exclusive concern with the environment and on to other issues such as human rights.

SHELL IN NIGERIA

A major case was Shell and its actions in Nigeria. In 1995 Ken Saro-Wiwa, a writer and opponent of the regime in power, together with eight colleagues, was tried and executed. They were accused of conspiring to murder several people killed in political disturbances in Ogonland in the previous year. These disturbances involved clashes between minority groups and the government and between the groups and Shell over alleged environmental despoliation of their region and over the distribution of government oil revenues. The convictions were the outcome of a trial that independent observers considered unfair. In spite of appeals from other countries, including UK Prime Minister John Major and Nelson Mandela, the executions went ahead. Protests against Shell broke out all over the world. In the short term the impact on Shell's business was relatively slight, in that at the end of the year its share price and profits stood at record levels. Nevertheless the impact was profound. The image of the company had been tarnished. Individual senior executives felt branded. The lessons were quickly learned and Shell produced its first Social Report in 1998. This was despite the fact that in 1997, John Jennings, the retiring chairman, had stated that the Board could not accept the demands of activists that the company should produce one.

Predictably, reactions to the report varied from seeing it as a public relations exercise to welcoming it as a first step on the road to transparency. The company now stated 'Shell companies will no longer form joint ventures where partners decline to adopt business principles compatible with ours.' This does not remove the dilemma of what to do about existing relationships. Shell remains in Nigeria, where it has been involved since colonial days. Oil companies face particular problems in that they have to operate in parts of the world where oil is to be found. Once they decide to go to a particular country they have to make a long-term commitment because of the nature of the exploration and extraction business and over time democratic regimes may be displaced by other kinds.

Meanwhile, in April 2001, the United States Supreme Court announced that it would allow a civil action to proceed in which Saro Wiwa's relatives would claim that Shell aided and abetted the writer's torture and death. In June 2009 the action was settled out of court.

NIKE

Another high profile human rights case in the 1990s was that of Nike, which focused public attention on the exploitation of labour in developing countries. In 1996 there were demonstrations by activists at the opening of the company's San Francisco store on the grounds that the company's products were produced under sweatshop conditions. At first the company's response was defensive. It argued that a poorly paying job was better than no job; that the issue of low wages in developing countries was not something any one company could do anything about and that protests should be directed to the UN; and that in any case Nike was dealing with the problem.

Nike was to some extent responsible for drawing the fire of activists to itself because of the high profile the company had built for itself and its brand. (It spent $280 million on advertising in 1994). Its promotional expenditure, involving millions of dollars in fees to sports stars to wear its products, contrasted sharply with the miserly wages paid to its employees and those of its contractors. The company was accused of ruthlessly moving contracts from country to country in search of lower labour costs.

Following worldwide concern over its activities, the Nike Board changed its approach. First it stopped the use of the hazardous chemical toluene. Also it began supporting research initiatives and conferences on international manufacturing practices and instituted some independent monitoring of its production sites. The Nike case led to the setting up of an independent monitoring service, the Apparel Industry Partnership and the Apparel, Footwear and Retailing Working Group of the NGO Business and Social Responsibility.

By the year 2001 Nike's products were being manufactured in 700 sub-contractors factories worldwide. No person under the age of 16 is allowed to work in any factories making apparel and none under 18 in factories making footwear. As well as internal teams that regularly visit these factories there are audits by PricewaterhouseCoopers. The factory sites and the results of the external audits are posted on the company's website. Nike has joined the Global Alliance for Workers and Communities that was set up in 1999. This group identifies workplace issues, highlights compliance problems and provides guidance for the funding of education programmes, health clinics and community programmes.

The company's Community, Environmental and Labour Affairs Department employed 90 people, with two Vice presidents of Corporate Responsibility – one to manage the team and one for external outreach and strategy. Hannah Jones of Nike (Jones, 2001) states that 'Nike believes that the integration of ethical behaviour and sustainable development into every aspect of society and business is fundamental and essential to the long term health of the world and to our business.'

She goes on to say that 'that's an easy, blithe statement to make, when the reality is complex, multi-faceted, and there are no easy, one stop answers available to put consumers' concerns to rest.'

The Kyoto Protocol

The Kyoto Protocol was adopted in Kyoto, Japan, on 11 December 1997 but did not come into force until 16 February 2005. The Kyoto Protocol is an international agreement linked to the United Nations Framework Convention on Climate Change. The major feature of the Kyoto Protocol is that it set binding targets for 37 industrialized countries and the European community for reducing greenhouse gas (GHG) emissions. These amount to an average of 5 per cent against 1990 levels over the five-year period 2008–2012

Recognizing that developed countries are principally responsible for the current high levels of GHG emissions in the atmosphere as a result of more than 150 years of industrial activity, the Protocol places a heavier burden on developed nations under the principle of 'common but differentiated responsibilities.'

One hundred and eighty-four Parties of the Convention have ratified its Protocol to date. The detailed rules for the implementation of the Protocol were adopted at COP 7 in Marrakesh in 2001, and are called the 'Marrakesh Accords.' (This agreement has been superseded by the Copenhagen Accord of 2009.)

In the UK, global warming was linked to the experience of the wettest winter (2000/2001) since records began, accompanied by widespread floods, The subject hit the headlines again in April 2001 when President George Bush announced that the United States would not ratify the Kyoto treaty. Soon afterwards Anita Roddick called for an international boycott of Esso petrol because of Exxon's support for Bush's action. The boycott was backed in the UK by a number of celebrities, including controversial artist Damien Hirst, comedian Rory Bremner, singer Annie Lennox, and Bianca Jagger, the former wife of the Rolling Stones singer.

The Anti-Globalization Movement

At the millennium the most public expressions of concern over the environmental and social impact of globalization took the form of mass demonstrations in several cities throughout the world. The violence accompanying these has been rightly condemned, but there was growing acceptance that the issues that were raised by the great majority of peaceful protestors were important and worthy of serious consideration. Books such as Naomi Klein's *No Logo* (2000) and Noreena Hertz's *The Silent Takeover* (2001) became international best sellers, exerting a powerful influence on peoples' attitudes to business.

No Logo has been described as 'the bible of anti-corporate militancy'. In it, Klein sets out her thesis under four headings:

- No space – an account of the power of global brands.

- No choice – concentration of power in retailing leading to restriction of consumer choice.

- No jobs – as investment switches from investing in production facilities and labour to spending on marketing, mergers and brand management.

- No logo – how and why there is a political reaction against global corporate power.

Klein's work is based on extensive research including field studies of working conditions in the developing countries. There is no doubt that she gives an accurate account of a great deal of corporate activity.

She begins with a graphic account of de-industrialization as it has affected the garment manufacturing district of Toronto where erstwhile factories and workshops are now being converted into loft style apartments or workshops and business premises for artists, graphic designers, yoga instructors or film producers. The few workers left in the garment trade are elderly and she contrasts this with the youth of the garment workers in countries like Indonesia who are working for sub-contractors of Nike, the Gap or Liz Claiborne, earning less than US$2 a day. Here and elsewhere in Asia she encountered working conditions very similar to those which prevailed in the factories and sweatshops of Britain and America around 100 years ago or in countries like Greece Portugal or Ireland less than 50 years ago.

She accuses multinational corporations such as Coca-Cola, Microsoft, IBM, McDonald's and, above all, Nike of being engaged in a process of 'mining the planet's poorest back country for unimaginable profits.'

The migration of much manufacturing from the developed to the developing world has undoubtedly led to the exploitation of labour markets characterized by low wages, poor working conditions and the suppression of trades unions, and the campaign inspired by Klein's work to improve these conditions is to be applauded. Nevertheless it must be recognized that the companies involved have had to face the stark alternative – either move manufacturing to areas of low-cost labour or go out of business, as has indeed happened in the case of many clothing and shoe manufacturing companies. Poor working conditions in Europe and North America in the past did not improve overnight. It took many decades of economic growth, productivity gains, the rise of organized labour, growing regulation of industry by governments and the leadership of a few pioneering progressive companies to produce the conditions that prevail today. Hopefully, the process of improvement in countries like Mexico or China can be worked through in a shorter time frame, but this depends at least as much on the policies and actions of national governments and intergovernmental agencies as on those of corporations.

Klein's central thesis is that as more people discover the brand name secrets of 'the global logo web' their outrage will fuel the next big political movement – a vast wave of opposition aimed at transnational corporations, particularly those with very high brand name recognition. She describes these companies as producers of brands rather than products. She is, however, mistaken in stating that brands were first developed as a means of enabling consumers to differentiate between mass-produced products that were virtually indistinguishable from each other. The brands I remember from childhood represented goods and products that were quite distinctive in their quality, and value for money. Names such as Cadbury's, Mars, Lux toilet soap, Ovaltine, Singer and Hoover were bywords for quality and better than a written guarantee. She also ignores the key role played in a manufacturing process by product development and design. Her description of what goes on is confined to two activities – making the product and marketing it. But before a product can be made – whether it is a computer chip, a running shoe or an automobile, it has to be designed and developed and it is in the quality of that design and the extent to which it meets consumer expectations that the true value of the associated brand lies.

It is possibly the case that strong brands can be built on the basis of advertising and image-building alone, and it is true to say that to associate a product with a particular lifestyle or set of aspirations can be an effective marketing tool, as in the case of Starbucks. In focusing as she does on Nike she has picked a soft target. In this case it may be justifiable to say that the brand is the product. People don't buy trainers, they buy Nike and all the associations of sporting excellence that have been built up around that brand. The contrast between the wealth of Nike shareholders and managers and, not least, the sport stars who sponsor the product on the one hand and the young persons who work in the many factories in the developing countries understandably makes people like Klein angry.

The process of building an image of a particular lifestyle or ideal around a product for marketing purposes is not, however, a new one. Why, when we have reason to celebrate, do we order champagne instead of sparkling sauvignon blanc? It is because clever marketing over many years has led us to associate the brand name 'champagne' with success and happiness. When we drink to the health of the happy couple at a wedding reception from bottles costing up to 10 times the cost of a good sparkling wine how many of us stop to think about the hourly wage of the grape pickers on the estates of the great chateaux? Brand symbols – logos – not only act as a means of instant recognition to the prospective purchaser, but also act as a badge of status.

The Millennium Goals

In 2000 world leaders set eight goals to be achieved by 2015. These were:

- end poverty and hunger

- universal education

- gender equality

- child health

- maternal health

- combat HIV/AIDS

- environmental sustainability

- global partnership.

The United Nations report on the Millennium Goals 2009 stated that major advances in the fight against poverty and hunger have begun to slow or even reverse as a result of the global economic and food crises. The assessment, launched by UN Secretary-General Ban Ki-moon in Geneva, warned that, despite many successes, overall progress had been too slow for most of the targets to be met by 2015.

The Copenhagen Summit

The first decade of the twenty-first century ended with the much heralded Copenhagen Summit on global warming, which was much hyped in advance and of which much was hoped. For the most part, peoples' hopes were not fulfilled.

One hundred and ninety-two countries were represented at the summit. All agreed that the atmosphere could only safely absorb a finite amount of greenhouse gas and that mankind had already used up most of its carbon budget

The Accord reached after two weeks of frantic negotiations agreed a set of objectives – such as the need to keep the temperature increase below 2°C – but did not make it clear how they would be achieved. The summit's most important goal was to set binding emission targets and on this it failed. Delegates spent two weeks debating a range of possibilities, but the Accord contained no specific targets, only an agreement for each country to submit more suggestions by the end of January 2010. The two biggest sources of emissions, the USA and China, were criticised for their failure to move beyond their opening bids on emissions. In the end, delegates only agreed to 'take note' of the accord, rather than formally to adopt it, but even then there were five countries who did not agree.

The rich countries came to Copenhagen prepared to offer poor nations a large sum of money in return for their signatures on an agreement which, in effect, would avoid any significant adjustments to Western standards of living. Under the Accord $20bn would go to developing countries over the following three years and $100bn annually by 2020. Many developing countries were willing to accept the deal but not all. Sudan and Venezuela led the resistance.

President Obama was accused of trying to impose the will of five nations on the rest of the world. However, Copenhagen might have ended without any statement at all had Obama not ignored the democratic process by holding exclusive talks with China, India, Brazil and South Africa. Many small nations protested that they only learnt of the Accord when President Obama announced it at a press conference.

UK Prime Minister Gordon Brown tried to strike a positive note, saying that the Accord represented a first step towards saving the planet from dangerous global warming.

Disenchantment over the outcome of the recent Copenhagen climate conference was 'justified,' said US President Barack Obama, speaking on PBS TV, 24 December 2009. However, he defended the little progress that was made at the meeting. 'The science says that we've got to significantly reduce emissions over the next 40 years. There's nothing in the Copenhagen agreement that ensures that that happens,' he argued.

But Obama added: 'What I said was essentially that rather than see a complete collapse in Copenhagen ... at least we kind of held ground and there wasn't too much backsliding from where we were.'

Business reaction to the outcome of the Copenhagen summit was generally negative, saying political leaders missed the opportunity to get billions of pounds of investment flowing into green technology.

The summit was the focus of demonstrations by people representing a wide range of NGOs and informal groupings of individuals concerned about climate change. However, the most frequently heard chant was 'System change, not climate change.' Among the more active protesters were many who saw capitalism as the root cause of climate change and other threats to human life on the planet.

Summary

The history of the sustainability movement highlights the very real risks of ignoring public concern about the impact of business on the environment, and the proven effectiveness of what may appear to begin as small, amateur campaigns against large multinational corporations and organizations. In an age of ever-increasing instant, global communications, the need for responsible, transparent, well-thought through strategies for dealing with sustainability issues becomes imperative.

The pioneers who first raised concerns about the impact of economic growth and globalization on the natural environment and on such things as human rights at the beginning of the second half of the twentieth century would no doubt have been bitterly disappointed by the lack of progress made by the time of the Copenhagen Accord. They would have seen it as 50 wasted years.

Postscript

As this book was going to press, news broke of the disastrous leak of oil from the BP drilling operation in the Gulf of Mexico, giving even more force to the feeling that fifty years have indeed been wasted.

7

Sustainability Issues in a Post-Scarcity World

Introduction

Chapters 3 and 4 outlined some of the limitless possibilities of the economics of abundance, some of them happening right now, others which are likely to occur in the next 50 years. It could be a good world to live in, where many of today's problems such as incurable diseases, famine, polluting methods of production and transportation, meaningless work and access to education have been solved. But that is an optimistic outlook; there is significant risk that that future may never arrive, or only in a severely compromised form that does not benefit the planet or significant sections of society. This chapter examines these risks in more detail.

What scale of risk are we talking about? Quite possibly nothing less than the catastrophic collapse of global society, leading to very large scale loss of life, damage to property and to the environment. This scenario could be precipitated by major events in any one of the components of what Tomorrow's Company have called the 'triple context':

- the environment

- the global economy

- the socio-political sphere.

In this chapter risk is discussed under these three headings for clarity, but this should not disguise their interconnectedness.

Environmental Risks

The word 'environment' covers an immense range of complex issues, among which the following interrelated topics are perhaps the most prominent:

- the emission of 'greenhouse gases' and global warming

- water shortages

- pollution of rivers and lakes

- destruction of the rain forests

- species facing extinction

- use of chemical fertilisers and pesticides

- exhaustion of non-renewable resources

- disposal of toxic waste and nuclear waste.

Each of these areas of concern has its own group of activists, its own NGOs, intergovernmental agencies and committees, and the field as a whole has been the focus of innumerable international conferences, not least the high-profile Copenhagen summit in December 2009.

The exigencies of space make it impossible to explore each of the above aspects of environmental sustainability in detail and so the discussion here will focus on just two of them: climate change and the potential exhaustion of non-renewable natural resources, two topics that have dominated discussion and aroused considerable controversy throughout the first decade of this century.

THE CLIMATE CHANGE CONTROVERSY

The Earth has warmed by 0.74°C over the last 100 years. Around 0.4°C of this warming has occurred since the 1970s. The recent Fourth Assessment Report (AR4) of the Intergovernmental Panel on Climate Change (IPCC) (IPCC 2007) asserted that human activity is the primary driver of the observed changes in climate. The report's main conclusions are as follows:

- The current scientific consensus is that the main human influence on global climate is emissions of the key greenhouse gases – carbon dioxide (CO_2) methane and nitrous oxide. The accumulation of these gases in the atmosphere strengthens the greenhouse effect. At present, just over 7 billion tonnes of CO_2 is emitted globally each year through fossil-fuel use, and an additional 1.6 billion tonnes are emitted by land-use change, largely by deforestation. The concentrations of these gases in the atmosphere have now reached levels unprecedented for tens of thousands of years.

- According to AR4, mean global temperatures are likely to rise between 1.1 and 6.4°C (with a best estimate of 1.8 to 4°C) above 1990 levels by the end of this century, depending on the level of emissions. This will result in a further rise in global sea levels of between 20 and 60 cm by the end of this century, continued melting of ice caps, glaciers and sea ice, causing changes in rainfall patterns and intensification of tropical cyclones.

There are, however, minority views held by some climate scientists and economists, which either refute the idea that climate change is occurring or argue that if it is occurring it is due to other factors, such as changes in the activity of sunspots. One person who has summarized the sceptics' position for the lay reader is former UK Chancellor of the Exchequer, Nigel Lawson (2008).

Yet another viewpoint is that of Professor Philip Stott of the UK School of African and Oriental Studies who argues that the billions of dollars which would be spent implementing Kyoto would achieve very little by way of temperature reduction, but could be better spent on clean water for the world or clearing the debt of all 41 of the world's poorest countries.

His views are echoed in a book by Bjorn Lomberg (2001) who, while putting forward the controversial opinion that current doom-laden predictions are unwarranted, goes on to suggest that actions taken by governments and environmental agencies could actually make matters worse.

Global warming, he asserts, will not reduce food production nor increase storms and hurricanes, but the cost of reducing it, estimated at some US$5 trillion, will damage world economic development and hit the developing countries hardest in terms of employment, industry and exports.

To complicate the picture, it also appears to be the case that there can be periods of no- or reducing- global warming within an overall period of increasing global warming. According to some records, there was no significant global warming between 1998 and 2008; or between 1981 and 1989, or between 1977 and 1985.

However, according to a number of recent studies the current lull in no way contradicts the fact that human emissions of greenhouse gases are causing long-term warming. The NCDC study in particular looked at both observed temperature records and at climate model predictions for the twentieth and twenty-first centuries. Their results indicated that climate change over the twenty-first century is likely to involve periods of a decade or two when the global average surface air temperature shows no upward trend or even slight cooling, while the long term trend continues to indicate warming.

So-called global warming sceptics are, however, getting more vocal than ever, and banding together to show their solidarity against the scientific consensus. Upwards of 800 sceptics took part in the second annual International Conference on Climate Change – sponsored by the Heartland Institute, an American conservative think tank – in March 2009. Keynote speaker and Massachusetts Institute of Technology meteorologist Richard Lindzen told the gathering that 'there is no substantive basis for predictions of sizeable global warming due to observed increases in minor greenhouse gases such as carbon dioxide, methane and chlorofluorocarbons.'

Most sceptics attribute global warming to natural cycles, not emissions from power plants, automobiles and other human activity. They argue that any warming from the growth of greenhouse gases is likely to be minor, and difficult to detect above the natural fluctuations of the climate. Among the possible natural explanations include increased output from the sun, increased absorption of the sun's heat owing to a change in the Earth's reflectivity, or a change in the internal climate system that transfers heat to the atmosphere.

But scientists have not been able to validate any such reasons for the current warming trend, despite exhaustive efforts. And a raft of recent peer-reviewed studies – many which take advantage of new satellite data – back up the claim that it is emissions from tailpipes, smokestacks and factory-farmed animals (which release methane) that are causing global warming.

A different kind of scepticism, however, is to doubt whether the rich countries can do much to arrest climate change as vast populations in the emerging countries struggle to raise their living standards.

At the World Economic Forum at Davos in 2004 the issue of sustainability came first in a delegate vote on the most important issues currently facing business – ahead of problems to do with the world's financial systems. Powerful arguments are now being put forward to demonstrate that doing good for the environment can be good for business.

The Intergovernmental Panel on Climate Change's (IPCC) 2007 report provides a clear basis for action by asserting that the evidence for global warming is 'unequivocal'. The advent of an American president who is committed to act, with a team of advisers who are not simply believers in climate change but advocates of tough measures to mitigate it, is accelerating the momentum for action.

In Europe, 'green' parties have had a considerable influence on European Community legislation. In 17 European countries there are 'green' members of national parliaments and in France, Belgium, Germany Italy and Finland they have taken ministerial positions.

In the UK, however, the Green Party is very much an outsider – to some degree because of Britain's electoral system which works in favour of the established major parties. As at June, 2010, all that the UK had to show politically were two Green Party MEPs out of 46 across the EU, two Green Party members of the Scottish Parliament and two members of the London Assembly.

In May 2009 a group of 20 Nobel prize-winning scientists, economists and writers took part in the St James's Palace Nobel Laureate Symposium on climate change. The symposium concluded that the United Nations climate summit in Copenhagen in December 2009 must agree to halve greenhouse-gas emissions by 2050 to stop temperatures from increasing by more than 2°C. While even a 2°C temperature rise will have adverse consequences, a bigger increase would create 'unmanageable climate risks', according to the St James's Palace memorandum, signed by 20 Nobel laureates in physics, chemistry, economics, peace and literature. In the event, the Copenhagen summit was only able to muster a statement that the temperature must not be allowed to rise over 2°C, without any commitment as to how that might be achieved.

Business leaders are similarly unenthusiastic: the 2009 PricewaterhouseCoopers Global CEO survey found that 40 per cent of CEOs were 'not at all concerned' about climate change. Only 7 per cent were 'extremely concerned', compared to 42 per cent who were 'extremely concerned' about the economic downturn. These figures suggest an understandable level of 'climate change fatigue' in the face of more pressing issues. Can they afford to be so laissez faire in the face of apparently overwhelming scientific evidence?

POST-SCARCITY AND CLIMATE CHANGE

The forces that are moving the developed world to a post-scarcity state are not only many and powerful, they are moving extremely fast. The worldwide web is doubling every two years. A super computer is now so cheap that an individual household could afford one (if it had a use for such huge computing power!). New sources of energy and new materials are fast being discovered and developed. The impact these forces are having and will continue to have on every aspect of life – the global economy, social and political systems and the natural environment – will be profound.

Climate change, by contrast, although its advance may be equally remorseless, will move relatively slowly. The rate of change to result, say, in a global average temperature rise of 4 degrees by the end of the century is an increase, on average, of .0044 degrees a year. The rate of change that new technologies will create will be exponential by comparison.

At the same time the continuation of economic growth over the next 90 years would enormously increase the wealth available to nations with which to tackle problems arising from climate change as they arise. China is already rich enough to be able to move over 300,000 people in order to forestall a future shortage of water. A little imagination enables us to envisage what might be possible in 10, 20, 50 years time. In this context the belief that we can save the planet by relatively small actions today, such as foregoing foreign holidays or bicycling to the office, seems scarcely credible.

Take for example, the problem of the contribution to greenhouse emissions by cattle. An article in *The Times*, June 11 2009 quoted a recent UN report, which stated that cows release more greenhouse gases than all forms of human transportation combined. Cattle produce some two thirds of ammonia emissions, which cause acid rain, and more than a third of all methane gas released as a result of human activity. Cattle eructate an estimated 60 million tonnes of methane globally every year and methane is 23 times more potent than CO_2 as a heat-trapping gas. The environmental impact of cattle is huge, particularly when the deforestation of land to make way for cattle is taken into account, plus the fuel burnt to make fertiliser to grow cattle fodder, and the 16,000 litres of water needed to produce a single kilogram of beef.

The UN report asserts that animal gases pose a big threat to the world's chemical balance. The simplest way to reduce the emissions would be to cut global consumption of meat and milk. Yet this is not feasible. People are too addicted to their steaks, beef burgers and cheese burgers. Consumption of red meat in the developing countries has risen by a third in the past decade along with growing affluence, and the production of milk and beef is set to double in the next 30 years.

Instead of trying to persuade people to change their dietary preferences, a combination of technological innovation, government incentives and public pressure should be used to ameliorate the situation by changing how cows are farmed and how beef is produced. Geneticists are working on ways of improving bovine digestion to reduce gas emissions and in the Netherlands farms have developed ways to heat manure and trap the methane in it to make electricity for the local grid. A recent report in *The Proceedings of the National Academy of Sciences* concluded that if 1 million cows were treated with a single hormone to increase milk production, the environmental effect would be equivalent to taking 400,000 cars off the road.

Meanwhile, scientists are attempting to produce synthetic meat in laboratory conditions using cell-culture technology. For example, the Dutch Government is sponsoring a £2 million project to try to cultivate pork flesh. Another approach involves changing cattle diet to render them less likely to emit gases. Groupe Danone found that cows emit less methane in the spring. Spring grasses are higher in omega-3 fatty acids, which seem to help the cow to digest better. Several experimental cattle farms have begun feeding the animals year-round on foods rich in omega-3, such as alfalfa and flax, rather than soy or other traditional fodders. Preliminary results suggest that the cows are healthier, produce more nutritious milk, and emit around 18 per cent less methane.

EXHAUSTION OF NATURAL RESOURCES

Despite the fact that the economies of the OECD countries today are variously described as post-industrial, knowledge-based, 'weightless', or information economies, or simply as the 'New Economy' or the e-economy, it remains the case that the most immediate and significant threat to their sustainability is the supply of essential raw materials and energy.

To focus on the energy supply situation alone, a sustained stoppage in the flow of oil from one or more of the world's major sources of supply would have a very rapid impact on the production and distribution of food and manufactured goods. The resultant unemployment and real hardships experienced by the populations of the main advanced industrial societies would ensure that economic collapse would be rapidly followed by social disintegration.

The most likely cause of such disruption is the unsettled political situation in the Middle East, where more than the survival of Israel and the Palestinian state is at risk. America's concern to reduce dependence on imported oil is no doubt fuelled by the anxieties created by this situation. In the context of such a relatively tangible and immediate threat the longer-term problems posed by global warming are likely to be pushed to one side.

The long-term solution to both global warming and the fragility of oil supplies is of course identical – on the one hand reduction in the remorseless growth in the consumption of energy based on fossil fuels and on the other the development of alternative energy sources. The former lies in the sphere of government, using such tools as energy taxes, development of public transport systems, research grants and regulation. The latter task falls mainly to industry – to the oil companies themselves and the automotive manufacturers in particular.

According to the International Energy Agency, if governments continue to pursue current policies the world's energy needs will be more than 50 per cent higher in 2030 than today, with developing countries accounting for 74 per cent, and China and India together for 45 per cent, of the growth in demand. Fossil fuels are forecast to account for 84 per cent of the increase. World oil reserves are sufficient to meet this level of demand, but coal's share will rise from 25 to 28 per cent.

China will become the world's largest energy consumer, ahead of the USA. Emissions of carbon dioxide will jump by 57 per cent by 2030. The USA, China, Russia and India alone will contribute two-thirds of this increase. Even under the IEA's more radical 'alternative policy scenario' CO_2 emissions stabilize only by 2025 and remain almost 30 per cent above 2005 levels. Dramatic changes in technology will be required, the most important of which will be towards carbon-capture-and-storage at coal-fired power plants.

According to Tony Hayward, the chief executive of BP, quoted in an article in *The Times*, 11 June 2009, global oil production will decline because of dwindling demand owing to gains in energy efficiency, not because of a scarcity of supplies of crude.

The *BP Statistical Review of World Energy* showed that, for the first time, total energy demand in poorer countries, including China and India, exceeded that of the wealthier nations in the Organization for Economic Co-operation and Development (OECD).

According to BP there are 1.258 trillion barrels of proven oil reserves left in the ground, enough to supply the world for 42 years at present production rates. The Review said that reserves of gas were sufficient for 60 years and coal for 122 years.

Jeffrey Sachs (2008) has calculated that changing to a sustainable energy system by 2050 would cost well under 1 per cent of annual world income.

In summary, therefore, energy shortages are only likely to lead to a catastrophic breakdown in civil society if the transition from oil-based technologies to alternative energy sources is mis-managed. The threats to economies and livelihoods resulting from climate change are real and serious and must be resolved, but are not so likely to derail post-scarcity abundance as shorter-term energy crises. The two issues are, of course, inextricably linked so resolving one is likely to resolve the other.

Global Economic Risks

The global economic system comprises a number of interacting sub-systems. That part of the system usually referred to as the 'real' economy, that is, the creation of wealth in the form of goods and services has recently been severely set back by the activities of that part of the system that has come to be known as the 'casino' economy.

The 'casino' economy of the global capital and foreign exchange markets is a virtual market place in which actors, both corporate and individual, serving their own self-interests, take actions which affect share prices, commodity prices, and interest and exchange rates regardless of the impact on governments or investors.

For example, a staggering £2 trillion is traded in the international foreign exchange markets every day, the greater part of it speculative in nature. While a small portion of the activity of the global capital and money markets is directly associated with the real economy of production and trade, the vast majority is composed of trades in the paper economy of short-term financial markets. This paper economy is enormous. The value of global financial securities greatly exceeds the value of annual world output of goods and services.

Professor Susan Strange (1997) was one of the first people to compare the speculative activity in the financial markets to a casino:

> The world of high finance today offers the players a choice of games. Instead of roulette, blackjack, or poker, there is dealing to be done – the foreign-exchange market and all its variations; or in bonds, government securities or shares. In all these markets you may place bets on the future by dealing forward and by buying or selling options and all sorts of other recondite financial inventions. Some of the players – banks especially – play with very large stakes. There are also many quite small operators. There are tipsters, too, selling advice, and peddlers of systems to the gullible. And the croupiers in this global finance casino are the big bankers and brokers. They play, as it were, 'for the house'. It is they, in the long run, who make the best living.

She goes on to observe that the big difference between ordinary kinds of gambling and speculation in financial markets is that one can choose not to gamble at roulette or poker, whereas everyone is affected by casino capitalism. What goes on in the back offices of banks and hedge funds 'is apt to have sudden, unpredictable and unavoidable consequences for individual lives?'

In recent times the distinction between the traditional banking system and the casino economy has become increasingly blurred as banks, building societies and insurance companies moved from their traditional role of custodians of peoples' savings and providers of capital into increasingly speculative behaviour.

THE WASHINGTON CONSENSUS

The dominant economic ideology of the last 25 years which has largely determined the nature of the global financial system is embodied in the so-called 'Washington Consensus'. It is an ideology that traces its roots to longstanding policies of the IMF and to adoption by the World Bank of ideas in vogue in Washington early in the Reagan administration concerning deregulation and supply-side economics, the policies of the Thatcher government in the UK and neo-liberal tendencies of the business community and the economics profession in the USA.

Among the favoured policy prescriptions of the Consensus is financial liberalization in both the developed and the developing countries. Domestically it is achieved by weakening or removing controls on interest and credit and by diluting the differences between banks, insurance and finance companies. International financial liberation involves removal of controls and regulations on both the inflows and outflows of financial instruments that move through foreign exchange markets. It is the implementation of these ideas and policies that is perhaps the single most important cause of the surge in global financial flows. An additional factor has been the influence of technological advances that have facilitated the growth of 24-hour electronic trading.

Many of the players in the financial markets buy financial instruments on very thin margins, based on loans obtained by pledging the assets as collateral. This is called 'leverage'. In turn, the borrowed funds are used to purchase other financial assets, multiplying the demand for credit and financial assets. As demand grows, more sophisticated financial assets are invented, including many forms of financial derivatives. A major portion of the accumulated debt remains serviceable only as long as the prices of most assets will rise or at least remain relatively stable. If prices turn down, they easily can lead to a chain-reaction. If investors respond instinctively like a herd, they will bring a far-reaching collapse that constitutes a crisis.

A notorious example of the influence of prominent players was the attack on British sterling in 1992 by George Soros' Quantum Fund. Believing that sterling was overvalued, the Fund quietly established credit lines that allowed it to borrow $15 billion worth of sterling and sell it for dollars at the then 'overvalued' price. Its purpose, of course, was to pay back the loan with cheaper pounds after they had depreciated. Having gone long on dollars and short on sterling, Soros decided to speak up noisily. He publicized his short-selling and made statements in newspapers that the pound would soon be devalued. It wasn't long before sterling was devalued; he made $1 billion in profit. The Quantum Fund's profits were at the expense of the British government, especially the Bank of England, and British taxpayers.

THE FRAGILITY OF THE FINANCIAL MARKETS

The fragility of the financial markets is due to three particular issues: asymmetric information, herd behaviour and self-fulfilling panics. Asymmetric information is a problem whenever one party to an economic transaction has insufficient information to make rational and consistent decisions. In most financial markets where borrowing and lending take place, borrowers usually have better information about the potential returns and risks associated with the investments to be financed by the loans than do the lenders. Moral hazard occurs when borrowers engage in excessively risky activities that were unanticipated by lenders and lead to significant losses for the lender. Yet another form of moral hazard occurs when lenders indulge in lending indiscriminately because they assume that the government or an international institution will bail them out if the loans go awry.

Yet another illustration of asymmetric information is the invention of ever more complex derivatives to shift risk around the financial system. The market for these products has been growing rapidly, both on futures and options exchanges (two of the several places where derivatives are traded). A product developer, for example, can take the risk in a bond and break it down into a series of smaller risks, such as that inflation will reduce its real value or that the borrower will default. These smaller risks can then be priced and sold, using derivatives, so that the bondholder keeps only those risks he wishes to bear. Enron sold a lot of these sorts of derivatives, booking profits on them immediately even though there was a serious doubt about their long-term profitability. There are many examples of huge losses incurred in derivative trading.

The Asian crisis of 1997–98 provides a good example. There were relatively few signals beforehand of impending crisis. All the main East Asian economies displayed in 1994–96 low inflation, fiscal surpluses or balanced budgets, limited public debt, high savings and investment rates, substantial foreign exchange reserves and no signs of deterioration. What then caused the herd-like flight from Asian currencies? No doubt several factors were at work. Opinions began to change among key lenders about the regulation of financial sectors in several Asian countries and their lack of transparency. Several important hedge funds reduced their exposure by shorting currency futures. The calling in of loans led quickly to deep depression in several Asian countries. It has been estimated that the Asian crisis and its global repercussions cut global output by $2 trillion in 1998–2000.

In the autumn of 1998, meltdown seemed very close. In addition to the Asian crisis the Russian government defaulted on its debts. The US stock market fell 20 per cent in August and September, and comparisons with 1929 began to occupy the headlines once more. In late September a major hedge fund, Long Term Capital Management, threatened collapse with potential losses of US$14 billion. Pessimistic and critical books appeared, such as Paul Krugman's *The Return of Depression Economics* (Krugman 2008) George Soros's *The Crisis of Global Capitalism* (Soros, 1998) and Peter Warburton's *Debt and Delusion* (Warbuton, 1998, reprinted 2005). Calls for greater regulation came from all sides – from politicians, central bankers and investment bankers as well as street level activists. A year or so later the storm had passed; the Asian economies bounced back and confidence was restored; calls for reform were once again voices crying in the wilderness.

The Asian crisis of 1998 apart, the 1990s was a decade of continually rising share prices and related investor confidence, the longest running bull market since the Second World War. It was also a period which saw a large number of financial collapses, scandals and cases of fraud. But as each new debacle outdid its predecessors in scale and complexity, the strength of the bull run and the confidence of investors remained unshaken. The general view was that the financial markets were not spinning out of control; bad apples would inevitably appear from time to time and would be dealt with, but the overall financial system was not seriously threatened.

At the turn of the century the markets experienced the so-called dot com boom and bust. For a while 'dot com' enterprises with no profit track record achieved billion dollar valuations and companies in associated IT and communications sectors were disproportionately valued in all the leading stock markets. So much for the efficiency of markets. Once realism had reasserted itself, bear markets returned for a time, but without provoking a serious loss of confidence.

In June 2001 the Bank of England issued a warning that financial regulators around the world should monitor the growing market for credit derivatives. Anxiety was growing that this relatively new form of financial instrument had not been tested during an economic downturn. A typical transaction would involve one institution being paid a fee to underwrite the risk that another institution would not be repaid money it was owed under a credit agreement with a third party. In this way commercial banks can, in theory, transfer the risks associated with the loans they make. The exposures created by these instruments naturally increase as credit risk grows within the economy.

In 2003, Frank Partnoy (2003), a former Wall Street trader turned university law professor, argued the case for an even more pessimistic viewpoint and asserted that the appearance of control in the financial markets is an illusion, and that there was a very real danger of a market meltdown. He pointed to a number of changes since the 1980s that had contributed to the growing fragility of the system. These include the growth of 24-hour trading, the deregulation of markets, the increasing complexity of financial instruments, the growth of private contracts (so-called 'over the counter' trades, which perhaps would be better described as under the counter trades), and the increased separation of ownership from control in large corporations.

Partnoy gives highly detailed and insightful accounts of some of the most notorious financial scandals and scams of the 1990s. He relates the exploits of traders who became legendary on account of the profits they made and the bonuses they earned – people like Frank Quattrone who, in the late 1990s was reputed to be earning $100 million dollars a year. He describes such illicit trades as the currency speculations carried out by Leeson and which led to the collapse of Barings. The sins of such august institutions as CSFB, Salomon Brothers, Bankers Trust, Merrill Lynch and Deutsche Bank are also well documented.

One of the most interesting cases he describes is that of the bankruptcy of Orange County, California, and how the treasurer's investment strategy led to losses of $1.7 billion. Instead of buying US Treasury Bonds he bought a form of derivative known as structured notes, mainly from Merrill Lynch. These contained complex formulae that in essence were a bet on interest rates remaining low. He not only bet $7.4 billion of Orange County's taxpayers' money, he borrowed about $13 billion and invested that in structured notes.

These trades were very profitable to Merrill which made $62.4 million from Orange County in 1993 and 1994 alone. The Orange County treasurer lost his bets when the Federal Reserve raised interest rates. Partnoy was also highly critical of the role played in this and other financial disasters by the credit rating agencies, Standard and Poors and Moody's. Not only did they give AAA ratings to the structured notes, thus enabling the treasurer to fit his large interest-rate bets within the technical limits of his investment powers, they gave Orange County's own bonds AAA ratings right up to December 1994 when the county filed for bankruptcy.

In many cases the lack of transparency in trading reflected ingenious ways invented by traders to enable their companies to avoid regulations. For example, Japanese insurance companies were prohibited from investing in equities, a rule that was highly frustrating as long as the Nikkei index continued to rise. Bankers Trust developed a form of security known as an equity derivative which enabled the Japanese to avoid this rule. It was, in effect, a bet on the Nikkei, and when the Japanese stock market declined a year later the insurance companies suffered substantial losses.

Probably the best known of all the financial debacles in the 1990s caused by the use of derivatives was that of Long Term Capital Management (LTCM). Known as the 'Rolls Royce' of hedge funds, LTCM was founded by an outstandingly successful trader, John Meriwether. He employed some highly qualified people including two Nobel Prize winners, Robert C. Merton and Myron Scholes. Investors rushed to put money with the team and banks were equally keen to make them unsecured loans. Beginning in April 1994, LTCM enjoyed a four-year run of very substantial profits. Banks that were selling complex derivatives to their clients began to pay LTCM to take on the more esoteric risks.

By 1997 the fund employed no less than 25 PhDs. It had about $4.7 billion of equity which it used to borrow $125 billion and enter into $1.25 trillion of derivatives. In August 1998 Russia defaulted on some of its debts, triggering a crisis in the markets as financial institutions that had borrowed to buy Russian bonds were forced to sell other investments to raise cash. In particular they were dumping stocks and bonds in emerging markets in Latin America, Eastern Europe and Asia. LTCM's computer models had assumed that losses in some investments would be compensated for by gains in others. At this time, however, almost every market went down and LTCM's position began to unwind rapidly. Faced with the prospect of the worst crisis the world had experienced in half a century, 14 major banks agreed to contribute $13 billion in return for a 90 per cent stake in the company. A massive crisis was avoided, but the downside was that others drew from the events the lesson that if you failed on a large enough scale either the government or the other players in the system would bail you out.

With scares like this in mind, Partnoy (2003) proposed a number of recommendations to help prevent serious damage to the investment system in the future:

- Treat derivatives like other financial instruments; that is, make them subject to the same prohibitions on fraud, the same disclosure requirements, the same banking regulations, and so on.

- Shift away from narrow rules which parties have been able to circumvent and adopt broader standards.

- Eliminate the 'oligopoly of gatekeepers', such as auditors, lawyers and especially credit-rating agencies.

- Prosecute complex financial fraud effectively.

- Encourage investors to control and monitor their own investments.

We now know that the warnings of Partnoy and others were disregarded. The remorseless growth of debt continued as did the practice of 'passing the parcel' of credit-related derivatives. The distinction between the banking system and the casino economy became blurred as banks, building societies and insurance companies moved from their traditional role of custodians of peoples' savings and providers of capital into increasingly speculative behaviour. As the sub-prime mortgage market crisis developed in the USA, first one card then another was pulled from beneath the house of cards.

In April, 2007, the American bank New Century Financial, which specializes in sub-prime mortgages, filed for Chapter 11 bankruptcy protection. As it sold on many of its debts to other banks, the collapse in the sub-prime market began to have an impact at banks around the world.

On the 14 September UK depositors withdrew £1bn from Northern Rock in what was the biggest run on a British bank for more than a century. They continued to take out their money until the government stepped in to guarantee their savings.

In March 2008, Wall Street's fifth-largest bank, Bear Stearns, was acquired by larger rival JP Morgan Chase for $240m in a deal backed by $30bn of central bank loans. A year earlier, Bear Stearns had been worth £18bn.

In July, Financial authorities stepped in to assist America's two largest lenders, Fannie Mae and Freddie Mac. As owners or guarantors of $5 trillion worth of home loans, they are crucial to the US housing market and authorities agreed they could not be allowed to fail.

In August, in one of the biggest losses in UK corporate history, the Royal Bank of Scotland (RBS) reported a pre-tax loss of £692 million in the first half, after writing down £5.9 billion on investments hit by the credit crunch.

In September, Fannie Mae and Freddie Mac were rescued by the US government in one of the largest bailouts in US history.

Later in the month Lehman Brothers filed for Chapter 11 bankruptcy protection, becoming the first major bank to collapse since the start of the credit crisis. Another major US bank, Merrill Lynch, also stung by the credit crunch, agreed to be taken over by Bank of America for $50bn. This was followed by the US Federal Reserve announcement of an $85bn rescue package for AIG, the country's biggest insurance company, to save it from bankruptcy.

In Britain, Lloyds TSB announced its intention to take over the country's biggest mortgage lender, HBOS, in a £12bn deal creating a banking giant holding close to one-third of the UK's savings and mortgage market. The deal followed a run on HBOS shares.

Also in the same month, in the largest bank failure yet in the United States, Washington Mutual, the giant mortgage lender, which had assets valued at $307bn, was closed down by regulators and sold to JP Morgan Chase.

The US House of Representatives rejected a $700bn rescue plan for the US financial system. On Wall Street share prices fell sharply, with the Dow Jones index slumping 7 per cent or 770 points, a record one-day point fall. However, in October, the US House of Representatives passed the plan.

Whilst these events were taking place, the collapse of the Ponzi scheme run by Bernard Madoff became another major scandal in 2009, but was a very small part of the of the global financial crisis, where the losses amounted to trillions. But it was symptomatic of the underlying causes of the global crash because his success depended on the failure of regulation, greed, lack of transparency and on very inadequate due diligence. Madoff's clients included top-rated banks, hedge funds and investment groups, primarily in New York, Florida, Texas and Europe. None of them worked out the secret of his apparent success, and warnings from a few suspicious investors were ignored by America's Securities and Exchange Commission.

Reporting on the credit crunch has focused on two things – the huge losses sustained by the financial institutions implicated in the crisis and the huge sums devoted by governments to bailing out the banks. Yet there have also been huge losses in terms of the destruction of real wealth as, one after another, manufacturing and service enterprises across the globe have been forced into bankruptcy and their employees thrown out of work. Plant and equipment have become idle and may never be brought back into use. Thousands of skilled workers may never again have the opportunity to employ their skills.

This is a very different scenario from Schumpeter's creative destruction, which is a function of innovation and technical change (see Chapter 5 for a more detailed discussion of Schumpeter's work).

Over the years the ongoing series of scandals and failures has served to undermine the level of trust in both the integrity and the competence of financial services institutions. These failures are systemic. In particular they flow from a culture combining greed, a cavalier attitude to risk, a lack of transparency, lack of alignment between the interests of investors and those of intermediaries and the failure to manage endemic conflicts of interest.

The global financial system currently serves the interests of senior employees and directors of financial institutions and speculators and their legal advisers rather than the interests of wealth-producing enterprises, savers or members of pension funds. The combination of greed, incompetence, fraud and the endemic fragility of a system based on confidence mean that savers face undue risk when entrusting financial institutions with their cash.

NEW REGULATORY REGIMES

In March 2009, following a request by Prime Minister Gordon Brown, the chairman of the UK's Financial Services Authority, Adair Turner, produced proposals for a new regulatory regime for the financial services industry. The report contained a dissection of the recent crisis, blaming governments, regulators and financial institutions for putting too much faith in the efficiency of markets. Key points were:

- The quantity and quality of capital in the overall banking system should be increased significantly above that required by the recommendations on banking laws and regulations issued by the Basel Committee on Banking Supervision. The new regime should require banks to increase their capital buffer in good times so they can reduce it in bad times.

- Banks need to increase by several times the capital they hold against their trading activities.

- A maximum gross leverage ratio should be introduced as a backstop against growth in balance sheets.

- No Glass-Steagall-type separation of banks that would ban commercial banks from engaging in more risky activities – because in part, it wouldn't be practical.

- A new European independent regulatory authority needs to be created to set standards and oversee national supervisors, but individual firms should still be regulated at a national level.

- 'Colleges of supervisors' to supervise complex, cross-border financial institutions.

- The FSA is to look more closely at UK units of foreign institutions.

- Regulators should be able to extend their powers to institutions that become bank-like or become so important they threaten stability, such as hedge funds.

- Codes on remuneration need to be created on a UK and global level. Regulators need to look at pay to ensure it doesn't encourage excessive risk-taking.

- Clearing and central counterparty systems need to be put in place for credit-default swaps.

The report also raised the question of whether mortgages need regulating to limit how much can be borrowed, and asked whether whole classes of products, such as credit-default swaps, need regulations on their design or use.

In August 2009 Turner said that the City had grown 'beyond a socially reasonable size' and that it was accounting for too much of the country's national output and absorbing too many of Britain's brightest graduates.

In particular he cited fixed-income securities, trading, derivatives and hedging as areas that have grown beyond socially optimal levels. He added that he would be in favour of City-specific taxes, such as a Tobin tax, if his proposed new rules on capital failed to shrink investment bank balance sheets and curb the more useless or reckless trading.

Tobin taxes were first proposed by the economist James Tobin in the 1970s as a way to curb speculation in foreign exchange markets and reduce volatility. However, such taxes could apply to other trading, including bonds, equities and derivatives.

The risk with such a tax is that trading would simply shift to more benign regimes and that the taxes might have the unintended consequence of reducing liquidity. Getting global agreement to such a tax would be very difficult.

On 17 June 2009, the US President Barack Obama unveiled his financial regulatory proposals which would give the Federal Reserve Board more power to regulate large, integrated Wall Street firms while also creating a new agency to crack down on abuses by mortgage and credit-card lenders.

- The key issues addressed include largely unregulated trading of complex financial instruments, including mortgage-backed securities, which dragged down some of the nation's largest banks and brokerages as the housing bubble of the mid 2000s collapsed and foreclosures soared. In addition, the proposal aims to tackle widespread criticism of generous pay and bonuses on Wall Street tied to lucrative but risky short-range trading strategies rather than long-term performance.

- The Obama administration's proposal aims to strengthen the Federal Reserve as the primary monitor of large integrated financial houses and, more importantly, to gauge the systemic risks posed by the connections between firms. The plan would have the Fed keep its eyes on a wider range of companies – such as the insurance giant AIG, which played a pivotal role in the meltdown of complex financial instruments – and would allow the government to seize a large financial firm that posed a risk to the wider system.

- At the same time, the White House is taking on the problems of individual consumers by proposing a new agency that would tackle some of the mortgage and credit card industry abuses. The new Consumer Financial Protection Agency would not only regulate those industries with an eye toward protecting consumers, but it could also require institutions to retain as much as 5 per cent of the loans they originate, to ensure that they carry an element of risk.

- Other key aspects of the Obama plan include better coordination among the key government regulatory agencies as well as first-ever federal regulations on hedge funds, an expanded role for the Federal Deposit Insurance Corp. (FDIC), and a proposal to combine two existing regulatory agencies into a new one called the National Bank Supervisor.

SUMMARY

The people who benefit from speculative financial movements are, for the most part, better educated and wealthier than the vast majority of fellow citizens. They have fewer connections to the real economy of production and exchange than most people. And their purpose in trading financial assets, again for the most part, is to make a profit quickly rather than wait for an investment project to mature.

People who do not participate directly in the buying and selling of short-term financial instruments are nonetheless influenced indirectly by the macroeconomic instability and contagion that often accompany interruptions in financial market flows. This is true for people both in developed and developing countries. In developed countries, the voracious appetite of financial markets for more and more resources and for the brightest graduates of the universities saps the vitality of the real economy – the economy that most people depend upon for their livelihood.

In developing countries, attracting global investors' attention is a mixed blessing. Capital market inflows provide important support for building infrastructure and harnessing natural and human resources. At the same time, surges in money market inflows may distort relative prices, exacerbate weakness in a nation's financial sector, and feed bubbles. As the 1998 Asian crisis attests, financial capital may just as easily flow out of, as into, a country. Unstable financial flows often lead to one of three kinds of crises:

- Fiscal crises. The government abruptly loses the ability to roll over foreign debts and attract new foreign loans, possibly forcing the government into rescheduling or default of its obligations.

- Exchange crises. Market participants abruptly shift their demands from domestic currency assets to foreign currency assets, depleting the foreign exchange reserves of the central bank in the context of a pegged exchange rate system.

- Banking crises. Commercial banks abruptly lose the ability to roll over market instruments (that is, certificates-of-deposit) or meet a sudden withdrawal of funds from sight deposits, thereby making the banks illiquid and possibly insolvent.

Although these three types of crisis sometimes appear singly, they more often arrive in combination because external shocks or changed market expectations are likely to occur simultaneously in the market for government bonds, the foreign exchange market, and the markets for bank assets. The vast majority of people in the developing world suffer from these convulsive changes over which they exercise absolutely no control.

The conclusion is that, despite the various attempts at fixes that are taking place, the whole system is fatally flawed. It is failing to meet the needs of savers; it is creating huge short-term pressures on company management teams and it is highly socially divisive because of the huge sums that top people earn in bonuses.

Looking to the future, one of two things must happen. Either there must be a radical cultural change in the financial world – a change which restores integrity to the system – or the system will wither and be replaced by another set of institutions that perform the necessary functions. In this respect, the global financial system poses as great a risk to post-scarcity abundance as mismanaging the transition from oil-based technologies.

Social and Political Risks

Concern about the social impact of economic growth well predates concern about its impact on the environment. Reforming industrialists and politicians of the nineteenth century campaigned against the exploitation of child labour, the employment of women in mines and excessive working hours. It was left to the poets to worry about the erosion of the Arcadian landscape in favour of those 'dark satanic mills'.

In the twentieth century, although the Brundtland report incorporated a societal element into the original concepts of sustainable development, the most widely held perspective in recent years has been one of environmental protection and resource conservation. A consequence of this is that, since the Rio Summit in 1992, sustainable development has been mostly linked to pending global environmental disasters such as global warming, the loss of biodiversity, resource conservation and so on.

Things are now changing and there is a growing appreciation of the social/political dimension of sustainable development. It is evident, however, from much that has been written on the subject, both by company representatives and people in NGOs or pressure groups, that there is considerable lack of clarity regarding what, precisely, is meant by 'social' in the context of sustainable development. There is confusion, too, as to what the implications for policy making are. It is much more difficult to set targets in the social field than in relation to such concrete issues as disposal of toxic waste or restriction of fishing quotas.

In my view the issue of social sustainability needs to be considered country by country rather than at a global level. The focus of concern should be on four things needed by a sustainable society – good governance, social cohesion, strong social institutions and a sound social infrastructure.

GOVERNANCE

In the fourteenth century Ambrogio Lorenzetti was asked by the chief magistrates of Siena to paint allegorical depictions of good and bad government and to represent the effects such regimes would have in the town and the country. The allegory of 'bad government' depicts assassinations, sacking, violence, poverty, famine and so forth, while the one of 'good government' shows prosperous cities, cultivated lands, well-being, wealth, joy and so forth. The overall meaning of the painting is clear: if the city is administered in a 'good' way, then the whole populace will benefit. The artwork is divided into four sections: the Allegory of Bad Government, represented by an evil man with horns dressed in black (like the Devil) who is surrounded by allegorical figures representing Cruelty, Discord, War, Fraud, Anger and Tyranny; the Effects of Bad Government on Town and Country in which the lands are uncultivated and the people are suffering from violence and thefts; the Allegory of Good Government, represented by an old, wise monarch who sits on a throne and is surrounded by allegorical figures like Justice, Temperance, Prudence, Strength, Peace, as well as the theological virtues of Charity, Faith and Hope; and finally, the Effects of Good Government on Town and Country in which the city of Siena is depicted as rich, prosperous, serene and tranquil. These remarkable paintings, which are on public view in the Palazzo Publico, where the magistrates held their meetings, serve better than any definition to indicate what governance is all about.

The World Bank (2009) gives ratings on six indicators of the standard of governance for 212 countries. The indicators are:

1.   voice and accountability

2.   political stability

3.   government effectiveness

4.   regulatory quality

5.   rule of law

6.   control of corruption.

The data also show how the situation has changed over time. Not surprisingly Somalia scores extremely poorly on all six criteria. The chart for Zimbabwe shows how standards have deteriorated between 1998 and 2008, particularly in respect of government effectiveness, rule of law and control of corruption. In sub-Saharan Africa the relatively high standard of governance in Botswana stands in sharp contrast with the very low standard in Angola. The developed country with relatively low scores is Italy, with low ratings for political stability, the rule of law and control of corruption.

The principal consequences of poor governance are widespread corruption at many levels of society, the existence of powerful organized crime groups, and neglect of the country's infrastructure. Poor governance in a number of African countries is the major barrier to the relief of poverty.

SOCIAL COHESION

A society characterized by an adequate level of social cohesion is one in which individuals and communities can co-exist peacefully and, while respecting others' particular beliefs, values and customs, work together to tackle social problems such as crime, drug trafficking and corruption. For social cohesion to be strong enough to support the social fabric within national boundaries, conditions in regard to social justice must be such that individuals and groups see themselves as having a real stake in society and hence are fearful of having something to lose if the social fabric should disintegrate. This implies a need for major steps to eliminate poverty and reduce inequality.

In today's world, respect for other peoples' beliefs, values and customs is a scarce commodity and the sustainability of the way of life of the developed nations is under threat from extremists representing alternative ideologies or religious fundamentalists. As nations hostile to the West gain nuclear capability, the threat of nuclear war may once again overshadow other issues. Groups of terrorists, often with the support of hostile regimes, are capable of carrying out massive acts of sabotage such as 9/11.

The main source of loss of cohesion in a number of countries is the failure of people from different ethnic or religious groups to learn how to embrace diversity, develop tolerance of differences and live together peacefully.

Gross inequality can also lead to a loss of cohesion. It can also have other negative social consequences. Wilkinson and Pickett (2009) studied the link between inequality and the quality of life in the developed countries. They found per capita GDP to be much less significant for the quality of life than the size of the gap between the richest and poorest 20 per cent of the population. The more equal the society, the better the record on life expectancy, infant mortality, obesity, crime, and literacy. The USA, which is the most unequal society in terms of the wealth gap between richest and poorest comes bottom on many of the measures, followed by Portugal and the UK. The Scandinavian countries have the highest scores for equality and for the well-being of their citizens.

SOCIAL INSTITUTIONS

Societal sustainability also requires the existence of strong social institutions of which the family and the local community are of key importance. These are the building blocks of a society, and to the extent that they crumble away so will the whole social fabric be in danger of disintegration. These basic institutions link in with trades unions, churches, clubs, voluntary organizations and groups such as Neighbourhood Watch to establish and reinforce the social mores and to work for the achievement of such goals as greater social justice or the preservation of the countryside.

In the past, where there were strong links between a business, (usually family owned) and a local community, as in the case of Bourneville (Cadbury's) or Port Sunlight (Lever Brothers) in the UK, the company was among the social institutions which, at local level, provided important constituents of the 'glue' that held communities together. That era of business paternalism now lies in the past, but for the sake of the sustainability of society, the links between business and the community may need to be revived.

SOCIAL INFRASTRUCTURE

A sustainable society needs also an adequate level of investment in the social infrastructure, in particular in housing, education and training, healthcare facilities, and the creation of employment opportunities. To achieve this calls for an adequate allocation of the nation's wealth to public investment projects, with the consequent implications for levels of corporate and personal taxation.

SOCIAL CAPITAL

All these things, but particularly strong community ties and a 'sense of civic engagement', fall under the heading of what the Harvard sociologist Robert Putnam (2000) calls 'social capital'. 'Whereas physical capital refers to physical objects and human capital refers to properties of individuals, social capital refers to connections among individuals – social networks and the norms of reciprocity and trustworthiness that arise from them.'

He has drawn attention to indicators of the decline of social cohesion in the USA. He cites, as an example, the decline from over 20 per cent in the 1970s to around 12 per cent in the early 1990s in the proportion of adults attending public meetings on town or school affairs. More recent work, however, indicates that there has been an increase in cohesion since 9/11, reflecting a tendency for people to draw together when they feel under threat.

Emile Durkheim, the great French sociologist, introduced the concept of 'anomie' in his book *The Division of Labour in Society*, first published in 1893. He used the term to describe a condition that was occurring in society such that rules governing how people ought to behave with each other were breaking down and thus people did not know what to expect from one another. Anomie, simply defined, is a state where norms (expectations of behaviours) are confused, unclear or not present. He observed that social periods of disruption (economic depression, for instance) brought about greater anomie and higher rates of crime and deviance and that sudden change also caused a state of anomie. If that process was observable in France in the late nineteenth century how much more intensely is it at work today?

Elkington (1997) also uses the concept of social capital and quotes Fukuyama (1995) who describes social capital as 'a capability that arises from the prevalence of trust in a society'. It is a measure of 'the ability of people to work together for common purposes in groups and organizations'. Fukuyama argues that differences in social capital explain wide divergences in well-being and economic performance between countries. One way in which this comes about is that where a country's social values are such that firms can rely on trust to support their business activities there are large benefits to be gained from lower transaction costs incurred in lawyers', accountants' and auditors' fees. In turn, the state responds to breaches of trust with excessive legislation and regulation.

Over the course of the next few decades the growth of abundance could, in a large number of countries, provide the resources needed to pull people out of the depths of extreme poverty and social deprivation and could provide the investment capital needed to deliver greatly enhanced social infrastructures and hence an improved quality of life.

However, in the past, economic growth has not necessarily delivered a better quality of life, according to a great deal of the evidence. In the UK almost every social indicator, such as chronic disease, crime, unemployment and divorce rates, has deteriorated since the 1950s. More recently the UK government statistical publication *Social Trends* has highlighted the widening gap between rich and poor, the high levels of homelessness amongst single parents and the instability of many relationships. A similar story is told in the USA which, although it has one of the highest average income levels in the world, fares worse than any other developed nation in terms of homelessness, infant mortality, drug abuse, murder, percentage of population on welfare and percentage in prison.

In its October 1997 review the UK National Institute of Economic and Social Research listed the 24 richest nations in terms of GDP per head, and then derived a quality of life ranking based on a combination of the level of GDP generated per hour of work and various social factors such as life expectancy, levels of education and degrees of unemployment, plus political and civil rights. Their conclusions quite clearly show a disconnection between quality of life and economic wealth.

The Economist Intelligence Unit (EIU) (2005) developed an index of the quality of life and calculated it for 111 countries. Nine quality of life factors were identified:

1.   material well-being

2.   health

3.   political stability and security

4.   family life

5.   community life

6.   climate and geography

7.   job security

8.   political freedom

9.   gender equality.

These nine variables were found to explain over 80 per cent of the variation in life-satisfaction scores of some 74 countries. GDP per capita was found to account for over 50 per cent of the inter-country variation in life satisfaction. However, in the developed countries there has been only a very slight upward trend in life satisfaction over several decades, despite the fact that living standards have improved very significantly.

The top five countries for quality of life in 2005, as measured by the EIU index, were: Ireland, Switzerland, Norway, Luxembourg and Sweden. The UK ranked 29th and the USA 13th. Of the countries covered by the study, the bottom five were Tajikistan, Nigeria, Tanzania, Haiti and Zimbabwe.

GROWTH OR DEVELOPMENT?

The use of the term 'development' instead of growth is significant. It implies that the process of wealth creation is concerned with broader goals than simply increases in per capita income. Wealth creation in this sense is not to be measured exclusively in financial terms or counted in numbers of cars or mobile phones produced; rather, it is to be measured in terms of the satisfaction of basic human needs – for a healthy diet, access to education and medical care, to clean air and non-toxic environments, freedom from political oppression and from crime. In other words, the benefits from abundance will depend on the uses it which it is put.

For nations that enjoy abundance the test of successful government should lie in measured increases in the quality of life as perceived by citizens rather than GNP growth. It implies a more equitable distribution of wealth. Perhaps above all it implies the need for peoples' values to change, to be less materialistic. How is this likely to happen? In the developed societies of the West and increasingly in other highly developed nations such as Japan, the closing decades of the twentieth century witnessed massive shifts in human values. Among the most obvious examples are those to do with race, sexuality

– particularly the decriminalisation of homosexuality in a number of countries – artistic freedom from censorship and considerable strides towards the acceptance of female equality. The early advocates of such changes were not only regarded as deviant; they were in many cases quite literally treated as criminals.

Today, radical protesters against the materialism of society and the abuse of power by big business are dismissed as cranks and idealists. Yet in many cases the values they espouse are ones which will become mainstream in the future. The elimination of gross differences in wealth and the quality of life, the acceptance of obligations to future generations and the goal of sustainable development will in the end become fully accepted and embedded as parts of both local and global-values systems. Far-sighted politicians and business leaders can see this and at the very least are swimming with the tide. A very few visionary leaders are ahead of the game.

Undoubtedly there is plenty of room for progress in improving people's quality of life, wherever they live in the world, and it is this is rather than economic growth as traditionally and more narrowly defined that is the essence of the social and economic dimensions of sustainability. This is discussed at more length in Chapter 9, which addresses the poverty trap in which millions find themselves across both the developed and developing world.

In terms of risk, however, socio-political issues have a great deal of potential to derail post-economic abundance. Politicians and business leaders do not have a good track record of ensuring fair and adequate distribution of resources across the globe, and many of the bitter conflicts of the late twentieth and early twenty-first centuries have their roots in these economic and social inequalities.

Sustainable Abundance

This chapter has looked individually at risks to post-scarcity abundance from the 'triple context' of:

- the environment

- the global economy

- the socio-political sphere.

It has shown that although climate change has a very high profile, there are perhaps greater and more immediate risks relating to energy supplies; civil unrest owing to the unequal distribution of wealth; and from a global financial system which operates in many respects like a giant game of poker.

However, the point of managing risk is as much about enabling good things to happen as it is about preventing bad things. And there is a good deal to play for in the post-scarcity economy. If no catastrophic events occur leading to a radical and persistent decline in the rate of world economic growth, world real incomes per head could rise 4.5 times by 2050 and world population by 40 per cent. This would mean a sixfold increase in global output. Much of the increase is likely to be concentrated in the developing world, China and India in particular, but the outcome in the developed countries would be to bring about an unquestionably post-scarcity state.

Is such an implied increase in consumption feasible? The answer is yes and no according to Sachs (2008) – yes, given important changes in incentives, technology and social and political institutions; and no, because the current system is unsustainable. Professor Sachs falls between those environmentalists who see no solution but to cut back consumption and those who believe growth is sustainable, given the right policies.

SACHS IDENTIFIES THREE GOALS

- The end of extreme poverty world-wide by 2025, including improved economic security for people on low incomes within the rich countries as well.

- Stabilization of the world's population at 8bn or below by 2050 through a reduction of fertility rates. This is obviously critical for the achievement of sustainability.

- Sustainable systems of energy, land and resources use that avert the most serious threats of climate change, species extinction, and destruction of ecosystems.

Sachs is optimistic on the supply of resource inputs, arguing that fossil-fuel resources, renewable energy and availability of fresh water should be sufficient to support continued growth over the next half century. This would almost certainly require a transition from mainly oil-based energy technologies to ones based on coal and renewables. The main challenge, in Sachs' view, is to make growth compatible with climate change. While he concedes that climate change is a huge threat, he also believes it can be dealt with at modest cost – less than 1 per cent of global income.

Sach's three goals are important but what is missing is the goal of providing a better quality of life for people in the context of viable and healthy communities. There is little point in raising the income level of poor Africans if the net result is an increase in drug taking, alcoholism, stress-related illnesses, loss of the sense of belonging, and so on. There is little point in saving people from dying of starvation to watch them dying from AIDS.

What is needed, therefore, as part of any policy framework for the future of society, is a clearer view of what constitutes progress and in what ways increasing abundance can be harnessed to promote it. Economic growth over the past decades has been linked in many countries to an increase in drug taking, alcoholism, crime and the breakdown of family life. It has not, in general, been linked to an improvement in any index of human happiness.

Human society has already evolved from mere survival, where almost everyone in a community had to contribute work to achieve enough to stay alive, to a point where, in the developed countries, the essentials to living are produced by a very small percentage of the population, and the rest either work on things that would not, in the past, have been regarded as essential, or are unemployed. Will society, in the future, be able to supply employment opportunities for all those who seek them? If vast numbers are to be unemployed, how will they occupy their time?

With the increase of the availability of free knowledge, will it affect how people learn? Will it mean that people have a smaller core of formal education where they learn how to learn by themselves? What will be the future role of formal educational qualifications and how will they be obtained?

Given that the pace of change is increasing, what will this mean for the incidence of mental illness, stress-related illness and loss of identity?

What role will the human interaction opportunities offered by web technology play in fostering and accelerating popular movements – for example, in bringing about increased democracy and bringing down oppressive regimes?

Will there be even more radical changes in society's mores? In a relatively short period of time the decriminalization of homosexuality in many countries has been followed by single-sex marriages. The Christian church has accepted women priests. A coloured person has become President of the United States. What comes next?

PART 3

The Poverty Trap

8

Poverty Across the Globe

Introduction

In Chapter 7 the risks to post-scarcity abundance from inequalities in the distribution of wealth were identified. They are serious risks, and are the underlying causes of many bitter conflicts today and in the past. Many commentators agree that there are enough resources, technologies and food available now to relieve poverty and inequality in every country in the world, but the process and timescale to achieve this seems to stretch into infinity. It is the biggest elephant in the room when discussing the limitless potential of post-scarcity abundance.

Poverty can be either absolute or relative. In the developing countries, millions live in conditions of absolute poverty, on the edge of starvation. Eliminating poverty at this level may well be the world's biggest problem. At the same time there is relative poverty on a large scale in the developed world, with millions of families struggling to meet the basic costs of housing, food, transport, heating and health care.

After a brief review of poverty in both the developed and developing worlds, this chapter goes on to look at the cause of poverty in the most extreme cases, in African countries, and at some of the possible solutions. Chapters 9 and 12 then go on to review a number of significant initiatives which are taking place, some of which involve collaborations between business, governments and NGOs to create sustainable solutions, tailored to local conditions and requirements worldwide.

World Poverty

As was mentioned in Chapter 1, the World Bank has warned that world poverty is much greater than previously thought. It has revised its previous estimate and now says that 1.4 billion people live in poverty, based on a new poverty line of $1.25 per day. This is substantially more than its earlier (2004) estimate of 985 million people living in poverty in 2004.

The Bank has also revised upwards the number it said were poor in 1981, from 1.5 billion to 1.9 billion. The new estimates suggest that poverty is both more persistent, and has fallen less sharply, than previously thought. However, given the increase in world population, the poverty rate has fallen from 50 per cent to 25 per cent over the past 25 years. The new figures still suggest that the world will reach its millennium development goal of halving the 1990 level of poverty by 2015.

The latest figures confirm that Africa and sub-Saharan Africa in particular, has been the least successful region of the world in reducing poverty. The number of poor people in Africa doubled between 1981 and 2005 from 200 million to 380 million, and the depth of poverty is greater as well, with the average poor person living on just 70 cents per day. The poverty rate is unchanged at 50 per cent since 1981. This is partly a reflection of the fact that population growth has been much faster in sub-Saharan Africa than in other parts of the world.

But in absolute numbers, it is South Asia which has the most poor people in the world, with 595 million, of which 455 million live in India. The poverty rate, however, has fallen from 60 per cent to 40 per cent.

China has been most successful in reducing poverty, with the numbers falling by more than 600 million, from 835 million in 1981 to 207 million in 2005. The poverty rate in China has plummeted from 85 per cent to 15.9 per cent, with the biggest part of that drop coming in the past 15 years, when China opened up to Western investment and its coastal regions boomed. In fact, in absolute terms, China accounts for the lion's share of the world's reduction in poverty. In percentage terms, world poverty excluding China fell from 40 per cent to 30 per cent over the past 25 years.

Poverty in the Developed World

UNITED STATES

The measurement of national income per head of the population (per capita gross domestic product or GDP) is a notoriously difficult exercise, even more so when comparisons between countries with different patterns of production and consumption are attempted. Suffice it to say that at the beginning of 2008, before the deep recession of 2008/2009 had set in, the major developed countries such as the USA, UK, Germany and France each enjoyed per capita GDPs in the region of $40,000. This level of income would certainly qualify them in the eyes of the early commentators such as Keynes and Chase as post-scarcity societies.

This wealth was not, of course, equally distributed. The wealthiest 1 per cent of Americans earned 21.2 per cent of all income in 2005, according to data from the Internal Revenue Service. That was up sharply from 19 per cent in 2004, and surpassed the previous high of 20.8 per cent set in 2000, at the peak of the previous bull market in stocks. The bottom 50 per cent earned 12.8 per cent of all income, down from 13.4 per cent in 2004 and a bit less than their 13 per cent share in 2000.

In America, national poverty data are calculated using the official census definition of poverty, which has remained fairly standard since it was introduced in the 1960s and is useful for measuring progress against poverty. Under this definition, poverty is determined by comparing pre-tax cash income with the 'poverty threshold', a level of annual income that adjusts for family size and composition. In 2007, according to the official measure, 37.3 million people, or 12.5 per cent of the total US population, lived in poverty.

Blacks and Hispanics have poverty rates that greatly exceed the average. The poverty rate for all blacks and Hispanics remained near 30 per cent during the 1980s and mid 1990s. Thereafter it began to fall. In 2000, the rate for blacks dropped to 22.1 per cent and for Hispanics to 21.2 per cent – the lowest rate for both groups since the United States began measuring poverty.

Recent trends in health care costs, health care coverage, and household income have contributed to growing disparities between different income groups in the United States. Many US workers have come to expect employers to contribute to employee health insurance which has been seen as an important part of overall compensation. However, recent economic trends have resulted in a growing disparity in health care coverage and affordability. A study by the McKinsey Global Institute (2009) identified three categories of workers that are emerging from trends in healthcare coverage and income growth.

The top-income category (earning on average $210,100 per annum) has enjoyed both rising incomes and growing employer-paid healthcare benefits, which have made their out-of-pocket spending on healthcare a relatively small portion of total spending. The higher-middle-income category (earning an average of $84,800 annually) and the lower-middle-income group (earning on average $41,500), have also seen increasing benefits and incomes – but at a much slower rate, making the uncovered portion of their healthcare costs increasingly expensive. In the bottom-income category (earning an average of $14,800 a year), incomes have not only been stagnant, but their employers are less likely to pay for their health insurance. This group is finding healthcare difficult, if not impossible, to afford.

Employers are spending more on health care per employee but for fewer employees. In 2005, employer-paid health benefits covered 22 per cent of households in the bottom-income group, contrasted with 56 per cent of the lower-middle, 81 per cent of the upper-middle, and 89 per cent of the top income group.

While some employers are offering more comprehensive benefits to attract and retain better workers, other companies have withdrawn the offer of employee health care benefits altogether; yet others have had to limit the number of employees eligible for benefits (for example, by including only full-time workers or those of a certain tenure). Employee contributions to insurance premiums have also been rising, discouraging some from taking up their employers' contribution

President Obama's 2010 Budget laid the groundwork for reform of the American health care system, most notably by setting aside a deficit-neutral reserve fund of $635 billion over 10 years to help finance reform of the US health care system to bring down costs, expand coverage, and improve quality.

Growing inequality indicates that the benefits of increasing abundance are accruing more to powerful elites than to the mass of the working population.

UK

In the UK, the most commonly used definition of low income is a household income that is 60 per cent or less of the median household income in that year. The latest year for which data are available is 2006/07. In that year, the 60 per cent threshold was worth £112 per week for single adult with no dependent children; £193 per week for a couple with no dependent children; £189 per week for a single adult with two dependent children under 14; and £270 per week for a couple with two dependent children under 14. These sums of money are measured after income tax, council tax and housing costs have been deducted. They therefore represent what the household has available to spend on everything else it needs, from food and heating to travel and entertainment.

In 2006/07, around 13 million people in the UK were living in households below this low-income threshold. This is around a fifth (22 per cent) of the population.

This 13 million figure is an increase of a million compared with two years previously. The increases over the last two years follow six uninterrupted years of decreases from 1998/1999 to 2004/05 and are the first increases since 1996/97.

The number of people on low incomes is still slightly lower than it was during the early 1990s but much greater than in the early 1980s. However, the proportions of children and pensioners who are in low-income households are both lower than a decade ago.

Clearly, therefore, significant numbers of people in these two rich societies are not experiencing post-scarcity conditions. Keynes' vision of abundance[1] is, for a significant proportion of the population, still some way in the future. This brings to mind Ackerman's comment quoted in Chapter 5 'Our economy is so set up that it creates goods at a higher rate than it produces income with which to purchase them.'

POVERTY AND AGEING POPULATIONS

Two trends are combining to create a special problem of poverty in the developed world. On the one hand the age structure of the population is changing, with relatively fewer young people and relatively more people over the age of 65;

---

1   See Chapter 5.

this trend is most strong in Japan and Germany, less strong in the USA. The second trend is that people are living longer as a result of improved nutrition and advances in medicine. The consequence is that it has become increasingly difficult for individuals or their employers to ensure a good standard of living in old age. The amount individuals need to save in order to ensure a comfortable standard of living in retirement has reached a level such that many people see it as unaffordable. At the same time actuarial calculations have identified huge deficits in corporate pension funds, with the result that many companies have closed schemes or severely restricted the benefits associated with them. Yet, looked at through a post-scarcity lens, much of the pessimism about the long-term impact of an ageing population may well be exaggerated, given that economic growth can lead to the creation of a level of wealth such that the needs of the elderly can be met without undue burden on the rest of society.

Poverty in a Post-Scarcity World

Clearly the world as a whole has a long way to go before the dream of post-scarcity can begin to apply to whole regions. However, if we take the same sort of timescale as that used to predict and assess the pace and impact of climate changes, it is highly possible that as a result of new technologies and continuing economic growth, vast regions of the world will have attained post-scarcity living standards by the end of the present century. It is possible to see this beginning to come about in both China and India. Africa will remain as the laggard region. The big questions, therefore, are whether or not the global economy can sustain the rate of growth in wealth creation which will make possible the elimination of extreme poverty, and whether or not this can be achieved without destroying the habitability of the planet in the process. The answer will depend not only upon mankind's ingenuity and adaptability but also on peoples' values and sense of social justice.

The Causes and Cures of Poverty

Paul Collier (2007) in his scholarly analysis of the causes and possible cures of poverty focuses attention on what he calls the 'failed' countries that are concentrated in Africa and central Asia, with a scattering elsewhere. These countries have made little or no progress in eliminating extreme poverty. Their growth rates have been negative in absolute terms and in relative terms massively below that of the rest of the developing world. The bottom billion of people in these countries are poorer than they were in 1970, and if nothing is done about them, they will gradually diverge even further from the rest of the world economy over the next couple of decades. Collier argues that we cannot accept a situation in which more than a billion people live in impoverished and stagnant countries.

In Collier's opinion, the problems these countries have are very different from those addressed for the past four decades in developing countries generally. Aid in its traditional form does not work well in these environments. Change in the societies at the very bottom must come from within. In all these countries, there are struggles between those trying to achieve change and entrenched interests opposing it. Much can be done to strengthen the hand of the reformers. But to do so will involve drawing upon a wide range of approaches.

Collier lists a number of factors which, taken together, lead to persistent extreme poverty.

THE CONFLICT TRAP

Some of the bottom billion countries are stuck in a pattern of violence, either a prolonged, civil war or a series of *coups d'état*. Countries with a high level of dependence on exports of valuable resources such as oil or diamonds are particularly likely to be conflict-ridden. Natural resources help both to finance conflict and to motivate it.

THE NATURAL RESOURCE TRAP

It might be assumed that the discovery of natural resource wealth would be a catalyst for prosperity, but this is only exceptionally the case. The 'resource curse' causes countries to suffer from the 'Dutch disease' (so-called because of the effects of North Sea gas on the Dutch economy), whereby resource exports cause the country's currency to rise in value against other currencies, thus making the country's other export activities uncompetitive.

THE LANDLOCKED TRAP

Landlocked countries incur much higher costs to import or export goods. Costs vary in ways that don't depend on distance. The transport costs for a landlocked country depend on how much its coastal neighbour has spent on transport infrastructure. Landlocked countries also depend on their neighbours for markets; if neighbours are economically stagnant or embroiled in civil war that will obviously affect trade.

THE TRAP OF POOR GOVERNANCE

Poor governance and policies can destroy an economy with alarming speed (Zimbabwe provides an obvious example). The leaders of some of the poorest countries are among some of the global superrich. Many of the politicians and senior public officials in the bottom billion are corrupt.

MIGRATION

The bottom billion are also integrating into the world economy through emigration. People are voting with their feet as well as their wallets. The author's research shows that these countries will haemorrhage their educated people – their human capital – to a far greater extent than their uneducated people. Emigration takes time to build up but it accelerates – it becomes easier once other family members have already moved.

The financial power of the diaspora is already making a difference, and Africans outside the continent are the biggest donors and financial contributors to African development. In 2003, according to the World Bank, remittances to Africa by non-resident Africans were estimated at US$200 billion, representing revenue greater than official aid and foreign direct investment for many African countries.

Notwithstanding the valuable role remittances play, the ongoing and sustained development of the continent also requires the skills and talents of expatriate Africans working in partnership with those at home to fulfil the potential of the continent.

The Role of Aid Programmes

Aid alone, says Collier, is unlikely to address the problems of the bottom billion. The G8 Gleneagles summit in 2005 committed to doubling aid to Africa but the additional aid will not, in his view, produce the hoped-for growth. Aid has tended to be more effective where governance and policies are already reasonable. Countries that are poorly governed have the greatest need but there comes a point at which money is ineffective in these environments. It is estimated that 40 per cent of Africa's military spending is actually financed by aid. Aid has serious limitations and will not be enough to turn the societies of the bottom billion around. The challenge is to complement it with other actions.

Trade Policy

There are, however, some interventions that are strikingly cheap. These include changes in developed countries laws that would benefit the bottom billion and the generation of international norms that would help to guide behaviour. For example, Western banks have taken deposits looted from the bottom billion societies, held them in great secrecy and refused to give them back to those countries. Collier argues that, if we made the reporting of potentially corrupt deposits a requirement of banking, and made the freezing and repatriation of those deposits much easier, it would not damage our financial system – we already do it if we suspect money has a link to terrorism or drug trafficking.

There are some aspects of OECD trade policy which Collier regards as indefensible, notably the protection of agriculture. Another dysfunctional policy is tariff escalation: the tariffs on processed materials are higher than on the unprocessed materials, making it harder for the bottom billion to diversify their exports by processing their raw materials before they export them. These are examples of 'policy incoherence', where one policy works against another. It is counterproductive to provide aid with the objective of promoting development and then adopt trade policies that impede that objective.

The fair trade campaign attempts to get higher prices for some of the bottom billion's current exports. According to the Fair Trade Foundation there are some 3,000 products, such as coffee, chocolate, fresh vegetables and flowers that are fair-trade certified.

Bottom-billion governments adopt high trade-barriers because they are one of the key sources of corruption. Governments confer protection on businesses owned by their friends and relations; running the protection system day-to-day can also be lucrative – becoming a customs officer is about the best job you can possibly get in these countries and people pay large bribes to become one.

Collier sums up by saying it is time to redefine the development problem as being about the countries of the bottom billion, the ones that are stuck in poverty.

Growth is not a cure-all, he acknowledges, but the lack of growth is a 'kill-all'. The failure of the growth process in the bottom billion is the overwhelming problem that we have to crack.

The Role of Education and Talent

In an address during the African Economic Conference in Addis Ababa, in November, 2007, the African Development Bank (AfDB) Group President, Donald Kaberuka said 'Africa can realize its dream – but it will do so largely via Africa's talent rather than its geology. A rich well-endowed sub-soil is clearly a major advantage, but it is not enough. And the absence of it is not necessarily a condemnation to poverty and dependence.' Kaberuka pointed out that 'neither India nor China's geology is particularly well endowed. But these are two peaceful and stable countries with highly talented people who have put science and technology at the centre of their agenda to overcome poverty.'

In May 2008, despite suffering from motor neurone disease which has left him almost completely paralyzed, the renowned physicist, Professor Stephen Hawking, made the journey to South Africa to launch a project backed by some of the world's leading high-tech entrepreneurs and scientists. It involves a £75m plan to create Africa's first postgraduate centres for advanced mathematics and physics.

Hawking was joined by eminent physicists and mathematicians including two Nobel laureates in physics, David Gross and George Smoot, and Michael Griffin, the head of NASA.

Neil Turok, founder of the project and professor of mathematical physics at Cambridge University, where he is a close colleague of Hawking, said the aim of the centres was to 'unlock and nurture scientific talent' across Africa. 'Apart from an African Einstein, we want to find the African Bill Gates and the Sergey Brins and Larry Pages of the future,' said Turok, referring to the founders of Microsoft and Google.

The 15 new centres will be modelled on the African Institute for Mathematical Sciences which was founded by Turok in Muizenberg, near Cape Town, four years previously. It has produced 160 graduates from 30 African countries, many of whom have gone on to take science doctorates. Another 53 will graduate shortly.

Turok decided to push for 15 more such institutes after winning the £50,000 Technology, Entertainment and Design prize in America earlier this year. He donated the money to the Institute. He has since been offered support potentially worth tens of millions of pounds. Google, the Gates Foundation and Sun Microsystems are among those that have expressed interest. 'The people who will make Africa rich are the brightest people because they will generate wealth,' Turok said.

In 2007 the Consultative Group on International Agricultural Research (CGIAR) Gender & Diversity Program launched an unprecedented $13 million effort to support the fast-tracking of careers of at least 360 African women in agricultural research. Participating countries include Ethiopia, Ghana, Kenya, Malawi, Mozambique, Nigeria, Tanzania, Uganda, and Zambia.

The Nairobi-based African Women in Agricultural Research and Development (AWARD) program is being funded with a four-year grant from the Bill & Melinda Gates Foundation. The grant represents the Foundation's belief in the importance of engaging women at every level in agricultural development. Today, women farmers produce 60 to 80 per cent of crops critical to feeding the people of Africa. Yet women comprise less than 20 per cent of agricultural researchers.

'Women bear much of the responsibility for cultivating crops in Africa and they face challenging and changing conditions,' said Rajiv Shah, director of agricultural development for the Bill & Melinda Gates Foundation. 'African women scientists can help bring practical, sustainable improvements to the African farm sector so smallholder farmers – most of whom are women – can build better lives for themselves and their families.'

In March, 2008 Cisco announced the launch of its Global Talent Acceleration Program (GTAP) facility in Johannesburg, South Africa. Part of an ongoing investment in the region, GTAP is a long-term Cisco initiative aimed at developing local next-generation local network consulting engineers for the company.

The Johannesburg facility is the second GTAP initiative to be launched in emerging countries, following the establishment of a facility in Amman, Jordan in November in 2007. The entire African region is experiencing tremendous growth in Information Technology (IT) and people are the heart of the boom. Finding the right talent to support this growth is becoming a critical challenge for governments and organizations alike. Instead of importing talent from other regions on a temporary basis, GTAP helps Cisco to provide customers with a long-term solution in the form of a highly skilled and well-trained local work force. The skills that GTAP provides to its graduates contribute to the local knowledge infrastructures that are critical for accelerating and sustaining economic growth.

Torque IT, a strategic Cisco partner in South Africa, is one of the first companies signed up to host and manage the program training facility at its premises in Johannesburg.

Entry- or associate-level candidates for the program are typically recent college graduates and mid- or professional-level students who have significant prior experience with Cisco networking. After the completion of training, students will generally make the transition to full-time employment with Cisco Advanced Services as Network Consulting Engineers (NCE's), working out of Cisco's regional service-delivery hub.

9

The Promise of Alternative Finance and Social Business

Introduction

There are three significant factors which are likely to bring about a step change in the way global poverty is addressed and eventually eliminated.

- First, the current failure of traditional capital markets models. The credit crunch has led to calls for system change in the global economy and the values and principles of social capital markets are being demanded: accountability, transparency, sustainability and governance. Social enterprises have a great opportunity to step in and help build the new world economic order.

- Second, it is increasingly being recognized that getting developing world populations actively involved as entrepreneurs via microfinance and growth finance is likely to be more successful in alleviating poverty than foreign-aid programmes.

- Tools are now available which make it increasingly possible to develop social business. Web-based platforms and offerings are available for all manner of social economic transactions including investing (SRI, public equity, social venture capital, debt, loans, microfinance, and others); philanthropy (from donations to mission-related investments); purchasing (goods and services marketplaces) and income generating (jobs, projects and ideas marketplaces).

My own view is that there are now so many powerful forces pushing for systemic change that it will not be long in coming. A powerful social movement has been set in motion. Recession may slow its progress but will not halt it. We are witnessing the early stages of the emergence of a new form of capitalism, one in which concern for social justice; human rights and the environment are seen as goals ranking in importance alongside profit shareholder value. John Elkington (2001) uses the metaphor of *The Chrysalis Economy* to describe what he calls the economic equivalent of an 'extraordinary natural process of metamorphosis' as the old economy mutates into a 'dematerializing, bit-driven new economy.' He goes on to say that 'Only if today's Corporate Locusts and Caterpillars can become Corporate Butterflies and Honeybees can we have any chance of creating truly sustainable forms of capitalism.' My own expectation is that such a form of capitalism will be more rather than less successful in wealth creation than that which existed at the end of the twentieth century. As it matures, however, we shall be using somewhat different definitions of 'wealth' from those we have used in the past, definitions that take account of the quality of life as well as material progress.

In this chapter the roles of alternative financial institutions and of social or hybrid businesses are reviewed as agents for change in the battle to improve the quality of living for those mired in the poverty trap described in Chapter 8.

Alternative Financial Institutions

Tender green shoots of new forms of wealth-creating organizations and new types of financial institutions are emerging. Some of the emerging models are as likely to be as profitable as more conventional companies, and most will be more adept at pursuing goals that so many conventional for-profit companies fail to reach: treating customers fairly, protecting the environment, creating a healthy workplace, and supporting the communities in which they operate.

MICROFINANCE

Financial inclusion offers the ability to alleviate poverty at a profit for its financiers, and its widespread acceptance is already lifting millions out of poverty. Micro-credit and financial inclusion are not new concepts. Early examples include the Chit funds in India, the Susus of Ghana and the credit institutions of the nineteenth century in Europe.

The difference today is that financial inclusion is a commercially viable proposition. Whether it is microfinance banking institutions in Africa, or injecting capital into a rural microfinance centre in Nepal, this is a business in a very real sense, yet it has a social purpose. It is based on economic common sense, experienced international business managers are driving it and, most importantly, it makes a profit, without having the maximization of profit as an objective. It offers the chance to unlock the full economic potential of some of the world's largest markets, and the effect of this cannot be underestimated.

However, there is a long way to go. Fewer than 20 per cent of people in many African countries have access to bank accounts, something that most people in developed countries take for granted.

Across Asia and Africa, access to finance is rightly seen as an essential contributing factor to sustainable economic growth. The work of microfinance institutions and development organizations plays an important role in helping the poorest in society. Large international organizations, particularly those in the financial sector, have a role to play alongside governments and microfinance institutions to catalyze the development of small enterprises.

GRAMEEN BANK

In 1974, Professor Muhammad Yunus, a Bangladeshi economist from Chittagong University, led his students on a field trip to a poor village. They interviewed a woman who made bamboo stools, and learnt that she had to borrow the equivalent of 15p to buy raw bamboo for each stool made. After repaying the loan, sometimes at rates as high as 10 per cent a week, she was left with a very small profit margin. Had she been able to borrow at more advantageous rates, she would have been able to build up some capital and raise herself above subsistence level.

Realizing that there must be something terribly wrong with the economics he was teaching, Yunus took matters into his own hands, and from his own pocket made loans to a group of basket-weavers. He found that it was possible with this small initiative not only to help them survive, but also to create the spark of personal initiative and enterprise necessary to pull themselves out of poverty.

Against the advice of banks and government, Yunus carried on giving out 'micro-loans', and in 1983 formed the Grameen Bank, meaning 'village bank' founded on principles of trust and solidarity. The bank is 95 per cent owned by the poor borrowers of the bank, 97 per cent of whom are women. The remaining 5 per cent is owned by the Bangladeshi government

Grameen Bank does not require any collateral against its micro-loans. Although each borrower must belong to a five-member group, the group is not required to give any guarantee for a loan to its member. Repayment responsibility solely rests on the individual borrower. The total number of borrowers in 2009 was 7.67 million. The bank has over 2,000 branches and a total staff approaching 25,000.

The size of the bank's operations is indicated by the fact that the total amount of loan disbursed by the bank, since inception, and up to and including 2008, is Tk418.90 billion (US$7.59 billion). Out of this, Tk374.50 billion (US$6.76 billion) has been repaid.

Projected disbursement for year 2009 is Tk75.00 billion (US $1091 million). End of the year outstanding loan is projected to be at Tk55.00 billion (US$800 million). The loan recovery rate is 98.32 per cent. The bank finances 100 per cent of its outstanding loan from its deposits and over 54 per cent of its deposits come from bank's own borrowers.

In 1995, the bank decided not to receive any more donor funds. The directors do not see any need to take any donor money or even take loans from local or external sources in future. The growing amount of deposits will be more than enough to run and expand its credit programme and repay its existing loans.

Ever since it came into being, the bank has reported profit in every year except in 1983, 1991 and 1992. It declared 20 per cent dividend for the year 2007. It also has created a dividend equalization fund to ensure distribution of dividends at attractive rates in the coming years.

There are four interest rates for loans: 20 per cent for income-generating loans, 8 per cent for housing loans, 5 per cent for student loans, and 0 per cent loans for beggar (that is, disabled, blind, and retarded) people, as well as old people with ill health. The bank has a special programme, called the Struggling Members Programme, to reach out to the beggars. About 108,741 beggars have already joined the programme. Total amount disbursed under this programme stands at Tk124.81 million. Of that amount of Tk91.60 million has already been paid off.

The Bank introduced housing loans in 1984. This programme was awarded the Aga Khan International Award for Architecture in 1989. Housing loans have enabled 665,568 houses to be constructed with each loan averaging Tk13,103 (US$191).

All interests are simple interest, calculated on declining balance method. This means, if a borrower takes an income-generating loan of say, Tk1,000, and pays back the entire amount within a year in weekly instalments, she'll pay a total amount of Tk1,100, that is, Tk1,000 as principal, plus Tk100 as interest for the year, equivalent to 10 per cent flat rate. The minimum interest for deposits is 8.5 per cent and the maximum rate is 12 per cent.

The bank provides larger loans, called micro-enterprise loans, for fast-growing enterprises. There is no restriction on the loan size. The average loan size is Tk 23,978 (US$348.92) and the maximum loan taken so far is Tk1.2 million (US$17,500) which was used to purchase a truck.

Scholarships are given every year to the high-performing children of Grameen borrowers, with priority on girl children. Up to December 2008, scholarships amounting to US$1,334,506 had been awarded to 69,990 children. Students who succeed in reaching the tertiary level of education are given higher-education loans, covering tuition, maintenance, and other school expenses. By December 2008, 30,948 students received higher-education loans.

On 13 October 2006 it was announced that Muhammad Yunus and Grameen Bank had been awarded the Nobel Peace Prize.

OIKOCREDIT

The Dutch hybrid organization, Oikocredit, is one of the world's largest sources of private funding to the microfinance sector. It also provides credit to trade cooperatives, fair-trade organizations and small-to-medium enterprises (SMEs) in the developing world.

Oikocredit offers a dual return to its investors – financial and social. In addition to earning modest financial returns, investors know that their money is being used to fight poverty, promote fair trade and help conserve the planet's natural resources.

TRIODOS BANK

Triodos Bank is one of Europe's leading ethical banks. Established in 1980 in the Netherlands, with a UK office following in 1995, Triodos Bank enables money to work for positive social, environmental and cultural change. Triodos offers a comprehensive range of banking services for social businesses, charities and groups along with a variety of savings accounts for individuals.

Triodos Bank is a public bank with thousands of customers and shareholders. Its principles and independence are guaranteed through a special share-holding trust which protects the social and environmental aims of the bank. The bank has offices in the UK, Belgium, Spain and the Netherlands as well as an international development investment unit which finances fair trade and microfinance in developing countries.

Triodos Bank has always been, and remains, about transparency and the realization of social, environmental and cultural objectives in day-to-day banking. This integrated approach has been fundamental to the bank since it was established in 1980. Triodos Bank has been a pioneer and still is a leading innovator in sustainable banking. It only finances enterprises which add social, environmental and cultural value – in fields such as renewable energy, social housing, complementary health care, fair trade, organic food and farming and social business. It also finances fair trade and microcredit organizations in developing countries. This is done with the support of depositors and investors who wish to contribute to social justice within the context of a more sustainable economy.

The Bank's mission is:

- to help create a society that promotes people's quality of life and that has human dignity at its core;

- to enable individuals, institutions and businesses to use money more consciously in ways that benefit people and the environment, and promote sustainable development;

- to offer its customers sustainable financial products and high quality service.

The company's key business principles are to:

- promote sustainable development

- respect and obey the law

- respect human rights

- respect the environment

- be accountable to stakeholders for its actions

- provide continuous improvement.

SUSTAINABLE BANKING AWARDS

In June 2009 the *Financial Times* and IFC, a part of the World Bank Group announced the winners of the 2009 FT sustainable bank awards. The awards recognize banks and related financial institutions that have shown leadership and innovation in integrating social, environmental and corporate governance considerations into their operations.

The nominees for the awards were chosen from 165 entries from 117 institutions across 42 countries. There were five categories:

- sustainable banker of the year (The winner was Triodos bank, Netherlands).

- emerging markets sustainable banker of the year (The winner was Itau Unibanco, Brazil).

- achievement in basic needs financing (The winner was Microensure, UK).

- achievement in banking at the bottom of the pyramid (The winner was Root Capital, USA).

- sustainable investor of the year (The winner was Global Environment Fund, USA).

Microfinance is not without its critics, however. An article in *The Times*, (29 April 2009) referred to the view of microfinance taken by Aneel Karnani,

Associate Professor of Strategy at the Ross School of Business at the University of Michigan. He argues that microfinance doesn't do that much to lift the poor out of poverty. He points out that those countries that have lifted people out of poverty have not done it through microfinance, but through the development of larger enterprises which create jobs – for example, in places like China and Vietnam. What is needed, in his view, is to create garment factories rather than creating individual entrepreneurs by giving them each a loan to buy a sewing machine.

GROWTH FINANCE

The success of microfinance has shown that it is possible to lend money in poor countries. However, it has long been thought that venture capitalists will not invest readily in enterprises in developing countries. The larger sums involved, and distant, unfamiliar economies have deterred regular investors. Yet 'growth finance' could be about to prove that assumption to be wrong.

Indeed, growth finance could achieve success on a scale well beyond the scope of micro-finance. Microfinance can raise families out of poverty, but growth finance could lift countries out of poverty.

Whereas microfinance provides loans from as little as a few dollars to would-be entrepreneurs, growth finance aims to provide credit of between $50,000 and $1 million to small and medium-sized enterprises in developing countries.

In 2009 a conference was held to launch the Aspen Network of Development Entrepreneurs (ANDE). The network aims to bring non-governmental organizations and investors together. The former will provide research and technical assistance to encourage the latter to invest funds and support businesses in emerging markets.

ANDE – which includes among its founders some of the largest philanthropic foundations in the world, including the Bill & Melinda Gates Foundation, the Rockefeller Foundation and the Shell Foundation, which hosted the event – aims to help to invest $750 million (£510 million) to assist small and medium-sized enterprises in the developing world.

Acumen Fund, another co-founder, invests in the types of projects that ANDE wants to support. It has invested $1.9 million into LifeSprings hospitals, which provides reproductive and paediatric healthcare to people on low incomes. Despite the low incomes, profitability comes from the potential scale of the market. LifeSpring will open 30 hospitals and franchise another 140 in the next three years. The company is looking to make a financial return, but is not profit-maximizing – that is what differentiates it. It exemplifies Yunus' view that we need a new sort of business which does not set out to be profit-maximizing, but is 'cause driven, rather than profit driven' (Yunus, 2007).

Social or Hybrid Businesses

Most of the non-governmental organizations working to relieve poverty and stimulate development do not recover their total costs and so have to spend a lot of time, money and energy soliciting donations. Their work is valuable, but the social business can be self sustaining and therefore able to do more than a charity in the long run. Social businesses focus on profit, without maximizing it.

Yunus suggests that there is nothing to stop social businesses spinning off traditional profit-based companies among the local poor populations by the upgrading of existing entrepreneurs. Such companies would cater for the poor according to their own cultural norms, but using the concepts of micro credit and appropriate pricing to serve their customers or possibly invite the community into the business, which could become a cooperative, actively seeking to make a profit within the conditions under which it operates.

Yunus suggests a number of sources from which social businesses might spring:

- Companies may want to extend the range of their corporate social responsibility initiatives.

- Companies may want to create social businesses as a way of exploring new markets, while helping the less fortunate.

- Foundations may increasingly see social business funding as a way of fulfilling their missions, particularly as the money will not be exhausted, even as it carries out social activities, because the whole idea of operating as a business is that the money needed is constantly replenished, if the project is well run.

- Successful entrepreneurs in profit-maximizing firms may reach a stage where they want to give back something to the societies which have enriched them or they just want to try something new. (Bill Gates, Warren Buffet, and George Soros come to mind.)

- Development donors may consider creating dedicated funds to support social business initiatives. The World Bank and regional development banks might create subsidiaries to support social businesses.

- Government agencies, for example, the UK Department for International Development (DFID), may create social business funds to support and encourage social enterprise.

- Retired wealthy persons, inheritors of wealth, or recipients of windfall gains may be inspired to create or support social businesses.

- Young, newly graduated people may choose careers in social businesses, motivated by the opportunity to have a part in changing the world.

Yunus believes that social businesses will quickly become a familiar fixture on the world business scene. He sees no reason why some people may not divide their investments between profit-maximizing and social businesses or work for different types of business at different times of their lives.

Examples of Social Businesses

THE DEVELOPMENT ALTERNATIVES GROUP

Development Alternatives is an example of a multi-agency approach to sustainable development in India. It is a non-profit organization and was established in 1983. Its activities cover the design and diffusion of appropriate technologies, environmental management systems and effective people-oriented institutions. It is concerned to bring about a sound balance among the basic prerequisites of sustainable development: social equity, environmental quality and economic efficiency.

Development Alternatives believes that the key to achieve this is the creation of sustainable livelihoods and that the basis of a better future is employment and the creation of self-employment opportunities. In particular the focus is on jobs that provide a decent income, produce goods and services for the local market, do not destroy the environment or the resource base, but enable the poor generally and women particularly both to contribute to economic development and to benefit from it.

There is considerable emphasis on innovation. To create sustainable livelihoods in reasonably large numbers, it is necessary to introduce innovative technologies, and create innovative institutions to achieve the widespread dissemination of environmentally friendly processes and technologies.

These technologies and market-based systems are basically designed to serve the interests of all, especially the rural artisan, cottage-based micro-entrepreneur, micro enterprises, small industries, farmers and landless labourers.

The group works through network partners to achieve mass dissemination of sustainable technologies and to demonstrate the feasibility of its models. It has set up a number of organizations such as Technology and Action for Rural Advancement (TARA) which manufactures and markets appropriate technologies to small enterprises.

Development Alternatives aims to carry out its work in a manner that is largely self-financing. This has been done through the sale of products and hardware technologies, provision of technical support through consultancies and training support to micro-enterprises and grassroots NGOs. It has provided such services in the fields of economic analysis, development of small-scale sustainable technologies, marketing, information and raising of finance. Project support has been received, particularly for research and design work, from Government of India agencies. Generous financial support has also been provided by a wide variety of donor agencies.

THE GREEN BELT MOVEMENT

The Green Belt Movement is one of the most prominent women's civil society organizations, based in Kenya, advocating human rights and supporting good governance and peaceful democratic change through the protection of the environment. Its mission is to empower communities worldwide to protect the environment and to promote good governance and cultures of peace.

It was started in 1977 by Dr. Wangari Maathai, the first African woman and the first environmentalist to receive the Nobel Peace Prize (in 2004). What began as a tree-planting programme to address the challenges of deforestation, soil erosion and lack of water is now a vehicle for empowering women. The act of planting a tree is helping women throughout Africa become stewards of the natural environment. By protecting the environment, these women are also becoming powerful champions for sustainable management of scarce resources such as water, equitable economic development, good political governance and peace.

More than 40 million trees have been planted across Africa. The result: soil erosion has been reduced in critical watersheds, thousands of acres of biodiversity-rich indigenous forest have been restored and protected, and hundreds of thousands of women and their families are standing up for their rights and those of their communities and so are living healthier, more productive lives. The success of the movement in Kenya has led to the setting up of the Green Belt Movement International (GMBI).

The mission of the Green Belt Movement International is to empower individuals worldwide to protect the environment and to promote good governance. Through its holistic approach to development, the Green Belt Movement addresses the underlying social, political, and economic causes of poverty and environmental degradation at the grassroots level. Its empowerment seminars help people make critical linkages between the environment, governance, and their quality of life. Participants develop a deep desire to better their own lives and communities. As they gain economic security, they are willing to protect shared resources such as forests, public parks, and rivers.

GBMI has developed four strategic goals:

1.   to strengthen and expand the Green Belt Movement in Kenya;

2.   to share the Green Belt Movement's programme with other countries in Africa and beyond;

3.   to empower Africans, especially women and girls, and nurture their leadership and entrepreneurial skills;

4.   To advocate internationally for the environment, good governance, equity and cultures of peace.

PATH

For an unacceptably long list of developing countries, including Afghanistan, Angola, Botswana, Lesotho, Liberia, Malawi, Somalia, and Zambia, life expectancy still wavers stubbornly around the 40-year mark. Three diseases, HIV/AIDS, TB, and malaria, disproportionately impact mortality and morbidity rates, though many developing countries have seen a rapid rise in the incidence of so-called Western diseases, including diabetes, cardiovascular disease, cancer and hypertension.

PATH, a not-for-profit organization specializing in global health, is taking a systems-approach to addressing these challenges, identifying critical gaps in healthcare systems. PATH establishes partnerships and leverages technology to develop solutions. Examples include the adaptation of food-industry technologies to develop a means of telling health workers whether the polio vaccine they plan to use has gone bad on its long journey from Europe to Africa. The vaccine vial monitors are printed directly on vaccine vial labels and darken with exposure to heat over time. This simple technology means no more uncertainty, no more waste. The organization's vaccines-work also involves partnership-based initiatives dedicated to helping vaccines from the laboratory into clinical development efficiently and quickly, both to combat malaria and the deadly streptococcus pneumonia which causes the deaths of up to 1 million children under age five each year.

ARAVIND

Dr. G. Venkataswamy (Dr. V) created Aravind in 1976 as an 11-bed eye clinic in an old temple city. Today, Aravind has grown into the largest and most productive eye-care facility in the world. It is completely self-sustaining and now treats over 1.7 million patients each year, two-thirds of them for free. From its beginning it developed a 'Robin Hood' business model of 'borrowing' from richer eye patients to fund operations of the poor. The business model is stated up-front and built into discussions about fees. It has proved entirely socially acceptable to those who pay.

WSUP

WSUP (Water and Sanitation for the Urban Poor) brings together companies (RWE, Thames Water, Halcrow Group, and Unilever) with NGOs (CARE, WaterAid, WWF) and government to develop commercial projects that: deliver a return (at around 7 per cent to 10 per cent designed to guarantee sustainability, not maximize profits) to commercial participants; promote community health; have a positive environmental impact; and are sustainable over the long-term.

Summary

All of these initiatives are expressions of a new type of organization with a blended purpose at its core: serving a living mission and making a profit or at least covering costs in the process. The essential framework of such a company – its ownership, governance, capitalization, and compensation structures – is designed to support this dual mission. And it is this design that enables companies to escape the pressure to maximize short-term profits and instead to fulfil a more fundamental purpose of economic activity: to meet human needs and be of benefit to life.

For the most part, these organizations are operating independently without significant involvement from large corporations. Chapter 12 looks in more detail how multi-national corporations can get involved, and the many benefits to them in participating in social enterprises.

PART 4
The Response of Business

10

The Business Response to Abundance

Introduction

When faced with major change in their lives people can respond in two ways. They can embrace change or resist it. The village blacksmith, who was drawn by curiosity to investigate the strange noise outside the smithy and saw his first automobile, could have reacted with fear, leading to resistance and denial, fearful that the car, by replacing the horse, would destroy his livelihood.

On the other hand he could have seen an opportunity, realizing that he would become more prosperous by selling his metal-working skills at a higher price by repairing cars. The same is true of companies. Faced with massive changes in the business environment – new technologies, globalization, shifts in consumer tastes and preferences, they can adapt or resist. History tells us that resistance is futile. Nevertheless it is the most common reaction.

This book has so far set out a vision of post-scarcity abundance. This chapter focuses on the impact of abundance on business activity and on the powerful global corporations and their traditional business models in particular.

Disruptive Business Models

The emergence of post-scarcity conditions is precipitating a number of new, disruptive business models. A 'disruptive business model' is one that wrong-foots existing companies in an industry sector to the extent that they are forced to concede leadership of that industry or, in the extreme, to see that industry decline and wither away.

The concept of disruptive business models was developed by J.L. Bower and Clayton M. Christensen in their classic 1995 *Harvard Business Review* article, 'Disruptive Technologies: Catching the Wave' (1995). There is an evident link with Schumpeter's concept of creative destruction (see Chapter 3).

Disruption may be the result of a new business model as in the case of easyJet (to be discussed later) or due to the introduction of a new technology or process. Examples of disruptive innovations include electric light bulbs, destroying the market for gas mantles; semi-conductors, destroying the market for thermionic valves; personal computers, destroying the market for, inter alia, typewriters; and digital photography, destroying the market for photographic film.

When a disruptive business model first appears on the scene it is often on such a small scale that the existing industry leaders take the view that it can be safely ignored – as was the case with IBM and the birth of Apple's PC or Borders in respect of Amazon.

Once it has become clear that the market for the new model is vast, it may be too late for the existing companies to respond effectively. A failure to respond may be due to a number of factors, among which bureaucratic inertia and denial are possibly the most important.

In the case of large multi-business corporations the response may be to exit from the particular industry sector under attack. Others may try to adopt the new model, but by starting late may find it difficult to succeed. If an existing industry leader has prospered over many years it will be likely that its cost structure is too high to enable it to adapt to the new model. It may be that to adapt will call for a radical change of culture which the existing company is incapable of achieving.

Some companies may try to have the best of both worlds. This was the approach taken by BA when threatened by the growth of 'no frills' airlines such as easyJet. BA set up its own 'no frills' operation, Go. This, however, was unsuccessful, largely for cultural reasons.

Some companies stay in denial until they are driven out of business. For example, in the UK, the collapse of the Woolworths store chain was precipitated by the credit crunch, but a major underlying factor was its failure to react to the threat posed by the rapid growth of 'pound shops' – stores in which every article was priced at one pound.

THE SWISS WATCH INDUSTRY

Although it dates back to the 1980s, the development of the Swatch remains one of the classic cases of a positive, adaptive response to a disruptive business model

In the 1970s the Swiss watch-making industry, world-renowned for its precision, quality watches, was in crisis. In just 10 years its export market had dropped by half, with Hong Kong and Japan now occupying the top spots. The Swiss craft-based industry could not compete with the lower-priced watches from Timex, Citizen, Seiko and Casio, which based their fabrication on a new technology – the quartz digital watch. The Swiss banks, to whom the watchmakers were indebted, called in Nick Hayek, an engineer, as a consultant to rescue the industry. Hayek saw that he could not solve the problem within the old paradigm of Swiss watchmakers based on craftsmanship. He came up with the idea of making plastic watches in many colours and styles and marketing them to the newly emerging fashion and life-style conscious consumer groups, positioning them at the low-price segment of the market and at prices lower than those of the products coming from Japan. The Swatch was launched in Zurich on 1 March 1983, with 12 models priced modestly between SFr39 and SFr50. It became an instant success in Switzerland. Some months later, the Swatch Group launched a major advertising campaign for its timepiece in the United States, the outcome of which was that 3.5 million Swatches had been sold by the end of 1984.

THE EUROPEAN AIRLINE INDUSTRY

Sometime around 1998, shortly after an article of his appeared in the magazine *Wired*, Kevin Kelly, author of *New Rules for the New Economy* (1998), was invited to speak to KLM executives in Amsterdam.

He argued in his talk that in the distant future nearly everything we make will be given away free. He ended by inviting his audience to imagine what might happen if they made their airline seats free. Getting on a particular flight would be free. A passenger would pay for everything else around that flight: the meal, their luggage, movies, taxes, and maybe even the reservation. A person who walked up with no reservation, no luggage, didn't want a meal, or rent headphones, might be able to fly for the cost of the taxes and airport fees if there was room. The cost of air transport per mile was heading toward the free anyway, he explained. They should get used to the idea. He added that even if they found this prospect too radical, they should begin to think in these terms because their competitors certainly would.

After some polite applause, a silver-haired gentleman put his arm around Kelly's shoulder and introduced himself. Kelly was not sure whether he was the chairman or the CEO. 'Young man,' he whispered into Kelly's ear, 'that was the most ridiculous talk I've ever heard.'

Budget airline easyJet is now a household name. Yet it is only just over 14 years ago that its first flight took off in 1995. In that time, easyJet has made flying affordable for everyone in Europe. The easyJet case has lessons and insights across a range of business and management issues, including strategy, business models and innovation.

Stelios Haji-Ioannou was a major factor in the early success of easyJet. He realized from the start that it was hard to make short-haul air travel glamorous. Instead, he wanted to declare the end of 'rip-off Britain' and offer consumers an airline with low-fare flights. The philosophy was simple: cut out the travel agent and the in-flight meals and pass on the savings to the customer. In the early 1990s Europe was being deregulated and he saw an opportunity to enter the airline business using a radically different business model. On a trip to the USA he was impressed by the low-cost operation run by Southwest Airlines. He admits that he copied Southwest's formula, believing he could operate a similar no-frills airline in Europe, attracting customers from trains and coaches as well as other airlines. Herb Kelleher, Southwest Airlines' founder, was his role model. Southwest transformed the US airline industry by making air travel affordable for ordinary people. It employs only a single type of aircraft to keep inventory and maintenance costs down. It also holds costs down by high utilization of aircraft and by operating economy class only, making boarding and turnarounds quicker. It also believes that, just because it offers low fares, there is no reason why customer service shouldn't be high.

The essential elements of the easyJet business model have always been fast turnarounds, no free lunches and enticingly low fares that rise as flights fill up. Nine out of ten easyJet flights are now sold via the Internet, a far higher proportion than for any traditional airline. The airline's cost control is legendary and it squeezes the maximum possible revenue from each flight.

Stelios believed that the world's biggest companies like Wal-Mart and McDonald's have succeeded because they sell low-cost products. He saw that, for years, the traditional airlines had conditioned people into believing that air travel had to be expensive. But he believed that if you give people a more affordable fare they would jump on an aeroplane as they would on a bus.

easyJet now carries more than 32 million passengers a year – great for the airline but not for the Green lobby which pointed out that aviation accounted for 7–11 per cent of Britain's harmful carbon dioxide emissions (it is estimated that a return flight from London to Florida produces CO_2 emissions equivalent to those produced by one year's motoring). The UK Government said it wanted to reduce the environmental impact of flights and controversially imposed a hike in air-passenger duty.

In response, easyJet insists it operates an 'environmentally friendly' airline: its low-cost model of fuller airplanes, direct flights and newer aircraft is greener than the 'hub and spoke' system of connecting flights operated by other airlines. easyJet has also introduced a new environmental code in its corporate social responsibility report as part of its mission to be 'green'. It says that its CO_2 emissions per passenger kilometre have fallen by 18 per cent since 2000.

THE LONG TAIL

The long tail is named after the type of power law curve that results when plotting the sales of CDs, computer games, books and other products, or the popularity of web sites. George Kingsley Zipf, professor of linguistics at Harvard, originally observed it in respect of the use of words in a language. There are a small number of words that appear very frequently: the, of, to, and, a, in, and so on. After that there is a steep decline, followed by tens of thousands of words that appear relatively rarely such as syllabub or asymmetry and so on. When the Zipf distribution is shown graphically these rarer words form a 'long tail' that tapers off to the right.

Chris Anderson, author of *The Long Tail* (2006) pointed out the greater significance of the long tail when something moves from the material world to the digital world. Anderson points out that in the real world, there are physical limits on how many CDs or books a shop can stock. In the same way there are only so many films a cinema can screen. The result is that very many films never make the big screen.

In the case of films on DVD, however, the economics are different. A movie that wouldn't fill a local cinema can still sell thousands of copies worldwide. According to Anderson's figures, for example, Netflix offers 25,000 DVDs. The 24,000 or so titles in the tail may not sell many copies each, but they add up. (Most of Amazon's sales are of titles the average bookstore simply does not have room to stock.)

GOOGLE

Google was incorporated by its founders, Stanford University graduate students Larry Page and Sergey Brin, on 7 September 1998. Eleven years later it was earning income in excess of $1 billion. Following a substantial acquisition programme, and a multibillion-dollar investment in building data centres, Google remains healthily profitable, earning a net income of $1.6 billion on $5.94 billion of sales in the third quarter of 2009.

The company's initial success was down to Page and Brin's insight in identifying a weakness in web search engines. In ranking results for a keyword search, traditional engines looked at the content of web pages, adding up, for example, the number of times a keyword appeared. Page and Brin realized that you would get a much better sense of the relevance of a page if you looked at the number and the quality of the other pages linking to it. Adding up links would give a better picture of a site's relevance. The superior results delivered by Google quickly drew the attention of web surfers and advertisers, and it quickly became the dominant search engine.

Whenever a company becomes extraordinarily successful in a short period of time, it naturally becomes an object of considerable interest to the media and to the business and academic communities, and comes to be seen as possibly offering a new model for business success. Since 2008, the features of the company's business model have been examined in articles in all the major business magazines, and business school professors have published case studies recording in detail how the company organizes and manages its product development and innovation.

Why does Google give away products like its browser and its operating system for mobile phones? The answer is that anything that increases Internet use is ultimately to Google's advantage, leading to increased advertising revenue.

The essential point about Google's business model is that it turns normal customer/supplier relationships upside down. The services that Google supplies to the public are not its products. Its product is the process of providing advertisers with an audience. Google's customers are companies with products they wish to bring to peoples' attention. This is why the services the public enjoy are free. The price for that free service, however, is an increasing invasion of privacy as Google becomes more and more adept at discovering things about its users that advertisers want to know. The more time that people and companies spend online, the more ads they see and the more money Google makes. At the same time, Google collects more data on consumers' needs and behaviour and can target its audiences more precisely, strengthening its competitive advantage in terms of what it can deliver to advertisers and further increasing its income.

As more and more products and services are delivered digitally over computer networks – entertainment, news, software programs, financial transactions – Google's range of potential contacts is expanding into ever more industry sectors.

An important source of competitive advantage for Google is its parallel-processing computer system. The system is able to carry out searches and other transactions at very high speeds. Because people demand quick responses from the software they use online, Google's system has provided it with a big advantage over rivals like Microsoft and Yahoo. The future competition among these companies will be fought as much on the power and efficiency of their equipment as on the attractiveness of their services.

Hal Varian is a professor at UC Berkeley's Haas School of Business and School of Information and is also Google's chief economist. Levy (2009) describes how, speaking at the annual conference of the American Economics Association, Varian described AdWords, Google's unique method for selling online advertising. AdWords analyses every Google search to determine which advertisers get each of up to 11 sponsored links on every results page. Varian called it the world's biggest, fastest auction, a never-ending, automated, self-service version of Tokyo's boisterous Tsukiji fish market which takes place every time a search is made.

The innovation process that Google has developed is the source of much of the interest that is focused on the company. That process appears to have three key features. First, Google believes in throwing lots of very bright people at innovation. In the different countries where it operates, it sets out to attract the best technical talent from the top universities.

Secondly, it places considerable emphasis on the ambience and pleasantness of the workplace. It provides its staff with very good quality food, games, free bus service, and other perks.

Thirdly, it organizes its product development staff into small teams and gives them considerable freedom in how they allocate their time and money. Following the example of 3M, Google allows its engineers to devote 20 per cent of their time to pet projects, with little or no supervision. The company's innovation system reflects its roots in the academic world. Google operates in much the same way that a science department operates in a big research university. It hires the smartest people it can find, allows them to pursue their particular interests in small collegial teams, but at the same time carefully monitors the progress and results of their work.

Google's success, therefore, can be attributed not to any one thing but to the way in which a number of things are combined in its business model. First and probably most important is the insight of the founders into the nature of the internet and the related economics of abundance.

Secondly there is the company's superb computer architecture. Finally there is the company's innovative culture. These elements, when put together, constitute a formidable business machine, finely tuned to the formula for success in a post-scarcity world.

Defensive Strategies

Companies that adopt a defensive posture in response to the falling prices that come with growing abundance employ a number of strategies to protect their prices and markets. These are by and large not new strategies – they are ones that companies have used over many years to protect their profitability. The various strategies in use include such things as branding, restriction of output, collusion between competing companies to fix prices, and action to protect trademarks, patents and copyright. The difference is that today these practices are being deployed on a much more widespread basis than hitherto, as the deflationary impact of abundance grows in force, and is felt over an ever wider range of industries.

BUILDING BRAND LOYALTY

Kotler (1993) defines brand as 'A name, term, sign, symbol or design, or a combination of these, which is intended to identify the goods or services of one group of sellers and differentiate them from those of competitors.'

According to Keller (2000) the world's strongest brands share a number of attributes:

- The brand image is aligned with the benefits that customers are seeking, whether these are reliability, quality, exclusivity, economy or service, or with social groupings with which consumers identify themselves, such as social classes, age groups or interest groups.

- The brand stays relevant. Without losing sight of their core strengths, the strongest brands adapt their image to fit the times. Gillette, for example, spends millions of dollars on R&D to ensure that its razor blades are highly technologically advanced. Yet at the same time, Gillette has created a consistent, intangible sense of product superiority with its long-running ads, 'The best a man can be,' which maintain relevancy to today's world through images of men at work and at play that have evolved over time to reflect contemporary taste and fashion.

- The brand makes use of and coordinates a full repertoire of marketing activities to build its strength. At its most basic level, a brand is made up of all the marketing elements that can be trademarked – logos, symbols, slogans, packaging, signage, and so on. Strong brands mix and match these elements to perform a number of brand-related functions, such as enhancing or reinforcing consumer awareness of the brand or its image and helping to protect the brand both competitively and legally. All of which, of course, is extremely expensive.

Coca-Cola makes use of many kinds of marketing activities in support of its global brand. These include media advertising (such as the global 'Always Coca-Cola' campaign); promotions and sponsorship (its extensive involvement with the Olympics). They also include direct response (the Coca-Cola catalogue, which sells licensed Coke merchandise) and interactive media (the company's website, which offers, among other things, games, a trading post for collectors of Coke memorabilia, and a virtual look at the World of Coca-Cola museum in Atlanta).

THE INTEL CASE

Intel provides an interesting example of the use of branding to support pricing structure in a technology component. The company was established in 1968 by three engineers, Robert Noyce, Gordon Moore and Andy Grove, when they left Fairchild Semiconductor to set up their own business.

To meet the requirements of a Japanese company manufacturing calculators they developed a microprocessor (the 4004) that performed the functions of 12 silicon chips and that could perform as fast as the Eniac, the fastest computer on the market at that time. Intel set about educating the engineering community in other uses for its microprocessors in products like traffic-light controllers, ovens and phones. Huge sales followed. A few product launches later in 1978 came the 8088 which was chosen by IBM for its first PC.

As more and more efficient microprocessors followed, more and more computer manufacturers incorporated Intel microprocessors into their products. However, Intel was relying on these manufacturers to convey to customers the benefits of using Intel products. As a result consumers knew very little about the company and its products. As consumers could now upgrade their machines by buying more advanced microprocessors it was becoming important that the company name and reputation became more widely known, so a marketing programme was developed for the purpose of building a distinctive brand.

At the same time Intel had to deal with the growth of intense competition and the consequent pressure on prices. The company AMD had been given a licence to manufacture Intel processors and began to market them using the same identification numbers as Intel. By offering the products at lower prices, AMD secured 52 per cent of the market by 1990. Intel had assumed its product numbers were protected trade marks and tried to stop AMD using them. However, AMD sued Intel for breach of contract and won.

Intel now realized that it had to create a strong brand to communicate to its customers what it believed to be the superior quality and performance of its products. It decided to take the radical step for a component supplier to address its campaign to the end user. The now familiar tagline 'Intel Inside' was adopted and shown inside a circle in the company's new logo.

Intel then offered to share the advertising costs of PC advertisements that included the Intel logo. By the end of 1991 some 300 PC manufacturers were engaged in joint advertising in this way.

In 1992 the company launched its first TV advertising campaign. It was now designating its models with names instead of numbers, starting with the Pentium.

To leverage the growing popularity of the brand the company started selling a range of other products, books, caps, T shirts, pens, key chains and dolls, all marked with the Intel logo.

In 2007 the Intel Corporation took another radical step when it released an advertising campaign featuring people dressed in silvery astronaut suits dancing to a song titled *Staying Alive*. Posters for the campaign featured a rainbow emerging from the logo of Intel's MMX microprocessor. This was just one more step along the way in the process of establishing the Intel brand as the only brand people would think of when microprocessors were mentioned. In the same year the company started advertising on the web.

Intel undoubtedly has had a well focused-R&D programme, but its 80 per cent dominance of the world market for processors and, by no means least in importance, the prices it is able to command, owe much to its sophisticated marketing.

In the Interbrand rankings of global brands in 2008, Intel ranked 7th. The value of its brand was estimated at $31bn. It ranked above such enduring consumer brands as McDonald's, Disney and Gillette.

In May 2009, the European Commission found leading computer chipmaker Intel Wednesday guilty of violating European anti-trust rules and ordered that it pay a fine of 1.06 billion euros ($1.45 billion). This is the largest fine the Commission has ever imposed. The Commission found Intel abused its dominant market position in the market for computer chips known as the x86 computer processing unit (CPU). Intel was accused of employing illegal anti-competitive practices to exclude essentially its only competitor, and that reduced consumer choice.

The Commission found that Intel awarded major computer manufacturers rebates on the condition that they purchase all or most of their supplies from

Intel and paid Europe's biggest computer retailer, Media Markt, to sell Intel-based PCs exclusively.

The Commission also found that Intel awarded payments to computer manufacturers so they would postpone or cancel the launch of products containing parts from its leading competitor AMD.

RESTRICTION OF OUTPUT

Another strategy aimed at maintaining scarcity and hence high prices is restriction of output. The most salient example is the restriction of oil production by the member countries of OPEC. Planning restrictions designed to conserve the countryside limit the supply of housing, which leads to rising house prices. In these cases, although the motives are different the outcome is to create scarcity. In the case of luxury goods an equally important motive is to maintain the air of exclusivity that surrounds their products.

Post-scarcity conditions bring a particular set of problems for companies that supply luxury goods. For the broad mass of consumers the main indicator of quality is its price. The message conveyed by the price tag may well be enhanced by sophisticated packaging and advertising that links the brand with prestigious people, but it is essentially price that equates with luxury and exclusiveness. The implication is, therefore, that although the prices of a wide range of goods may be falling, the suppliers of luxury items cannot afford to lower their own prices.

However, as affluence in the general population rises, more and more people aspire to own a Rolex or a Louis Vuitton bag. This implies a growth market for such products, yet this raises another set of issues. On the one hand if the luxury item begins to move into the mass market, it loses one aspect of its appeal – its exclusivity; on the other hand if price remains a barrier, consumers will be attracted by counterfeit or substitute products, particularly if they are very sophisticated ones.

How do companies that own luxury brands cope with this situation, particularly in the context of economic recession? The textbook answer is to cut costs and restrict production, but try to avoid cutting prices, since price-cutting will endanger the value of the brand.

But the reality for many companies is that they have no choice. Luxury and premium brands have grown so much – and reached so far into the mass market – that their owners cannot choose from a menu of cutting costs, output or prices. All are required. Prices, however, are cut discreetly, in outlet shops rather than in the principal shopping malls or airport shops. Costs are cut by seeking new sources of cheap labour. Luxury retailers in the USA are holding 'stealth sales' for their most prized customers as a way to boost earnings without diluting the value of their brand with public discounts or clearance offers. Whispered discounts are offered to shoppers at the point of sale, emails are sent to select individuals informing them of time-limited special deals, or inviting groups of clients to attend exclusive social events where they will be offered cut-price goods. Also, luxury goods companies have always tried to control distribution channels and limit discounting by selling through branded stores, but few of them control distribution channels sufficiently to stop powerful retailers discounting on their behalf.

PRICE FIXING

The least sensible way for companies to try to arrest an ongoing decline in prices for its products or services is to engage in a price-fixing conspiracy with its competitors. Yet this is exactly what some companies that are household names have done.

It is a crazy thing to do for three reasons. First, it is a criminal activity. Not only does the company face a very substantial fine when the offence is discovered, the company's senior executives face the risk of prison sentences.

- In April 2009 a senior executive of Hitachi was indicted in America for price fixing in respect of LCD screens supplied to Dell. His company, Hitachi Displays, was fined $31m. LG Sharp and Chingwa Picture Tubes were also fined. Executives from both these companies were fined and given prison sentences.

- In the UK, retail giants Argos and Littlewoods were fined a record £22.5m by the trading watchdog Office of Fair Trading (OFT) for fixing the prices of toys and games. A third conspirator, Hasbro was granted full leniency because it provided crucial evidence that initiated the investigation.

- Three cargo airlines have agreed to pay fines totalling $214m for their roles in a global conspiracy to fix prices for air freight. These penalties are the latest to be imposed following a probe by the US Justice Department that has led to the prosecution of 15 airlines and total fines in excess of $1.6bn. Three executives, from British Airways, Qantas and SAS pleaded guilty and received prison sentences.

- In addition to the air cargo investigation, British Airways was fined £121.5m in July 2007 by the UK Office of Fair trading for its role in a conspiracy with Virgin Atlantic to fix passenger fare surcharges. Virgin Atlantic and its executives avoided prosecution because they were granted leniency deals for being the first to volunteer information.

The second reason it is not very sensible, of course, is the huge damage to a company's reputation, bringing with it a loss of trust and the inevitable impact on revenue.

Finally, price fixing agreements are inherently unstable, with the consequence that the chances of discovery are very high. As suggested by the Prisoner's Dilemma game, all collusive agreements of this kind tend to fail because although price fixing is in the interests of the group of conspiring companies as a whole, it is not a profit-maximizing strategy for each individual firm. Thus the temptation to break ranks and cheat is very strong. Another source of instability is that if the cartel succeeds in keeping prices high this will enable new entrants to the market to compete successfully and establish themselves.

Many business leaders who speak of the positive role of market forces in creating prosperity risk imprisonment and their company's reputation by trying to prevent market forces operating in respect of their own company's products or services.

PATENTS, COPYRIGHT LOGOS AND TRADEMARKS

Companies can and do employ a range of legal devices to protect the prices of their products and services. These include patents, trade-marks, logos and copyright. Customers, however, find ways to fight back against these, as will be discussed in the next section.

Counterfeit Products and Piracy

According to an article in *Business Report* (Nov 12, 2007) the international trade in counterfeit goods is growing rapidly and, according to the International Chamber of Commerce, is worth $650 billion per annum. According to the World Customs Organization (WCO), which groups 170 customs administrations who collectively administer 98 per cent of international trade, counterfeiting and piracy account for about 7 per cent of global commerce.

Counterfeit and pirated goods are now produced on an industrial scale. According to research by the European Commission, the trade in some counterfeit goods is more profitable than drug trafficking. In 2004, the WCO reported more than 4,000 seizures involving about 166 million goods that were either counterfeit or pirated. It estimates that 43 per cent of available computer software is pirated.

Counterfeiting is not a purely economic issue. About 30 per cent of medication in the emerging nations is fake. Fake meningitis vaccines killed 2,500 people in Niger, counterfeit cough syrup killed 89 people in Haiti and fake antimalarial tablets killed 30 people in Cambodia.

Luxury items are no longer the sole focus of counterfeiters, with technology products, cigarettes and cigars, cosmetics, medication and household items joining the list. Not all counterfeit goods are cheap or poor quality versions of the originals. The high quality of some fakes often makes identification impossible without technical expertise. The counterfeit goods market responds to a powerful force of demand: consumers can buy an item for a fraction of the retail price, often without sacrificing quality.

The huge box-office success of *Slumdog Millionaire*, a rags-to-riches story of a Mumbai street boy, is set to become one of the most counterfeited movies of all time. The black market of counterfeit DVDs was flooded with illegal copies of the film, which won seven British Academy Film Awards (BAFTAs). In the UK, pirate versions were already being sold in London for £1 to £2.50 each, while it was still on current release. Within days of the release of the 3D film Avatar in January 2010, close to 1 million illegal downloads had occurred.

According to the BBC (5 Dec 2008) at Christmas time in 2008, UK parents were warned about fake imported Nintendo games consoles which could be a fire hazard and pose a danger to their children's safety. UK Revenue and

Customs said it had seized hundreds of counterfeit Nintendo DS and DS Lites, which were discovered to contain dangerous power adapters. Nintendo confirmed it had not produced the potentially dangerous adaptors. Several UK consumers had ordered the consoles after being attracted by the much cheaper price. Many had been bought for £40 instead of the usual £100 retail price.

One in eight British customers have recently had an experience of buying a fake watch, counterfeit handbag or other items, according to a study reported by InfoNIAC (23 July,2007). The conclusion is obvious – fake products are becoming more and more socially acceptable. Shoppers have considerably changed their attitude towards fake products, no longer feeling ashamed to admit, for example, that they wear a replica watch.

The study concluded that Burberry, well-known for its camel, red and black check fabrics, has become the number three in counterfeit sales, following leather goods producer Louis Vuitton and Gucci. As found by the study, about 1 million people acquired a fake Louis Vuitton product.

SOFTWARE PIRACY

According to the BBC (5 Dec 2008) Microsoft has launched 63 separate lawsuits against people peddling counterfeit software on auction sites. The legal action targets sellers in 12 nations including the USA, UK, Germany and France. Most of those Microsoft has targeted have been selling fake 'Blue Edition' versions of Windows XP.

Microsoft said the operating system was proving popular on auction sites as it is reaching the end of its commercial sales cycle. Windows XP stopped being installed on new PCs at the end of June 2008 to make way for Vista, the newest version of Windows. While Microsoft has claimed strong sales for Vista many businesses and consumers have shunned it in favour of the older software. Research by Microsoft into the quality of fake software sold on auction sites found that 34 per cent did not install properly and 43 per cent contained tampered codes that could expose buyers to identity theft or other attacks.

In pursuing auction sellers Microsoft has found that the trade in counterfeit software is now global. One of the cases it is handling spans four continents and involves peddlers in New Zealand selling Chinese copies of XP to customers in Australia, North America, the Netherlands, New Zealand and the UK.

FILE SHARING

File sharing has grown in popularity with the growth of high speed internet connections, and high-quality MP3 audio format. File sharing per se is perfectly legal with many legitimate uses; however, there is a substantial number of people who upload and download files containing copyright material without permission, thus infringing copyright. Despite the existence of various international agreements there are still sufficient differences between countries' laws to cause significant difficulties in protecting copyright. Recent years have seen a growth in litigation by industry bodies against a number of file sharers.

Current copyright law and enforcement may not be adequate to deal with rapidly developing new technologies and uses. The large number of individuals engaged in file sharing of copyrighted material means that copyright holders face problems relating to mass litigation and the accumulation of evidence. According to Wikipedia a number of studies have found that file sharing has a negative impact on sales of CDs.

In March 2007, the *Wall Street Journal* reported that sales of CDs in America had dropped 20 per cent in one year, the drop being attributed to the way people were getting their music. Today, more music than ever is getting into the hands of its consumers for free. A recent report by the International Federation of the Phonographic Industry suggested that of the download transactions which are now the world's default mechanism for the distribution of new music, 19 out of 20 are illegal.

According to G. Richard Shell, in a prescient article in Knowledge@ Wharton, suing customers is not a winning business strategy. Industries have a completely different strategic relationship with customers than they do with rivals. And this sort of strategy does not play well in the court of public opinion.

He draws a parallel with what happened 100 years ago, when the leading automobile manufacturers in 1903 tried to put down the threat of cheap, mass-produced cars by suing consumers who bought Henry Ford's automobiles. In 1903, when Henry Ford launched the Ford Motor Company, automobiles were high-priced, custom-made playthings for the rich. The major manufacturers had acquired a strategic property right very much like the recording industry's copyrights on recorded songs. It was called the Selden Patent and it gave its owners the exclusive right to sell self-propelled vehicles powered by internal combustion engines. A group of powerful companies had purchased it and formed an association to enforce it. Nearly every car company fell into line to pay royalties to the Association for the privilege of making and selling cars.

The association particularly did not like Ford's idea of driving prices down to where average people could afford a car. So it refused to license him. For Ford, it was either exit the industry or fight the Selden Patent in court. He decided to fight. The litigation lasted from 1903 until 1911 and included hundreds of lawsuits against Ford's customers to deter them from buying 'unlicensed vehicles.'

When the big companies started suing ordinary people who were just trying to buy a cheap car, public sympathy shifted against them. Ford won on appeal in 1911 when the court ruled that the Selden Patent covered only cars made with a special type of engine.

This story has important lessons for the recording industry. First, you will never win your market by suing your customers. Instead, you will simply alienate a generation of buyers. Shell gives an example of suing a 12-year-old girl in New York for downloading songs.

The second lesson is that no legal rule is strong enough to overcome a radical technical innovation. The Internet is designed to transfer data at zero marginal cost, so people want to download all kinds of things, including songs. Ultimately, no copyrights can stop that.

Thirdly, innovation always drives the down prices of yesterday's technology. Shell argues that the way to respond to the plight of the CD is not to sue internet-users. It is to find new ways to make money on music. Seven years after Shell's article, this is beginning to happen.

Nevertheless, the music industry was still using the courts in 2009. In June The Universal Music Group, owned by Vivendi, and other record labels were awarded $1.92 million in the retrial of a Minnesota woman accused of swapping music over the Kazaa internet service. The federal jury in Minneapolis said the woman, Jammie Thomas-Rasset, 32, of Brainerd, should pay $80,000 for each of the 24 songs that were posted on the site.

Anderson (2009) makes the point that piracy happens when customers perceive that the marginal cost of production and distribution of a product is significantly lower than the asking price. In such cases the only thing that can sustain the price is intellectual property law, copyright or patents. If people are willing to ignore the law the price can drop radically. The economic incentives to break the law are very considerable, with the result that piracy is unstoppable – in Anderson's view it is more like a natural source than a deviant social behaviour that can be controlled by legislation.

Summary

The inescapable conclusion is that, in the future, successful companies will be those which recognize that the economics of abundance will increasingly determine the market conditions within which they are operating. This recognition will lead to the adoption of different business models, involving different customer propositions, and in particular propositions which embrace sustainability.

The companies that will fail are those which attempt to prevent market forces operating and which try to create scarcity in the face of growing abundance.

11

The Business Response to Sustainability

Introduction

The sustainability of the economic, social and environmental systems of the world will be determined to a considerable extent by the decisions and actions of the board members and/or owners of the world's largest corporations. Of the 500 largest companies, 182 are based in Europe, 156 in the USA, 64 in Japan and 29 in China.

To what extent can these companies be a force for good in terms of contributing to the sustainability of the planet and the well-being of its inhabitants? What contribution can they make, acting either independently or in collaboration with governments and NGOs, to the maintenance and improvement of economic development and social capital in the societies in which they operate?

Business organizations, particularly the larger global ones, have wide-ranging impacts on our lives; they provide us with goods and services, they provide millions with jobs; they play roles in public services such as education and health. We entrust our savings to them. In sum, they enter into almost every aspect of our lives.

How companies are run and what objectives they set are, therefore, matters of concern to all of us and we should have an interest in who owns and controls them. Those who exercise control over companies can decide what they make, what they do, where they work and whom they employ as well as deeper issues such as what values they have, how they treat their employees, contractors and suppliers and whether they seek to play a positive role in society as a whole.

The Ownership and Control of Companies

A study carried out by Tomorrow's Company (2008) set out to ask a number of questions about companies:

- Who owns them?

- Who is actually in control?

- In whose interests is that control is exercised?

- And for what purposes?

- What are the implications of changing patterns of ownership for such things as wealth creation, wealth distribution and sustainability?

The report points out that the owners of shares in companies fall into a number of categories, and different schemes and approaches have been devised to enable them to manage their shareholdings using sustainability principles.

INSTITUTIONAL SHAREHOLDERS

Institutional investors have a fiduciary responsibility to individual investors, pension funds, insurance companies and other types of institution to manage funds for long-term value and tend to adopt a balanced risk profile. There are initiatives, however, such as the Principles for Responsible Investment (PRI), that are designed to encourage institutional investors to take sustainability issues into account. In early 2005 the United Nations Secretary-General invited a group of the world's largest institutional investors to join a process to develop the principles. Individuals representing 20 institutional investors from 12 countries agreed to participate in an Investor Group. The Group accepted ownership of the Principles, and was given the freedom to develop them as they saw fit.

The Group was supported by a 70-person multi-stakeholder group of experts from the investment industry, intergovernmental and governmental organizations, civil society and academia. The process, conducted between April 2005 and January 2006, involved a total of five days of face-to-face deliberations by the investors and four days by the experts, with hundreds of hours of follow-up activity. The Principles for Responsible Investment (PRI) emerged as a result of these meetings.

The PRI reflect the core values of the group of large investors whose investment horizon is generally long, and whose portfolios are often highly diversified. However, the Principles are open to all institutional investors, investment managers and professional service partners to support.

There are various types of signatory to the Principles – asset owners such as pension funds, investment managers and a miscellaneous group of service providers. To date there are around 200 signatories in the asset owner group and another 250 investment managers. By 2008 the PRI signatories had over $13 trillion under management.

In some countries institutional investors are pulling out of investment in particular companies or industry sectors, an example being AXA, the giant French insurer, pulling out of investments in companies that make cluster bombs and landmines. In the UK there has been government pressure on pension funds to use their ownership in order to hold companies accountable. There are a few funds that do restrict their investments to companies that they perceive to be pursuing sustainability objectives. One example is Generation Investment Management, founded in 2004 by Al Gore and David Blood.

PRIVATE EQUITY

Private equity (PE) firms have been growing in scale and reach. Whereas hedge funds look for undervalued or overvalued companies in order to buy or sell their stock, PE firms look for undervalued companies in order to transform the company itself. PE investors generally look for medium-term turnarounds, typically over 4–5 years. However, some PE firms, such as Permira and Warren Buffet's Berkshire Hathaway, are keeping their acquisitions and managing them for longer-term growth.

For example, Permira's website states that the company's ambition is to build stronger and more valuable businesses, which involves a concern for their long-term sustainability. In consequence, 'consideration of the social and environmental impact of our funds' activity is embedded into our day-to-day operations, the funds' investment process and the way we think about the governance of the funds' portfolio companies'.

Permira has a set of business principles to guide the behaviour of its staff and to underpin the way it operates. All partners and employees of Permira are expected to conduct their activities in accordance with both the letter and the spirit of these principles.

Advocates of PE argue that it tends to restore the links between ownership, financing, control and stewardship of a company and frees companies from short-term pressure to report ever increasing profits. However, this has to be balanced with a recognition that in many cases the PE investor's priority is a profitable exit within a decade. PE owners tend to insist on the high standards of environmental, social and governance performance needed to comply with laws and satisfy responsible investors – they have been identified as a very positive force in India, for example. But they may not always aspire to making long-term contributions to sustainability

SOVEREIGN WEALTH FUNDS

Sovereign wealth funds (SWFs) have grown rapidly in recent years. Initially seen as threats, they aroused concerns over issues of national security, the most high profile example being the proposed takeover of P&O by Dubai Ports World (DPW), involving P&O's six US ports. US lawmakers sought assurances that SWFs had no political goals while the EU also threatened to restrict SWF investments if they did not disclose more information about their intentions. After interventions from the OECD and IMF, SWFs agreed to a set of principles including a statement that 'investment decisions should be based solely on commercial grounds, rather than to advance, directly or indirectly, the geopolitical goals of the controlling government.' Since the credit crunch of 2007, however, the atmosphere has changed considerably as SWFs have poured billions into support for Western banks and financial institutions. Thus far the contribution of sovereign wealth funds has tended to be that of a patient long-term owner with dispersed but stable holdings. They strengthen the ability of managements to take a long-term view and appear to be primarily motivated by the prospect of financial return on the assets at their disposal, rather than by national or geo-political considerations or by sustainability issues An exception is Norway's Government Pension Fund, which does apply social responsibility criteria to its investments.

GOVERNMENTS

States continue to be influential owners of companies, but there is huge variation in the extent to which sustainability issues are taken into account. After almost 20 years when the globalization of capital and the privatization of state-owned enterprises have been the dominant trends, recent years have seen an increase in measures to constrain the impact of foreign ownership, particularly for industries deemed by politicians to be of national importance, whether on economic grounds or ones of national security. The credit crunch has recently led to an upsurge in state ownership of financial sector enterprises and key manufacturing companies, albeit on a temporary basis.

FAMILIES AND FOUNDATIONS

In many listed companies, the founding family influence is still strong, well-known examples being Ford in the USA, Sainsbury's in the UK and Fiat in Italy. Novo Nordisk provides an example of a family handing over to a foundation with principles that kept the family's values alive in the company. The company has adopted an ambitious charter that spells out the company's values and commitments, including ensuring that all products and services 'make a significant difference in improving the way people live and work.' Each year the company board must report to the Foundation which controls it shares on how it is ensuring that operations are 'economically viable, environmentally sound, and socially productive'.

In cases where the family firm is a private business with no outside shareholding, the company's approach to sustainability issues will be a function of the personal values and priorities of the family members.

EMPLOYEES

One relatively unusual but very stable model is the employee-owned company. Employee-owned companies have tended to be strong on social and environmental issues.

One of the best-known examples is the John Lewis Partnership PLC, with £6.8 billion (about US$10 billion) in revenues in 2007. It has a stated purpose of serving the happiness of its employee-partners. It is the largest department store chain in the UK, and also owns 200 Waitrose supermarkets. It is 100 per cent owned by its 69,000 staff members, among whom all profits are shared each year. It is overseen by an unusual bicameral governance structure: the company has a traditional board of directors as well as a second employee-based governing body, the partnership council, directly elected by employees. The partnership council in turn elects 5 of the 12 board members. The council also influences policy and holds management to account, since it has the formal power to dismiss the chairman.

MUTUALS AND COOPERATIVES

In these types of organization ownership is vested in suppliers or consumers. It is a very old type of business organization, but is enjoying a renaissance owing to the increased interest in operating sustainably. The cooperative model of ownership, which dates to the mid nineteenth century, was conceived as an alternative to the shareholder-based ownership model that developed at roughly the same time. The defining feature of the cooperative model is that these companies are owned and controlled by the members they serve. Members might be customers (as in a credit union), producers (as in a farmers' cooperative), homeowners (as in a housing cooperative), employees, or the community.

Cooperatives exist in many countries and have a membership in the region of 800 million people. In Spain, the Mondragón Corporación Cooperativa is the nation's seventh-largest industrial concern. More Americans hold memberships in co-ops than hold stock in the stock market. Rabobank Group in the Netherlands and the Springfield ReManufacturing Corporation in the USA are two examples of companies that have prospered by drawing on the commitment and engagement of their shareholder-customers and shareholder-employees respectively.

However, as Marjorie Kelly (2009) points out, stakeholder ownership also has its flaws. Cooperatives have failed to match the growth of shareholder-owned companies partly because they lack access to capital. On the other hand, when employee ownership is matched with involvement, businesses can achieve results that would be considered near-impossible in conventional companies.

Kelly quotes as an example the Cooperative Regions of Organic Producers Pool (CROPP), better known by its brand name Organic Valley, a producer-owned marketing cooperative in La Farge, Wisconsin. CROPP is owned by the 1,200 organic family farms that produce the dairy, eggs, and meat it distributes.

The company's mission is to save the family farm, which means paying as much as possible to farmers. With 2007 revenues of $433 million, Organic Valley stewards one of the nation's four largest organic brands.

HEDGE FUNDS

The term 'hedge fund' is generally used to describe private, largely unregulated capital funds whose managers bet on falling as well as rising assets, 'hedging' one type of investment with another, typically covering a position on a stock expected to rise by short-selling one expected to fall. By their nature, hedge funds make many short-term investments and drive up turnover of stock. Hedge funds are seen to be interested in creating value from movements in share prices, and in gaps between price and value – rather than from changes in the actual performance of the company. It is easy to dismiss hedge funds as speculative gamblers but arguably they are positive for investors if they either expose deficiencies in a company's management or highlight hidden strengths that others have not spotted. It is certainly widely assumed that hedge funds do not put sustainability issues very high on their agenda.

The Influence of Owners

The influence that owners of shares can bring to bear on sustainability issues depends to a great extent on the degree to which owners take a long-term view of the assets they control and are prepared to act responsibly with regard to these critical issues.

In some countries, such as the UK and USA, where companies have widely dispersed shareholdings, ownership duties often tend to be neglected while ownership rights tend to be delegated to intermediaries and are as a result heavily diluted. The result is to leave the boards and executives of companies with a very high level of control, providing they continue to deliver performance in terms of earnings per share.

However in many companies in continental Europe, where there are one or more major block holders, such as foundations, families or banks, shareowners are often deeply involved in company affairs. Typically, shares are divided into voting and non-voting shares and control is exercised by the shareholder or shareholders owning the majority of the voting shares. This approach effectively separates the issues of ownership and control. The owners of 'B' shares do not get a vote, exercise no control, but get a share of the economic benefits. The 'A' shareholders appoint the chairman and CEO. In reality a major block holder is often in full control.

Asian countries exhibit a range of other models. State influence persists in China; Japanese companies commonly have small cross-holdings with many other companies, while privatization of state-run companies in some former Eastern bloc countries has led to the concentration of assets in the hands of relatively few powerful shareholders.

While block holders with substantial holdings can move a company purely through their voting strength and influence, minority shareholders with smaller stakes can influence the decisions of a company through activism, campaigning and generating publicity. There are some types of activists with a financial motivation who may campaign for or against mergers, acquisitions or other strategic moves. There are also sustainability activists who take small stakes in companies in order to call attention to what they regard as socially irresponsible actions, often through resolutions tabled at annual general meetings. For example Amnesty International USA has launched two new actions targeting Google and Microsoft, demanding that the Internet giants stop aiding repression of free speech in China.

Thus the variations in patterns of ownership are considerable, leading to similar differences in the locus of control and hence of a company's approach to questions of sustainability.

Reporting on Sustainability Issues

A range of approaches to company reporting of performance across a wide range of issues has been developed recently; these have in common the twin aims of providing a broader-based set of performance measures than the traditional financial ones and of creating greater disclosure and transparency in relation to corporate activities. The new methods are variously known as social reporting, triple-bottom line reporting, social audit, social and ethical accounting or inclusive reporting.

Sometimes these terms are used to mean the same thing; that is, a report that covers the economic, environmental and social performance of a company may be called simply a social report; sometimes the various terms are defined more narrowly.

One of the first companies to produce a form of social report was General Motors. In 1971 the company convened a conference with prominent educators and representatives of foundations and investment institutions 'to explain the progress General Motors has made in a number of areas of public concern and to obtain the participants' thoughts as to the Corporation's activities and goals in these areas.' The topics covered included automobile emissions, industrial pollution, minority opportunities and automotive safety. Following the conference the company published the first in a series of reports covering a wide range of environmental and social issues.

The number of major companies now producing similar reports has been growing rapidly since the millennium. Several NGOs and a number of consultancies working in this field offer guidance to companies embarking upon the process of broad-based reporting. The advice they offer is very similar and it is summarized below:

- A guiding statement of purpose, vision and values.

- The starting point should be a clear vision of the path to sustainable development and the goals that will support the achievement of that vision, together with a clear statement of the organization's underlying values. This vision must link closely with the organization's business strategy and not be seen as something apart from it. It is the role of leadership to develop the vision and articulate it. Top management commitment to the process and active engagement in it is essential.

- An inclusive or holistic approach to the range of issues to be addressed.

The report should be inclusive, adopting a systems approach, involving a review of the whole range of the organization's activities and processes, and their economic, environmental and social impacts and the interactions between them.

- An inclusive approach to stakeholder involvement.

Stakeholder dialogue is essential to establish the issues to be reviewed. The process should encompass a wider range of stakeholder groups than those engaged in direct transactions with the company.

- Adequate scope

    This implies a time horizon long enough to respond to needs of future generations as well as those current to short-term decision-making. The scope of the report should include not only local but also long-distance impacts on people and ecosystems. It should reach back into the supply chain and forward to the ultimate use and disposal of the organization's products. It should also cover joint ventures and other business alliances.

- Practical focus

    The selected indicators and assessment criteria should be clearly linked to the vision and values. A mid course should be steered between a comprehensive report and the need to be sharply focused on the key issues. Standardised measurements should be used wherever possible to permit comparison and benchmarking. Measurements should be evaluated in relation to targets, reference values, ranges, thresholds, or direction of trends, as appropriate.

- Transparency

    The methods and data that are used should be accessible to all. All judgements, assumptions, and uncertainties in data and interpretations should be made explicit.

- Verification

    Independent, qualified assessors should verify the accuracy and comprehensiveness of data.

- Effective reporting and communication

    Reports should be designed to address the needs of the audience and set of users. Reports should be designed for simplicity in structure and use of clear and plain language; they should be stimulating and capable of capturing audience attention. The internet should be used for reporting. Reports should as far as possible be in real time rather than confined to annual reviews. They should be forward-looking rather than focused on the past. They should be the basis for dialogue rather than one-way communications.

- An ongoing process

  A capacity for repeated measurement to determine trends should be established. Goals, methods and indicators should be revised as new insights are gained. There should be a clear feedback process leading to performance improvements.

- Institutional capacity

  Continuity of assessing progress toward sustainable development should be assured by clearly assigning responsibility and providing ongoing support in the decision-making process, and by providing institutional capacity for data collection, maintenance, and documentation.

According to research by Ethical Investment Research Services (EIRIS), company reporting on sustainability issues has risen significantly over the past 10–20 years, influenced by a range of factors, including increasing regulation, NGO activism and the socially responsible investment movement. The study concluded that responsible business practices are increasingly being adopted by companies worldwide though there are significant differences between regions, as follows.

European companies have well-developed responsible business practices across a broad range of issues, reflecting a sophisticated responsible investment market, NGO pressure and a strong regulatory environment.

Although Japanese companies are characterized by strong performance on environmental issues, they need to make progress on other issues to match European levels.

A matter for concern, however, is that other than a core of companies which have adopted responsible business practices, North American companies lag significantly behind their European counterparts across all the areas researched.

European and Japanese companies were found to be clear leaders with respect to managing environmental impacts.

Nearly 75 per cent of European companies operating in high risk countries have developed a basic or advanced human rights policy compared with less than 40 per cent of North American companies. Also over 50 per cent of European companies have adopted a basic or advanced supply chain policy. However, fewer than 20 per cent of North American companies have done so. The low proportion of US companies achieving an advanced grade may be explained by the frequent omission of freedom of association and collective bargaining from their human rights policies.

Across all regions, with the exception of Europe, the majority of companies with a significant degree of reliance on global supply chains show little or no evidence of having a supply-chain labour standards policy.

Community involvement can range from simple donations of money to donations of expertise, time and resources and is widely used in all regions of the world as a means to build reputation. Differential tax rates and incentives for charitable giving between different countries play a part in affecting the average amount donated from country to country.

Major system change, however, cannot be brought about simply by the isolated actions of individual companies trying to be a force for good. Nor will it result from advocacy and campaigning, however persuasive. It calls for change in that 'network of diverse causal relationships within which companies are enmeshed'. If companies' efforts are to be fully effective they need to reach out and work to change the system, doing so in collaboration with other companies as well as with governments, international agencies, NGOs, and others.

Companies Working Together

THE WORLD BUSINESS COUNCIL FOR SUSTAINABLE DEVELOPMENT

The World Business Council for Sustainable Development (WBCSD) was formed in 1995 and is a coalition of some 200 international companies united by a shared commitment to sustainable development defined as environmental protection, social equity and economic growth. Its members are drawn from 30 countries and more than 20 major industrial sectors. The WBCSD also benefits from a thriving global network of national and regional business councils and partner organizations.

The Council's objectives are to:

- be a leading business advocate on sustainable development;

- participate in policy development to create the right framework conditions for business to make an effective contribution to sustainable human progress;

- develop and promote the business case for sustainable development;

- demonstrate the business contribution to sustainable development solutions and share leading edge practices among members;

- contribute to a sustainable future for developing nations and nations in transition.

In order to achieve this, the Council focuses on four key areas:

- energy and climate

- development

- the business role of social responsibility

- ecosystems.

THE GLOBAL REPORTING INITIATIVE (GRI)

The Global Reporting Initiative (GRI) was established in late 1997 with the mission of developing globally applicable guidelines for reporting on the economic, environmental and social performance, initially for corporations and eventually for any business, governmental, or non-governmental organization. Since then, GRI has developed the world's most widely used sustainability reporting framework. This framework sets out the principles and indicators that organizations can use to measure and report their economic, environmental, and social performance.

The cornerstone of the framework is the sustainability reporting guidelines. The third version of the guidelines – known as the G3 Guidelines – was published in 2006. Other components of the framework include sector supplements (unique indicators for industry sectors) and protocols (detailed reporting guidance) and national annexes (unique country-level information).

Sustainability reports based on the GRI framework can be used to benchmark organizational performance, demonstrate organizational commitment to sustainable development, and compare organizational performance over time. To date, more than 1,500 companies, including many of the worlds leading brands, have declared their voluntary adoption of the guidelines worldwide. Consequently the G3 Guidelines have become the *de facto* global standard for reporting.

Investors Acting Together

In recent years there has been an upsurge in activism by small groups of shareholders intent on influencing companies in particular directions. In the USA, large public pension funds such as Calpers and TRIAA-CREF have used their significant voting power to bring pressure on companies to improve their corporate governance.

One key question for the future, therefore, is whether shareholder engagement will grow. Today some shareholders are fully committed to engagement, for example the BT Pension Scheme, acting through Hermes Equity Ownership Services. They can see a clear link between sound sustainability policies and long-term financial health. Others may be engaging on sustainability issues simply because it is currently seen as the thing to do.

Awards and Citations

The Business Ethics 100 Best Corporate Citizens list was developed and first published in 2000. It has since gained international recognition as an indicator of best practices in the area of corporate social responsibility

The methodology for the list was developed by Marjorie Kelly, then Editor of *Business Ethics* magazine, and Samuel P. Graves and Sandra Waddock of Boston College. Together they created a scoring system that ranked companies according to financial, environmental, social, and governance performance. The methodology has evolved slightly since the list was first created.

The list is produced each year in conjunction with KLD Research & Analytics, the leading authority on social research and indexes for institutional investors. Environmental, social, and governance performance data for the 100 Best Corporate Citizens list comes from SOCRATES, KLD's comprehensive online database of environmental, social and governance research.

The CR Reporting Awards (CRRA) are the only annual, global online CR reporting awards. The programme was developed in 2007 to identify and acknowledge the best in corporate non-financial reporting. The CR Reporting Awards are managed by Corporate Register.com – the CR resources website and providers of an online directory of CR and sustainability reports.

Taking September 2007–October 2008 as the reporting period, 2,000 companies with relevant CR/sustainability reports published during this time were invited to participate. However, to make the voting process more manageable only the first 120 entries were accepted. The reports were divided across 9 award categories, with some reports entered into multiple categories. The winner for 2008 was Vodafone, and the runners up Coca-Cola and Dell.

Validation Processes

In 2008 some 3,000 companies published a corporate social responsibility (CSR) report to document their policies and performance on key issues, including environmental and social activities. Of these, around 750 included a third-party assurance statement addressing the report's credibility and completeness.

Assure View is a company which publishes information about the CSR validation industry. Their *CSR Assurance Statement Report* offers an independent, comprehensive overview of CSR report auditing. The report outlines who uses assurance, who provides assurance and what methods are used.

While CSR reporting has now become a basic business expectation, as long as the majority of CSR reports are not independently assured, serious doubts remain as to the meaning and reliability of these non-assured CSR reports. Of those reports which do include an assurance statement, Assure View points out that there are hundreds of assurance providers operating, and in the absence of a common language there is confusion as to which of the many assurance approaches provides the most credibility and certainty. Some standards and guidelines are emerging, but are far from being accepted across the board.

Socially Responsible Investment (SRI)

The last decade has seen the growth of ethical or 'socially responsible' investing, driven by growing public concern over a wide range of issues, including the impact of companies' activities on the environment, cases of fraud and misfeasance, and human rights abuses. Socially responsible investors (SRIs) and ethical funds boycott companies whose activities they oppose and favour companies with strong records of responsible behaviour. The value of responsible investment funds has grown dramatically in the last 10 years, with around USD 4 trillion of funds incorporating an analysis of ESG factors now being managed globally.

As of 2007, there were 260 socially screened mutual fund products in the USA, with assets of $201.8 billion, compared to just 55 SRI funds in 1995. This type of investment had a heyday in the late 1990s, particularly in the USA, when total assets under management using these strategies rose from $640bn in 1995 to $2.16 trillion in 1999, according to the Social Investment Forum. Since then the growth of SRIs has been less rapid though still robust, with SRI funds under management growing to $2.71 trillion by 2007.

Responsible investing has also been boosted by initiatives such as the Dow Jones Sustainability Index which records the financial performance of companies who are also leaders in embracing opportunities and managing risks deriving from economic, environmental and social developments. Discussing the rationale for the index, Dow Jones says 'A growing number of investors are convinced that sustainability is a catalyst for enlightened and disciplined management, and, thus, a crucial success factor.'

Another booming initiative is the Carbon Disclosure Project, whereby major investors join together to ask around 3,000 leading companies to provide data on their carbon emissions and efforts to address climate change. Launched in 2000, the project originally drew support from investors with $4.5 trillion under management. Today it embraces over 300 investors with around $41 trillion under management – about a third of the world's total invested assets.

Corporate Irresponsibility

The history of big business is littered with example after example of acts of commission and omission such that if they had been committed by individuals would have resulted in heavy fines and in some cases terms of imprisonment. Yet although we speak of corporate crime the truth is that these crimes were in fact committed by individuals. The perpetrators were members of boards of directors and/or the owners of companies who, whether by calculated purpose or passive assent, were party to the decisions involved.

The current focus on the word corporate in the phrase corporate social responsibility (CSR) masks the fact that corporations cannot take decisions and cannot therefore be said to act either responsibly or irresponsibly. If there is irresponsibility it lies at the door of the human beings who take the decisions.

The list of companies that have been found guilty of irresponsible behaviour, whether in a court of law or in the court of public opinion, includes some of the most highly regarded and long-established businesses, the directors of which are or have been respected and honoured in their countries.

The list includes downright fraud, neglect of health and safety, exploitation of workers in poor counties, pollution of the environment, antitrust behaviour and price fixing, and abuse of human rights. Among the world-class companies that have been successfully prosecuted in recent years are Enron, BA, Intel, Microsoft, Hitachi and Qantas.

Despite protestations about increasingly responsible corporate behaviour, there is a constant flow of news items that tell of the attempts of companies to lobby against regulation, to collude to fix prices or to defend such practices as the high level of sugar and saturated fats in food products aimed at the children's market.

There is little doubt that this Jekyll and Hyde behaviour is to a considerable extent due to intense pressure from powerful institutional investors to produce results – and results here and now, not in the medium or long term. The implication of this is that the investment community shares with company boards the responsibility for any actions that have a negative impact on the planet or on society. However it is very difficult to bring this responsibility home to individual fund managers.

So, can directors of companies claim that they are trapped in a system which gives them very little room for manoeuvre? Can those responsible for investing billions on the part of millions of individual beneficiaries make the same claim?

The answer is that the system is indeed at fault and is unsustainable; its cumulative, negative impact on the sustainability of the wealth-creating system as a whole is such as to imperil its survival. This does not, however, adequately excuse the behaviour of company directors or the lack of concern by investors for issues other than maximizing shareholder value.

One evident flaw in the present system is that when a company is found guilty of breaking the law and a fine is levied, the burden of paying the fine usually falls, not on the decision-makers, but on the shareholders. (The only assets possessed by a company are, of course, shareholders' funds; when we read a headline which says, for example, company X is fined $100m dollars, the headline should read 'the shareholders of company X were fined $100m.')

In most cases the company directors involved feel no pain; in consequence they are not deterred from infringing the law on future occasions.

In the relatively rare cases where the court imposes a prison sentence on an officer of the company it is not usually the case that the officer indicted is the CEO or chairman.

The system could be nudged in the direction of greater corporate responsibility by the simple process of requiring members of boards, including NEDs, to be held jointly responsible for paying any fines from their personal assets. Even more so, in the more serious cases if they were to face greater risk than at present of receiving custodial sentences they would hesitate, for example, before such acts as conspiring to conceal the dangerous side effects of a new drug.

Social Responsibility and the Pharmaceutical Industry

SCHERING-PLOUGH

According to an article in the US journal *CMAJ*, 24 October 2006, Schering-Plough Corp., the US pharmaceutical manufacturer perhaps best known for its anti-allergy medication Claritin, agreed to pay US$435 million in fines to settle criminal and civil charges that it illegally promoted several drugs. The agreement was reached with the US Justice Department, which also alleged the New Jersey-based company had defrauded Medicaid, the government health care programme.

The case marks the third time in the last five years that the company, which has annual sales of approximately US$10 billion, reached a multi-million settlement with the government. One of the largest health care fines ever meted out by the Justice Department, it brought to US$1.3 billion the total paid by Schering-Plough as a result of the settlements.

According to the government, Schering-Plough engaged in illegal sales and marketing practices involving several cancer drugs by promoting their use for treatments not government-approved at the time.

Although it is illegal for pharmaceuticals to promote drugs for non FDA-approved treatments, doctors have no such restrictions. According to the Justice Department, Schering-Plough paid doctors honoraria, directed prestigious and lucrative research grants their way, placed them on well-paying medical advisory boards and treated them to lavish dinners and other forms of entertainment in return for prescribing the drugs for non-approved (off-label) usages.

The Justice Department also alleged that Schering-Plough defrauded Medicaid of US$4.3 million in the late 1990s by overcharging the agency, which provides health insurance to the poor and disabled, for the systemic antihistamine Claritin RediTabs.

While Schering-Plough said the off-label promotions were isolated incidents, the government said they were part of a national plan that the pharmaceutical company's staff were trained to enact.

The company's website includes a statement on business integrity and compliance with laws and regulations impacting the company's global business operations and the approach taken to ensure compliance, including policies and procedures, training, auditing and monitoring, an anonymous reporting hotline, an investigations process, and application of discipline.

PFIZER

According to *The Times* (3 September 2009), Pfizer, the major US pharmaceutical company, was ordered to pay $2.3 billion (£1.4 billion), America's largest healthcare fraud settlement, for making false claims about four prescription medications.

The money included $102 million to be divided between 11 whistleblowers, former employees who became concerned that the company was asking them to break the law and mis-sell certain drugs – Bextra, Geodon, Zyvox and Lyrica.

Pfizer had pleaded guilty in 2004 to an earlier criminal charge of improper sales tactics. The case involved the company's use of 'off-label promotion', in which it marketed the four prescription medications for treatments that did not have the approval of the US Food and Drug Administration.

Pfizer's website has a statement about responsibility, which claims that the company is continually striving to lessen its impact on the environment, nurture a workplace of diversity and inclusion, conduct responsible business practices, and uphold the highest ethical standards in everything from research and development to sales and marketing.

In the governance arrangements for both Schering-Plough and Pfizer, the posts of chairman and chief executive are held by the same person. This is generally regarded as poor governance practice.

These two cases no doubt help explain why there is considerable scepticism in relation to the pharmaceutical industry's claim to be responsible and ethical.

A Question of Leadership

Companies will act responsibly and contribute to sustainability if those who exercise control (company directors and shareholders together) have the vision to see that our collective future is inextricably tied to sustainability and the courage and will to act accordingly.

STEWARDSHIP

The approach to leadership that is required is well summed up in one word: *stewardship*.

The UK's Eden Project – the creation of two vast biodomes in a disused china-clay quarry – provides a superb example of vision translated into action. In the words of the project's initiator, Tim Smit, 'Eden isn't so much a destination as a place in the heart. It is not just a marvellous piece of science-related architecture; it is also a statement of our passionate belief in an optimistic future for mankind.' The achievement of Smit's vision called for it to be shared by a large team of specialists in areas of expertise ranging from drainage systems to long-term finance; it required an act of faith and the will to overcome seemingly insurmountable obstacles; it involved a set of shared values and provides a good example of what is meant by stewardship.

> *We are also here to show that environmental awareness is about the quality of life at all levels. The environment is shorthand for issues that impact on us in a thousand ways every day, from the food that we eat and the clothes that we wear to the weather we enjoy or suffer. Most of all we wanted Eden to be a symbol of what is possible when people put their mind to the challenge of regeneration and restoration.*

In the business sphere, Block (1993) has argued the case for replacing our traditional concepts of leadership with the new concept of stewardship. Most of our theories about making changes, he asserts, are clustered around the idea of leadership and the role of the leader in achieving the transformation of organizational performance. In his view, this pervasive and almost religious belief in leaders actually slows the process of genuine transformation.

Stewardship, Block argues, is about 'the willingness to be accountable for some larger body than ourselves – an organization or a community. It is to do with 'our choice for service over self-interest', with being 'willing to be deeply accountable without choosing to control the world around us'. Stewardship is to do with the long-term survival of the organization and with its contribution to the wider society. It provides an ethical foundation to the leader's role.

At the heart of the stewardship concept lies that of service and self-interest. Today our doubts about our leaders are not so much about their talents as about their integrity and trustworthiness. For Block, the 'antidote' to the seductive, but ultimately destructive, force of self-interest is to commit and adopt a cause – the cause being the purpose and vision of the organization.

According to Manz and Sims (2001), a business leader who exemplified the stewardship concept is Dennis Bakke, co-founder of AES Corporation. AES is an international power company founded in 1981 that now has a turnover of over $3billion and operates over 140 power plants in some 46 countries. Bakke argued that 'the purpose of business and the purpose of AES is stewarding resources in order to meet a need in society'. Bakke believes that 'the stewardship of the earth and its resources for the benefit of all is a primary responsibility of mankind.'

INTERFACE

Another such is Ray Anderson, Chairman of Interface, a US carpet manufacturer. Interface is the world's largest manufacturer of commercial floor coverings and as a company has a long-standing commitment to not only becoming fully sustainable but also to becoming a 'restorative' company, that is, one which enhances the environment rather than depletes it Interface has set itself the goal of achieving zero waste by 2020. Teams have been set up using the acronym QUEST which stands for Quality Utilizing Employee Suggestions and Teamwork. These teams look at sources of waste and come up with ways to reduce and finally eliminate them.

Ray Anderson sees his company's mission as leading 'the second industrial revolution'. Until the mid '90s the company was content to comply with environmental legislation. But then customers and distributors began asking what Interface was doing about the environment. This was 1994, two years after the historic Rio Earth Summit. Interface's experience was not unique. Most companies and their customers were paying more attention to the environmental impact of their actions.

But Anderson, at one time co-chair of President Clinton's Council on Sustainable Development, had had an epiphany, and his response was like few others. In an address to a task force convened by Interface employees, he challenged them to make Interface a sustainable, even restorative company.

Anderson presented the company's employees with a seven-point plan:

- eliminate waste, with zero waste as a goal

- generate benign emissions to both the biosphere and lithosphere

- use renewable energy (Interface just recently inaugurated a plant that uses only solar energy)

- close the loop on waste, with less energy used to recycle and reuse than to extract the resource

- use resource-efficient transportation

- get suppliers, employers, and all the links moving in the same direction

- take cradle-to-cradle responsibility – that is, upstream and downstream supply-chain management.

One of Interface's ways of approaching new business thinking is the innovative Greenlease scheme for commercial customers. Greenlease recognizes that no customer actually wants to buy a heap of nylon fibres and glue; what they really want are the benefits provided by the carpets' warmth, appearance and texture, not the carpet itself. Customers would also welcome an alternative to a carpet that gradually wears out and then has to be disposed of (at a substantial environmental cost) and then replaced at a significant capital outlay.

The way Greenlease works is that a company leases carpet services from Interface, getting the benefit of new carpet tiles which are regularly inspected by Interface and automatically replaced when they become worn, effectively creating a carpet which consistently provides a high standard of presentation and function. Interface continue to own the carpet and any recovered worn carpet is rejuvenated or recycled into new carpet without the need to call upon virgin resources. It is in the interests of Interface to make the carpet go round in cycles as many times as possible, re-engineering and reformulating the production process to aid recyclability. From the customers' viewpoint, initial capital outlay and its resultant effect on cash flow is removed and the cost of providing a constant standard of carpeting to the business is truly reflected in their accounts.

ECOVER

Another business driven by sustainable leadership ideals is Ecover, an international company active in the production of ecological detergents and cleansing agents. It was founded in 1980 in Belgium. Ecover defines its mission as providing effective, sustainable solutions for the hygienic needs of people. This company has been a trendsetter in sustainable practices from the beginning – it marketed a phosphate-free washing powder even before phosphates were branded as a problem.

Since then Ecover, under the ownership of Jørgen Philip Sørensen CBE, has developed into the world's largest producer of ecological detergents and cleansing products. Besides its headquarters in Malle, close to Antwerp in Belgium, Ecover has sites in the United States of America, the United Kingdom and Switzerland, and its products are marketed in more than 20 countries.

Ecover's environmental policy is not only demonstrated by the products it sells; it is also an integral part of the company's business operations. Acting in the spirit of the externally audited ISO 14001 standard, Ecover has extended its environmental policy to all departments of the company, from production to marketing. One of the most striking results is the world's first ecological factory, which has a green roof extending over more than 6,000m². That building was put into service in October 1992. It received extensive press attention at the time, and it draws more than a thousand visitors every year.

Ecover has been awarded recognition and prizes on many occasions for its special contributions and achievements in the field of environmentally sound, sustainable development. Perhaps the most prestigious recognition was being named to the Global 500 Roll of Honour of the United Nations Environment Program, which was awarded to Ecover as early as 1993.

Ecover is a company that aims to optimize economic value, while regarding the environment as an inseparable part of the economy. Negative impacts on the environment are reduced by means such as stimulating and conducting research on new technologies and raw materials. In the social area, Ecover regards job performance as a means to foster the social wellbeing and personal development of its direct and indirect employees.

It has developed strong brands in the following specific areas:

- detergents and cleansing agents

- personal care products

- accessories for healthy houses and ecological quality of life.

In its in-house laboratory, Ecover develops ecological products that are claimed to be equal to conventional products in terms of effectiveness. The company takes ecological, economic and social aspects into account from the origin from his raw materials till the biodegradation of his final products. Strict criteria are employed as guidelines for all business operations, from selecting raw materials through production methods to full decomposition of the end products.

The raw materials for Ecover products are based on vegetable and mineral resources, which have two major advantages:

- They are renewable. That means they can be grown again or replenished and are inexhaustible.

- They offer an unlimited range of possibilities. Even the plastics used by Ecover are derived from vegetable materials.

By using renewable sources of materials, Ecover avoids creating environmental burdens and health risks.

In order to make this all work smoothly, the company has developed and introduced an environmental management system to ensure that the ecological character of Ecover is maintained at a high level in the production process as well.

Ecover's Environmental Handbook forms the basis for this environmental management system. It describes the measures that are taken to continually improve environmental management at Ecover and reduce environmental and safety risks in and around the factory. The environmental management system was set up in accordance with the recognized ISO 14001 standard, and it was certified by an external certification agency in December 2000. Since then, it has been controlled annually be external auditors.

Summary

Chapters 10 and 11 have outlined ways in which mainstream public and private organizations can survive and thrive in a post-scarcity world of abundance by considering new ways of doing business and putting sustainability at the heart of their operations. However, for millions of people caught in a poverty trap in some of the poorest countries on earth, these measures are unlikely to help them improve their quality of life. Chapter 12 addresses their plight, and some of the steps that are being taken to bring some equality to their lives.

12

The Business Response to Poverty

Introduction

Business is increasingly being seen as the partner of choice for resolving long-term poverty issues, but the challenge is to find ways of working together that satisfy the requirements of all stakeholders. This chapter reviews recent research and thinking in the area and looks in particular at new proposals for global development organizations, designed to spread risk and organize social investment more efficiently.

What Can Business Do?

In January 2009 the Ashridge Business School in the UK published a research study on the question of what business can do to alleviate poverty in the developing world.

The study builds upon earlier work by a number of other academics, notably Prahalad (2004) who suggested that from the many small amounts of disposable income available in the poorest countries a 'fortune' could be made. This would result from achieving very large volumes of sales while accepting small profit margins.

Pralahad argued that that there are huge potential profits to be made from serving the 4–5 billion people on under $2 a day – an economic opportunity he values globally at $13 trillion a year. The win for the poor of being served by big business includes, he says, being empowered by choice and being freed from having to pay the currently widespread 'poverty penalty'.

In shanty towns near Mumbai, for example, because they buy such small amounts, the poor pay a premium on everything from rice to credit – often 5 to 25 times what the rich pay for the same services. Driving down these premiums can make serving the bottom of the pyramid more profitable than serving the top, he argues, and points to a growing number of leading firms – from Unilever in India to Cemex in Mexico and Casas Bahia in Brazil – that are profiting by doing precisely that.

An alternative approach suggested by others would be for business to assist local communities in the poorer countries to increase their economic activity and in this way create markets for the goods and services of global companies. Global companies could help impoverished communities to establish small businesses and learn to acquire what the Shell Foundation has called 'business DNA'.

Yet others argue that any progress by the poorer countries will only come about by partnerships with global companies who are prepared to be involved commercially, but would be satisfied with less than profit maximization. They would see their involvement as a contribution to society and as a means of reducing the dangers of unrest, war and terror that spring from vast numbers of people feeling economically deprived.

As was noted in Chapter 9, Nobel prize-winner Muhummad Yunus, founder of Grameen Bank in Bangladesh, argues the case for a 'social business' to combine a degree of philanthropy with business acumen.

These various ideas have stimulated a great deal of debate as to their practicality and appropriateness. Some people question whether companies should become involved in any activity that is not solely devoted to wealth creation through profit for its shareholders. Prahalad considers that profit for companies and benefit for the populace of the poor nations are not incompatible.

The Ashridge study examines the various perspectives and on the basis of interviews, telephone discussions, and wide-ranging internet and literature search, sought to identify working models by which progress in alleviating poverty could be made.

The research looked at the extent to which companies have sought to work at the 'bottom of the pyramid' and at the style of the different approaches. Some companies have helped by employing local people and bringing prosperity to whole areas as by-products of their normal business, sensitively carried out as 'good citizens'. Others have aimed to sell specific products and services adapted to the needs of people on very low incomes at affordable prices and often in small quantities.

In other cases local entrepreneurs have been encouraged to set up small businesses, often as part of the supply chain of the company; local stores have been franchised for the sale of a company's goods; local people have been trained as salespersons, and microcredit and savings group opportunities have been set up to enable people to afford products and services; agricultural and technological advice has been proffered as part of an ongoing business relationship.

Non-governmental organizations (NGOs), both not-for-profit and those which engage in commercial activity to help fund their charitable activity, have played a significant role in developing opportunities for companies wishing to invest in the developing world.

The Ashridge research reviewed more than 50 global companies with interests in developing countries who positively influence the development of these countries by their commercial activities. A wide range of different relationships are involved and the companies are guided by their core competencies in deciding the nature of their investments.

To these global companies, the report adds another category – that of some large and small companies in the developing countries themselves – companies that are taking the plight of their fellow citizens seriously, combining philanthropy with commercial principles, sometimes charging the wealthy in ways that cover the costs of serving the destitute, sometimes providing microcredit, and working through self-help groups. The report gives some 50 examples of such local companies.

The activities of these two groups of companies are analysed and three working models of how companies can engage with the poorer communities are described as follows:

- The 'provider model', which works on normal business principles, where the company determines what products and services reflect their core competencies and offers them for sale.

- The 'empowerment model', where the company listens to the interests of the potential customers and adapts its products to the needs as seen by the customer. The small companies in developing countries who do business with the poorer section of the populace would probably lie in this category.

- The 'partnership model', in which the company enters into a joint venture with a local community to co-create a business to be decided upon by both parties and to be run jointly until the community representatives are able to take full control, while 'ambassadors' are sent out to co-create similar businesses in other communities. The area covered by the new businesses is secondary to the fact that they are learning how to run a business – any business. This model, known as the 'BOP Protocol' (BOP standing for 'bottom of the pyramid'), is very appealing in its call for dialogue and joint ownership of the outcomes, but the report raises the question as to whether enough companies would be able to put so much effort into such a rigorous approach as to make a big enough difference in the short term to the plight of poor communities.

The authors emphasize the importance of the NGOs in enabling companies to work in line with any of these models. NGOs have the knowledge and experience to work within a variety of cultures. Companies need the help of the NGOs to open doors in order to be successful in their relationships with local communities.

The report includes a case study of the project in Uganda in which the *Guardian* newspaper, Barclays Bank and the African NGO AMREF are cooperating to improve life in Katine district, seeking to learn from the experience and then to disseminate new knowledge.

It identifies a number of areas which need attention if wider business success is to be achieved in collaboration with poorer communities in ways which benefit both sides.

- Greater emphasis could be placed, in literature, the financial press and other media and political speeches and action, on the potential for business of the developing world.

- More thought should be given to whether businesses have a role in society apart from wealth creation, because of the enormous power large global companies possess.

- If they wish to gain and maintain a good reputation, it is in the interest of companies to be seen to be contributing to society. It is also in the self-interest of all businesses to have a stable world in which to operate.

- A degree of altruism and philanthropy is not inconsistent with the profit motive. Awareness of this might assume greater significance if companies conclude that there is not a 'fortune' to be made at the bottom of the pyramid.

- The increasing harmony and cooperation between NGOs and companies is to be welcomed. Companies would do well to seek the advice and cooperation of the NGOs when they are thinking of getting involved in the poorer parts of the world.

- Individual companies should consider setting up a specific unit to engage in work with needy populations, on a commercial basis, but without profit maximization being insisted upon.

- Companies could seek ways of coordinating their efforts in the BOP so that a number of interwoven problems are addressed simultaneously. To achieve such coordination a start could be made by the initiative of one company seeking out others who could complement their efforts. Equally, a simple system in the hands of one of the international institutions, foundations or government departments could be developed, as long as bureaucracy was kept to the minimum.

- Possibly, a government department could appeal for companies with different core competencies to form a coalition for dealing with the needs of specific communities.

- Any company deciding to move towards working with the BOP would need to recognize the need for careful and painstaking preparation; it would do no good just to go in on impulse or intuition.

- Companies in countries where there is a significant number of people living at the bottom of the pyramid could, as some of them are already doing, recognize a special responsibility toward those in their own backyard living in dire poverty.

- The role of small local companies can be significant in its own right and as a basis for the wider contribution from larger companies.

The research concludes that much good work is being done in many locations by businesses using commercial approaches. But the overall global effect is still very limited, given the scale of the need. However, lack of action is not an option. If the people who constitute the bottom of the pyramid are to be left in their current state, business itself is likely to suffer from the consequences in terms of social and political instability and the depletion of vital natural resources.

The most significant finding of this study is that investment in the bottom of the pyramid is currently too random to make the considerable integrated changes that are needed by poor communities. Individual firms deal with a very limited range of poverty related problems, which means that unless other firms complement their actions by investing in other areas of need, people will continue to suffer and die in large numbers.

The authors of the report take the view that ultimately there is not a fortune to be made at the bottom of the pyramid – only a modest profit. It means that those companies who decide to work with the bottom of the pyramid must inevitably do so with a measure of altruism.

In an interview published on the website Knowledge@Wharton, October 2009, Pralahad argued that companies are indeed taking up his ideas and that many more are successfully operating in poorer countries. He gives the wireless cellular phone industry as an example, claiming that some two and a half billion 'bottom of the pyramid' people are now connected to the system and that all the companies operating in these countries are making money. In India alone there are more than 12 million new subscribers a month. Prepaid cards have become the norm and networks of small shops which download minutes to the phones have sprung up. In Kenya, people who do not have access to bank accounts are using the phones to transfer cash via text encrypted text messages.

Businesses Need to Collaborate to Earn Legitimacy

A relatively optimistic view of the possibility of a corporate solution to global poverty has been put forward by George Lodge, Emeritus Professor at Harvard Business School and a former Secretary of Labor for International Affairs in the Eisenhower and Kennedy administrations and Craig Wilson, formerly a consultant economist for the World Bank, currently working for the International Finance Corporation in Bangladesh (Lodge and Wilson 2006). They believe that multinational organizations have the capabilities and resources needed to build investment, stimulate economic growth and create jobs in poor countries. Moreover, they argue that MNCs can do so profitably and sustainably. But, because MNCs lack legitimacy and in order to share risk, they suggest that a collective approach is better than an individual company going it alone.

The authors trace the decline of corporate legitimacy reflecting such things as revelations of large-scale abuse in corporate governance. They point out that there are changing public expectations about the impact of global companies on society, and that maximizing shareholder value is no longer enough. Corporations are being pressed by governments and NGOs to contribute to solving such problems as environmental damage, epidemic diseases, child labour, and developing-country poverty.

Some of the more thoughtful and far-sighted corporate leaders are responding to the threat posed by the decline in their legitimacy by searching for ways to meet such expectations, provide environmental leadership, reduce global poverty and make the world a better place, while still satisfying their shareholders.

An example is Grameen Danone Foods Ltd, a collaborative enterprise involving a 50–50 joint venture between Groupe Danone – the US$16 billion multinational yogurt maker – and the Grameen companies founded by Muhammad Yunus. The mission of Grameen Danone Foods is to bring affordable nutrition to malnourished children in Bangladesh with a fortified yogurt, under the brand name Shokti Doi (which means 'yogurt for power' in Bengali, the country's language).

Like a conventional business, Grameen Danone must recover its full costs from operations. Yet, like a non-profit, it is driven by a cause rather than by profit. If all goes well, investors will receive only a token 1 per cent annual dividend, with all other profits being ploughed back into the business. The venture's primary aim is to create social benefits for those whose lives the company touches. For example, the first Grameen Danone factory, which opened in November 2006, was deliberately built small, as a prototype for community-based plants that would provide jobs across Bangladesh.

As far as poverty reduction is concerned, the collective response of MNCs to date has been sporadic, poorly organized, and inadequate. The question, say the authors, is how to coordinate the actions of the many interested parties and achieve the desired objective.

MNCs are both targets for opponents of globalization yet can also form part of the solution to the huge challenges faced by the world. They are under attack from a wide range of organizations such as Amnesty International, Friends of the Earth, and Oxfam International which have enlisted the support of many governments and gained a lot of influence in international organizations such as the UN, the World Bank and the International Monetary Fund (IMF).

At the same time NGOs are encouraging, assisting, and pressuring the more progressive corporations to increase globalization's benefits and diminish its costs. This includes pushing MNCs to increase and improve the contribution they make to the reduction of global poverty. Some NGOs now work closely with MNCs and some NGOs pursue their objectives in cooperation with them. The Washington-based Center for Global Development (CGD), for example, focuses on the effectiveness of international aid and the reduction of poverty in developing countries. CGD has developed an index for measuring and ranking the performance of a set of rich countries with respect to global development and poverty reduction.

Some smaller NGOs or local branches of international NGOs work at the country level with MNCs in developing countries. The authors argue that MNCs find these local partnerships easier to enter, more likely to produce results, and less subject to posturing than collaboration with large, global NGOs. As these working-level partnerships between MNCs and NGOs become more commonplace, there is a convergence of objectives between these two very different types of organization. MNCs are taking more notice of social objectives; NGOs are becoming more business-oriented.

There has been a shift towards the development of partnerships between big business and development institutions. There are two reasons. MNCs, while hearing the calls for greater involvement in development, see they don't have the legitimacy or often the expertise to do what is asked of them. International and governmental agencies realize they don't have the resources or a mechanism for making sustainable business-based improvements to people's lives. This indicates the gap in the 'international development architecture'.

Pressed by NGOs and international leaders such as the UN Secretary-General to contribute more effectively to social improvements, MNCs have undertaken a wide variety of initiatives. The authors list the range of company responses: corporate social responsibility initiatives; industry codes of conduct; accession to agreed sets of behavioural principles; collaboration with the UN and other intergovernmental agencies; sustainable development initiatives; and 'innumerable' international councils and committees. However, they take the view that none as yet has made a substantial impact on global poverty.

MNCs are, however, increasingly interested in making sure their initiatives are efficient, make the most of the investment, and have a sustainable impact.

Linking MNCs, NGOs and Government Agencies

In recent years, most international development organizations have made poverty reduction a top priority. The authors outline the current structure of governmental agencies and organizations devoted to international development to reveal a gap that needs to be filled if progress is to be made towards meeting the widely endorsed eight Millennium Development Goals set in 2000 for achievement by 2015:

- end poverty and hunger

- universal education

- gender equality

- child health

- maternal health

- combat HIV/AIDS

- environmental sustainability

- global partnership.

Regrettably, the United Nations report on the Millennium Goals (2009) stated that major advances in the fight against poverty and hunger have begun to slow or even reverse as a result of the global economic and food crises. The assessment, launched by UN Secretary-General Ban Ki-moon in Geneva, warned that, despite many successes, overall progress had been too slow for most of the targets to be met by 2015.

International development agencies, owned, funded and controlled by the governments of rich countries, are broadly concerned with development and poverty reduction but their connection to MNCs is weak and variable. The agencies and their NGO counterparts have belatedly realized that MNCs can considerably augment their own disappointing efforts to reduce global poverty. While they have tried to develop more partnerships with business, they have failed to harness effectively the collective power of MNCs.

Lodge and Wilson review the main agencies to see where there is 'traction' on the issue of poverty and where the gaps lie.

- The World Bank. Provides project and structural adjustment loans, technical assistance, policy advice and knowledge services to poor and middle-income countries with the aim of reducing poverty. It normally works with and through national governments. MNCs rarely, however, participate in developing these strategies – in contrast to the involvement in the process of NGOs.

- The International Finance Corporation. The IFC is the part of the World Bank that interacts most closely with MNCs. Referred to as the 'private-sector' arm of the World Bank, the IFC invests in private, profit-making enterprises in developing countries, offers advice and support to developing country governments for improving the investment climate. Its Strengthening Grassroots Business Organizations Initiative (SGBI) targets smaller, community-driven businesses to provide them with technical skills and 'patient capital' believing these are the most effective way to meet the local community's objectives.

- The Organization for Economic Cooperation and Development. The OECD covers a wide range of governance, macroeconomic and industrial issues affecting its 30 rich country members and 70 poor country associates. It is ahead of other international institutions in advocating an increased role for MNCs in development.

- The United Nations. The UN coordinates the activities of its various agencies and employs its strong convening capacity to pull together individuals and groups for discussion and agreement on policies. MNCs have only been included in these discussions in recent years. In 2000, at the UN Millennium Summit in New York, world leaders issued the Millennium Development Goals which place eradicating extreme poverty and hunger as the number one goal.

- The UN Global Compact. Conceived in 1999 by Kofi Annan, the UN Secretary-General, to bring together the world's largest MNCs to encourage voluntary adoption of universal basic standards on human rights, labour standards, the environment and anti-corruption. It has set up a voluntary framework of 10 principles to guide business action in developing countries. While the Compact's initial thrust was to reduce the impact of large corporations, it has shifted to looking for ways that MNCs can make a greater contribution to development, while insisting that governments provide the necessary structure and support.

- The United Nations Development Programme. The UNDP, the development arm of the UN, focuses on crisis prevention and recovery, AIDS, poverty reduction, and democracy and governance. While it struggles to fund its programmes, it maintains the lead role in the UN's efforts to achieve the Millennium Development Goals. Under its Growing Sustainable Business for Poverty Reduction (GSB) initiative, it is forming partnerships with MNCs (such as ABB, EDF, Ericsson, Shell and Total) to reduce poverty in developing countries. Under the GSB initiative, these global firms have agreed to explore and pursue commercially viable project that have maximum impact on poverty reduction in the world's poorest countries. The authors suggest this is a model for the future.

- National government organizations. The efforts of developed
country governments to enlist their corporate sectors in development
are limited, though they all have bilateral development agencies and
channel considerable development resources through international
development organizations. USAID, the American international
development agency, has a Global Development Alliance with
30 MNCS to assist developing countries. France legally requires
companies to report on the social, economic and environmental
consequences of their activities.

The position taken by the authors is that the only way to change the system
is incrementally, locality by locality, using the skills, knowledge and access to
the world markets that only global corporations can provide. Only business
can help reduce poverty, and only if it is an integral part of its profit-making
activities, not as a 'pro bono sideline'. Only if poverty reduction is profitable will
it be sustainable. What are needed are more investment and more jobs; global
firms have the means and reach to bring small local businesses into being, with
the output of the smaller firms being demanded by bigger, normally foreign
firms.

Poverty reduction requires what the authors call 'engines of change' and
they believe that the most efficient and sustainable engines of change are
corporations. Examples include DaimlerChrysler's involvement in Brazil's
poverty-stricken northeast where it cooperated with a community development
project to build a high-tech factory making car seats from locally-sourced raw
materials; Nestlé's dairy operation in Panama involving several thousand
farmers to produce powdered milk; the Shell Foundation which is working in
Africa to support local enterprises that reduce poverty.

Lodge and Wilson set out some preconditions for a successful MNC-led
poverty-reduction mechanism:

- It must have a 'demonstrable and measurable' positive impact that
encourages independent replication by other firms.

- It needs the mandate to investigate and document the profound
effect that MNCs have on reducing global poverty.

- Its activities must be sustainable and therefore profitable.

- It should enhance corporate legitimacy by carrying the stamp of approval of the UN or another intergovernmental organization and a representative selection of NGOs.

The authors outline various options for businesses to consider if they decide to incorporate the objective of reducing poverty into their operations. For example:

- Companies can measure the magnitude of their impact on poverty. Where firms can show they have helped to reduce poverty, it should lessen political risk and improve corporate reputation.

- Helping host economies manage more proficiently the payments that flow to them in royalties, taxes, and so on. ExxonMobil, for example, works with host governments, NGOS and the World Bank to establish dedicated accounting systems for managing inflows to government treasuries of resource rents.

- Providing better and cheaper products for the poor, as advocated by Prahalad. Companies such as Hewlett-Packard, Cemex (Mexico) and Merck have all made money by modifying their products, services and marketing mix to turn poor people into customers.

- Removing company efforts on poverty alleviation from public affairs and corporate responsibility departments and positioning them as part of mainstream company operations.

- Improving the types of incentives for MNCs when making investment decisions. A company that cuts carbon emissions might be able to obtain a 'carbon credit' which has a positive financial value and therefore constitutes a positive incentive to seek and measure improvements. At present, there is no such equivalent 'poverty credit' which would encourage companies to invest in poor countries.

The authors say there is evidence that companies who have innovated to improve environmental safeguards, eco-efficiency, organizational health and safety, and cultural and heritage protection, have benefited from better political support and higher profits at lower risk. The same, they say, will be true for companies that play an explicit role in poverty alleviation.

Their analysis of the problem leads Lodge and Wilson to propose that a new institution be created by a select group of corporate leaders in cooperation with representative NGOs and the United Nations to address directly the issue of corporate involvement in poverty reduction.

The proposed World Development Corporation (WDC) would be a non-profit corporation established under the auspices of the UN to harness the skills, capabilities and resources of leading global firms to reduce poverty and improve living standards in developing countries. Working closely with existing international development agencies such as the World Bank, the IFC, and NGOs, it would be managed by representatives of a dozen or so MNCs at the invitation of the Secretary-General of the UN. The partners might invite other MNCs to become financial and technical contributors to the WDC. Shareholders would provide the initial capital which would be augmented by funds from OECD governments and other development agencies.

In terms of benefits for MNCs, it would help safeguard their investments in poor countries against political instability. It would be a vehicle through which local suppliers and markets could be developed. It would offer MNCs a collective approach to development that both lowers risk and increases the chance of success.

Perhaps the most important benefit for MNCs, in the eyes of the authors, is that the WDC would greatly enhance MNCs' legitimacy as they prove their effectiveness in meeting community needs.

The paradox is that in order to revive its legitimacy, the corporation is expected to do what is in many cases illegitimate in that it involves acting independently of local laws customs and institutions. It therefore needs help. The answer is to give the corporation the legitimacy it needs that can be bestowed by the UN, the NGOs and the communities it serves, and to provide it with sufficient public resources to enable it to serve community needs and reduce poverty, without threatening its survival as a profit-making institution.

There is a very long way to go to eliminate global poverty, but these initiatives and many others like them will increase the likelihood that post-scarcity abundance will benefit everyone rather than a privileged few.

PART 5

System Change

13

The Prospect for System Change

Introduction

Today, beyond any doubt, the desirability of system change is widely accepted. There is a growing consensus about the need to tackle three urgent problems at a global level.

- First, there are environmental sustainability issues and the threat of climate change in particular. The possibility of significant global warming over the course of the present century is, of course, an important issue. The aim of systemic change in respect of these matters can be summed up in the phrases sustainable growth and sustainable consumption.

- Secondly, there is growing consensus of the need for system change in the field of global finance and in particular that part of the financial sector that has been designated the casino economy.

- Thirdly there is seen to be a need for system change in relation to inequality and poverty.

How System Change Comes About

Frank Dixon (2007) points to rising awareness that systemic issues are a primary driver of growing problems with the functioning of the free market and declining environmental and social conditions and that there is an increased emphasis on the need for system change.

System change efforts, he argues, can be broadly categorized as mid-level or high-level. Mid-level system change work focuses on sector- or issue-specific areas (that is, transportation, hunger, climate change, and so on). High-level system change (HLSC) involves addressing the systemic factors which act so as to create negative social, economic and environmental outcomes. These factors include institutions, accepted conventions, rewards systems, and outdated mindsets

Dixon advocates an approach called sustainable systems implementation (SSI), a collaborative approach that engages system-change experts and leaders from business, government and civil society in dialogue and action for the purpose of driving effective HLSC. The approach seeks to identify key system-change leverage points and raise awareness of the most promising system-change strategies already developed but not widely implemented. It involves taking a true whole system focus and rendering complex ideas and strategies down to simple terms and concepts, with the goal of greatly expanding public awareness and action.

It has generally been the case that tackling the whole system at once has been regarded as too difficult. This has caused system-change efforts to be focused on improving system sub-elements, often without adequate consideration of the whole system. System-change programmes developed with this approach usually have low to no effective implementation. Dixon does not suggest that human systems could or should change at once. Instead the approach suggests that consideration of the whole system should inform, guide and coordinate improvements in system sub-areas. While this approach is complex, it probably is the most effective way to evolve human systems into more sustainable forms.

This is eminently sensible advice and the emphasis on the need for collaboration between experts in different fields and different institutions is very pertinent.

The Fear of Change

As a starting point, when considering the prospect of system change, we must accept that the vast majority of the world's population have a vested interest in the perpetuation of the existing system. This is obviously true of the general populace as well as the elites of the prosperous countries of North America, Western Europe, Australasia and Japan. In these countries investors are fearful of any change which might threaten their savings, companies are protective of their existing markets and business models, employees are protective of their jobs, and consumers cling to accustomed lifestyles. In the emerging economies such as China and India people aspire to the benefits of the system and eagerly await the day when they, too, will enjoy them. In the poorer countries the political and business elites who hold the reins of power are huge beneficiaries of the system, while the poorest of their citizens and employees cling to their jobs or other sources of income, however pitiful, rather than risk starvation. The fear of change, of the unknown, is universal.

The Inevitability of System Change

Nevertheless, as has happened countless times over the centuries, the system *will* change as the evolution of human society continues to unfold. Institutions that become dysfunctional wither and die and new institutions take their place. System change is inevitable and remorseless and in the end is strong enough to sweep vested interests aside. Indeed, system change is a continuous process as new technologies interact with the economy and with changing social attitudes and lifestyles. It only becomes apparent when the cumulative impact of incremental changes makes it clear that a tipping point has been reached and that fundamental change has taken place, as was the case with the Industrial Revolution. Relatively small incremental changes act as early warning signals but are mostly ignored.

The process cannot be halted or reversed, but it can be influenced by large-scale interventions as evidenced by such past events as the abolition of slavery, the New Deal and the break-up of the Soviet bloc. The institution of slavery was economically hugely important and the fortunes and livelihoods of many thousands of people depended on it. Despite this, sooner or later the forces of social and economic change would have done away with it. This process was hastened by advocacy on the part of Wilberforce and others, by political will and by military force. In the modern world the trend is in the direction of greater concern for the environment, greater concern for human rights and the reduction of gross inequality. These things will be brought about more speedily as a result of fresh advocacy, political action and, as in the cases of Iraq and Afghanistan, the use of military force.

System Change, Sustainability and Economic Growth

There are now many powerful forces pushing for system change in the interests of environmental sustainability. A powerful social movement has been set in motion, one which is powerful enough to strongly influence political decisions at both national and international level and is having a considerable influence on the allocation of resources. However, many of those who are working to achieve these goals are vehement in their opposition to continuing economic growth. The opposition seems to be based on several different grounds.

One is revulsion at the materialistic values of modern society in the developed world and a wish to see society return to a less material, perhaps more spiritual or at least more balanced set of lifestyles. Given some of the negative effects of affluence this can be sympathized with. However, it is a pipe dream. The engines that drive economic growth – new scientific knowledge, technological change, human ingenuity and the desire for improvement in living standards are too powerful.

A second basis for opposition to growth is the belief that further economic growth will lead to the acceleration of the deterioration of the environment and the using up of valuable non-renewable resources. Yet it is only as a result of continued economic growth that the world will be able to produce the resources needed to tackle issues such as climate change and poverty. More economic growth means more abundance – more food being produced, more efficiently and at lower cost. It means more and cheaper goods and services for people in poor countries – from bicycles to schools and hospitals. It means more victories over disease and better preventative health care resulting in lower infant mortality. It means the ability to fund the research that will result in substitute materials, new sources of energy, and new ways of capturing carbon.

'No growth' is not the answer. But what is needed is 'qualitative growth' as distinct from the concept of quantitative growth used by economists.

Most economists still measure a country's wealth in terms of its gross domestic product (GDP). This is a metric in which all economic activities that have a monetary value are added up, while all non-monetary aspects of the economy, such as voluntary work, are ignored. Expenditures incurred in treating accident victims or people suffering from alcohol abuse, are added as positive contributions to the GDP and the growth of this narrow, purely quantitative index is accepted as the sign of a healthy economy. (GDP does not include cash transactions in the so-called 'black economy' which in some countries can amount to very significant sums, nor does it account for such non-monetary transactions such as barter or gifting.)

Simon Kuznets, creator of the current system of national accounts, warned in 1934 that such a limited, one-dimensional metric should not serve as an index of overall social progress. Nevertheless, the goal set by the politicians controlling most national economies is to maximize growth of their countries' GDP thus defined.

The economists' view of growth been increasingly challenged, notably at the second UN Earth Summit in Rio de Janeiro in 1992, when some 170 governments agreed to correct it. Why has the ubiquitous use of GDP persisted since then?

One reason is that there has been strong resistance to the notion that companies and government agencies include on their balance sheets social and environmental costs which they have been accustomed to externalizing to taxpayers, the environment, and future generations. However, growing concerns about global climate change and pollution are now leading to fresh calls for change and strong pressure for internalizing such costs in accounting for company performance as well as in national accounts.

Also, the Kuznets system has two merits – it is relatively simple and purely quantitative, whereas attempts to develop a widely accepted metric of qualitative growth involve greater complexity and the exercise of qualitative judgement. Different groups of experts are coming up with different solutions.

The UN has developed a metric, the Human Development Index (HDI) which includes measures of such things as poverty, health, gender equity, education, social inclusion and environment.

Fritjof Capra and Hazel Henderson (2009) raise a key issue: how can we transform the global economy from a system striving for unlimited quantitative growth to one which is more sustainable without generating human hardship through more unemployment? They argue that we need to make a distinction between 'good' growth and 'bad growth'. The distinction would, however, call for judgement by politicians not all of whom would be likely to share Capra and Henderson's values. By bad growth the authors mean growth that is based on fossil fuels, involves toxic substances, depletes natural resources and damages the earth's ecosystems. This definition of 'bad' is confined to the raw materials and the production process involved. But what about 'bad' products – weapons systems, tobacco, pornography, junk food and so on? In the end growth will supply increasing amounts of what consumers, including governments, want, influenced, of course, by advertisers, lobbyists, the media and the force of public opinion.

A third school of thought assigns the ills of the modern world to the ideology of the market and the operation of the invisible hand. The alternative of state control of the economy has been tried and failed many times. In Russia and in China in the 1950s and 60s it resulted in huge suffering, famine and loss of personal freedoms. Many of the problems that are associated with market forces occur largely because they are not allowed to operate. Corporations, either singly or in cartels, attempt to fix prices rather than let them be set by the market; governments erect tariffs against foreign goods in order to protect domestic industries; hedge funds use super computers to enable them to receive market information fractions of a second ahead of their competitors. The distortion of markets and market abuse are rife.

Finally, there is the anti-globalization movement. In one sense, globalization is not something one can be for or against. Globalization is simply something that has been developing over centuries in response to improvements in communication and transportation. The objections relate not to globalization as such, but to the ways in which global capital markets and the removal of barriers to free trade often operate to the disadvantage of the least powerful nations.

Adapting to Post-Scarcity Conditions

Although the need for system change is widely accepted, there is little recognition of the need to adjust to post-scarcity conditions and to base policies and decisions on the principles of the economics of abundance rather than on the economics of scarcity. When both politicians and economists consider anything other than the immediate future they address issues of what is or will be affordable in the context of hidden assumptions based on the assumed scarcity of raw materials, goods and services rather than on their abundance.

At this stage we do not know exactly how an economy based on abundance would function. For example, as the cost of producing things falls ever closer to zero, what kinds of pricing policies will companies deploy in their efforts to protect profits? What will be the role of household savings? What will be the implications for fiscal policy? What will be the balance between private and public consumption? Will the benefits of advances in productivity be shared with the populations in the developing countries? Above all, will abundance in all senses of the word – abundance of talent, abundance of knowledge, abundance of information and abundance of goods and services – be effectively deployed in the interests of sustainability – social as well as environmental?

Increased wealth could be used to improve the quality of life, via improved healthcare, access to clean water, better education, adequate housing, the elimination of poverty and access to the arts. It could also be used to enable great strides in science and technology, much of which could be focused on achieving environmental sustainability.

At the same time there is a grave danger that greater affluence will largely be drained into pure private consumption coupled with the escalation of weapons systems and both in the context of continued or even enhanced levels of inequality. There a very real danger that as more and more societies attain the levels of per capita GDP currently obtaining in the USA, they will allocate sizeable amounts of that wealth to the development and acquisition of weapons, and nuclear weapons in particular, with all that implies for world peace.

Given a free choice the majority of consumers will choose to own and drive more cars, to eat more red meat, to accumulate more possessions, rather than willingly devote more of their income, via taxation, to the public good. Politicians will continue to be preoccupied with the exercise of military power. Abundance is therefore a serious threat to sustainability if such tendencies are allowed to go unchecked.

If the benefits of abundance are to outweigh the negative effects a far higher level of international cooperation will be called for than it has been possible to achieve hitherto.

There are many questions to which we cannot yet know the answers. In its detailed characteristics the future is unpredictable. Nevertheless the broad path that development will take during the next 20 to 30 years is beginning to become clear and to be signalled by the various early warning signs that this book has explored.

References

Akerlof, G.A. and Shiller, R. 2009. *Animal Spirits. How Human Psychology Drives the Economy, and Why it Matters for Global Capitalism*. Princeton, NJ: Princeton University Press.

Anderson, C. 2006. *The Long Tail*. London: Random House Business Books.

Anderson, C. 2009. *Free: The Future of a Radical Price*. London: Random House Business Books.

Ashridge Business School. 2009. *A Role for Business at the Bottom of the Pyramid* (on line). Available at: www.ashridge.org/Website/IC.nsf/wFARATTA/A%20Role%/20.

Bell, D. 1972. *The Coming of Post Industrial Society*. Harmondsworth: Penguin Books.

Berube, D.M. 2006. *Nano Hype. The Truth Behind the Nanotechnology Buzz*. New York: Prometheus Books.

Block, P. 1993. *Stewardship*. San Francisco: Berrett Koehler.

Bottomley, G. 1912. *To Ironfounders and Others*. London: Constable.

Bower, J. and Christensen, C.M. 1995. 'Disruptive Technologies Catching the Wave', *Harvard Business Review*, January–February 1995.

Capra, F. and Henderson, H. 2009. *Qualitative Growth*. London: Institute of Chartered Accountants of England and Wales (ICAEW) and Tomorrow's Company.

Carson, R. 1962. *The Silent Spring*. New York: Houghton Mifflin.

Chase, S. 1934. *The Economy of Abundance*. Port Washington, NY: Kennikat Press.

Collier, P. 2007. *The Bottom Billion: Why the Poorest Countries are Failing and What Can Be Done About it*. Oxford: Oxford University Press.

Dixon, F. 2007. *The Business Case for High Level System Change* (on line). Available at: www.CSRwire.com.

Drexler, K.E. 1986. *Engines of Creation. The Coming Era of Nanotechnology*. New York: Anchor Books.

Drucker, P.F. 1969. *The Age of Discontinuity*. New York: Harper Row.

Durkheim, E. 1984. *The Division of Labour in Society*. New York: The Free Press.

Economist Intelligence Unit (EIU) 2005 *Quality of Life Index* (on line). Available at www.economist.com/media/pdf/QUALITY_OF_LIFE.PDF.

Elkington, J. 1997. *Cannibals With Forks*. London: Capstone.

Elkington, J. 2001. *The Chrysalis Economy*. London: Capstone.

Feynman, R. 1959. *There's Plenty of Room at the Bottom*. Paper presented the annual conference of the American Physical Society, at the Californian Institute of Technology. Available at: www.zyvex.com/nanotech/feynman.html.

Ford, H. 1929. *My Philosophy of Industry*. Montana: Kessinger Publishing Company.

Fukuyama, F. 1995. *Trust; the Social Virtues and the Creation of Prosperity*. London: Hamish Hamilton.

Fuller, Buckminster R. 1972. *Utopia or Oblivion. The Prospect for Humanity*. Harmondsworth: Penguin Books.

Galbraith, J.K. 1969. *The Affluent Society*. Boston: Houghton Mifflin.

Hertz, N. 2001. *The Silent Takeover*. London: William Heinemann.

Hirsch, F. 1976. *Social Limits to Growth*. Cambridge, MA: Harvard University Press.

Intergovernmental panel on climate change (IPCC). 2007. Fourth Assessment Report (on line). Available at: www.ipcc.ch/

Jarvis, J. 2009. *What Would Google Do?* New York: Harper Collins.

Jones, H. 2001. 'Responding to stakeholders Concerns in the New Economy; Nike's Experience', in *Perspectives on the New Economy of Corporate Citizenship*, by S. Zadek, Copenhagen: The Copenhagen Centre.

Keller, K.L. 2000. 'The Brand Report Card', *Harvard Business Review*, January, 2000.

Kelly, K. 1998. *New Rules for the New Economy*. London: Fourth Estate.

Kelly, K. 2008. *Better than Free. The Technium* (on line). Available at:www.kk.org./ thetechnium/archives/2008/01/better_than_fre.php.

Kelly, K. 2009. *A New Kind of Mind. The Edge* (on line). Available at:www.edge. org/q2009/q0 9–1.html.

Keynes, J.M. 1963. 'Economic Possibilities for our Grandchildren', in *Essays in Persuasion*, New York: W.W. Norton.

Khosla, V. 2009. The World Must Put its Faith in Technology. *Sunday Times*, 29 March, 2009.

Klein, N. 2000. *No Logo*. London: Flamingo.

Kotler, P. 1993. *The Practice of Marketing*. Englewood Cliffs, NJ: Prentice Hall.

Krugman, P. 2008. *The Return of Depression Economics and the Crisis of 2008*. Harmondsworth: Penguin Books.

Lawson, N. 2008. *An Appeal to Reason: A Cool Look at Global Warming*. London: Duckworth Overlook.

Levy, S. 2009. Secret of Googleconomics; Data-fuelled Recipe Brews Profitability. *Wired*. May 22, 2009.

Lindsey, B. 2007. *The Age of Abundance*. New York: Harper Collins.

Lodge, G. and Wilson, C. 2006. *A Corporate Solution to Poverty*. Princeton, NJ: Princeton University Press.

Lomberg, B. 2001. *The Skeptical Environmentalist. Measuring the Real State of the World*. Cambridge: Cambridge University Press.

McKinsey Global Institute 2009. *Accounting for the Costs of US Health Care: a New Look at Why Americans Spend More* (on line). Available at: www.academyhealth. org/files/2009/monday/jensene/pdf.

Manz, C.C. and Sims, H. Jr. 2001. *The New Super Leadership*. San Francisco: Berrett Koehler.

Masnik, M. 2006. *The Economics of Abundance is Not a Moral Issue. Techdirt* (on line). Available at: http;//www.techdirt.com/articles/2006.

Meadows, D.L. 1972. *The Limits to Growth. A Report of the Club of Rome's Project on the Predicament of Mankind*. New York: Universe Books.

Minsky, H. 1986. *Stabilizing an Unstable Economy*. New York: McGraw Hill.

Nair, A.J. 2007. *Introduction to Biotechnology and Genetic Engineering*. Hingham, MA: Infinity Science Press.

National Institute of Economic and Social Research (NIESR). 1997. *Annual Review*. London: NIESR.

Packard, V. 1960. *The Waste Makers*. Harmondsworth: Penguin Books.

Paltridge, G.W. 2009. *The Climate Caper*. London: Quarter Books.

Partnoy, F. 2003. *Infectious Greed. How Deceit and Risk Corrupted the Financial Markets*. London: Profile Books.

Pestel, E. and Mesarović, M. 1974. *Mankind at the Turning Point; the Second Report to the Club of Rome*. New York: Dutton.

Phoenix, C. 2005. *Developing Molecular Manufacturing* (on line). Centre for Responsible Nanotechnology (CRN). Available at: www.crnano. orgdeveloping.htm.

Pilzer, P.Z. 1990. *Unlimited Wealth*. New York: Crown Publishers.

Pralahad, C.K. 2004. *A Fortune at the Bottom of the Pyramid. Eradicating Poverty through Profits*. Wharton, PA: Wharton School Publishing.

Putnam, R. 2000. *Bowling Alone*. New York: Simon and Schuster.

Reich, C.A. 1970. *The Greening of America*. London: Allen Lane.

Romer, P. 1986. 'Increasing Returns and Long-Run Growth', *Journal of Political Economy*, 94(5). (Oct. 1986), pp. 1002–1037.

Romer, P. 1990. 'Endogenous Technological Change', *Journal of Political Economy*, 98(5), pp. S7 1–102.

Sachs, J. 2008. *Common Wealth: Economics for a Crowded Planet*. London: Allen Lane.

Samuelson, P. and Nordhaus, W.D. 1985. *Economics*. 12th edition. New York: McGraw-Hill.

Schmidt, S. 2008. *The Coming Convergence*. New York: Prometheus Books.

Schumpeter, J. 1942. *Capitalism, Socialism and Democracy*. New York: Harper.

Shell, R.G. 2003. *Suing Your Customers. A Winning Business Strategy?* (on line). www.Knowledge@Wharton. October 22, 2003

Smith, Adam. 1776. *The Wealth of Nations*. London: Methuen and Co.

Soros, G. 1998. *The Crisis of Global Capitalism*. New York: Public Affairs.

Strange, S. 1997. *Casino Capitalism*. Manchester: Manchester University Press.

Sussex University Science Policy Research Unit. 1973. 'The Limits to Growth Controversy', *Futures*, 6(1), Special Issue.

Theobald, R. 1961. *The Challenge of Abundance*. New York: Mentor books.

Toffler, A. 1980. *The Third Wave*. New York: William Morrow.

Tomorrow's Company. 2007. *Tomorrow's Global Company*. London: Tomorrow's Company.

Tomorrow's Company. 2008. *Tomorrow's Global Talent*. London: Tomorrow's Company.

Tomorrow's Company. 2008. *Tomorrow's Owners*. London: Tomorrow's Company.

United Nations. 2009. *The Millennium Development Goals Report*. New York: United Nations.

Vogt, W. 1948. *Roads to Survival*. New York: William Sloane Associates.

Warbuton, P. 2005. *Debt and Delusion*. Princeton, NJ: World Metaview Press.

Wilkinson, W. and Pickett, K. 2009. *The Spirit Level. Why More Equal Societies Almost Always Do Better*. London: Allen Lane.

World Bank. 2009. *Governance Matters* (on line). Available at: http.//info. worldbank.org/governance/wgi/sc_asp.

World Commission on Environment and Development. 1987. *Our Common Future*. Oxford: Oxford University Press.

Zadek, S. 2001. *The Civil Corporation*. London: Earthscan.

Index

If you have found this book useful you may be interested in other titles from Gower

Integral Economics:
Releasing the Economic Genius of Your Society
Ronnie Lessem and Alexander Schieffer
Hardback: 978-0-566-09247-3
e-book: 978-0-566-09248-0

The Economics of Abundance:
A Political Economy of Freedom, Equity,
and Sustainability
Wolfgang Hoeschele
Hardback: 978-0-566-08940-4
e-book: 978-0-566-08941-1

Making Ecopreneurs:
Developing Sustainable Entrepreneurship
Edited by
Michael Schaper
Hardback: 978-0-566-08875-9
e-book: 978-1-4094-0123-0

Visit **www.gowerpublishing.com** and

- search the entire catalogue of Gower books in print
- order titles online at 10% discount
- take advantage of special offers
- sign up for our monthly e-mail update service
- download free sample chapters from all recent titles
- download or order our catalogue

For Product Safety Concerns and Information please contact our
EU representative GPSR@taylorandfrancis.com Taylor & Francis
Verlag GmbH, Kaufingerstraße 24, 80331 München, Germany